We are
the people
our parents
warned us
against

Nicholas von Hoffman began his writing career as a newspaperman in Chicago. He is also the author of *Mississippi Notebook*, *Make-Believe Presidents*, *Organized Crimes*, and *Citizen Cohn*.

# We are the people our parents warned us against

## NICHOLAS VON HOFFMAN

ELEPHANT PAPERBACKS
Ivan R. Dee, Inc., Publisher, Chicago

First ELEPHANT PAPERBACK edition published 1989 by Ivan R. Dee, Inc.,
1169 South Plymouth Court, Chicago 60605. Manufactured in the United States
of America.

ISBN 0-929587-06-5

Grateful acknowledgment is made to H-B Publications, San Francisco, for
permission to quote from the *Haight-Ashbury Songbook* by Ashleigh Brilliant.

**TO SAUL ALINSKY**
*with more gratitude and love than I can say*

In the summer of 1967, youth drew attention to itself by clustering in large numbers in most major American cities, where they broke the narcotics laws proudly, publicly, and defiantly. At the same time, they enunciated a different social philosophy and a new politics, and perhaps even mothered into life a subculture that was new to America.

This book tries to describe what happened in the Haight-Ashbury section of San Francisco. For it was in the Haight that whatever happened, happened most vividly and so intensely that it drew international attention to itself.

Names and identities have been changed when necessary to avoid embarrassing people. Where thoughts are attributed to people, the method used was not divination; they told me afterward what they were thinking.

NICHOLAS VON HOFFMAN

*Washington, D.C.*
*February 1968*

I want to thank my son, Alexander, who visited the Haight and spent many hours giving me the insights of a sensitive sixteen-year-old; Bill German, for allowing me the use of the *San Francisco Chronicle* offices and for many other favors; Elaine Mayes, for prowling over the Haight with me for days and sharing her ideas; Johann Rush and Michael Alexander, for doing the same; Susan Dooley, for invaluable editorial advice; Larry Stern, the *Washington Post's* National News Editor, for encouraging and standing behind an unorthodox project; Ben Bradlee, the *Post's* Managing Editor, for doing the same and for getting out from behind his desk and looking at the scene with his own eyes; and Mrs. Margaret Weiskopf, who typed this manuscript.

We are
the people
our parents
warned us
against

### 1,000 TEST LIFE STRAIN IN SHELTER

**Athens, Ga., Aug. 27 (UPI)—One thousand volunteers, ranging in age from six months to 80 years old, entered a makeshift underground fallout shelter yesterday to see if they can withstand the strain of living together for 24 hours.**

The fog came every day and destroyed the sunshine, and then the Haight was left to itself. News from the outside world sparked discontinuous. It flashed through the airy water like a stoned head flashes on a mandala, or on the nervous face of a straight. The fog and drugs filter out precision, leave a mood, an apocalyptic premonition.

### GUARD BUYS AD TO RESTORE IMAGE

**Washington, Aug. 30 (AP)—National Guard officers have hired a Madison Avenue advertising agency in a $50,000 effort to counter criticism of the Guard's performance in recent big city riots.**

### NO MORE HEROES

**American youth has no heroes. More than 50 per cent of U.S. youngsters, 16 to 23 in age, hold no living American in high regard. That statement is based on a Parade Magazine poll of 2,100 young people.**

### BAD SPOT FOR BIRD NEST HAIRDO

**Sunderland, England, Aug. 29 (Reuters)— Sea gulls attacked a woman at a bird sanctuary near here yesterday, apparently mistaking her new hair style for a nest.**

In the mornings before the fog came the Haight was straight and bright. That was the best time. Then the gray vapor would move across Golden Gate Park like liquid in slow-motion photography; it would curl up over itself from the fog belt of the Sunset District, penetrating through the branches and leaves of the trees topmost on the hills and pouring itself down on Parnassus Avenue where the rich hips lived; it would move up Haight Street following the trolley bus wires. The low sky would promise the coming of a hard, hailing summer storm, for the fog would bring wind and it would be cold. There was no storm. Never. Yet people adjusted their coats against the rains that would not come until October and tried to make images of the lights refracted before them in the fog.

There were reports of bats dying of unknown causes in the Carlsbad Caverns of New Mexico and of people dying of known causes in Vietnam, Nigeria, Detroit, and Bolivia. These were the reverberations from the other side of the fog, the mountains and the sea, wicked emanations from the world of Maya, from the oneiric life of American illusion. The prophets, the seers, and the magicians of the Haight knew that on their side of the mountain, where the fog blinded people from distraction, it was the center of the good vibrations, the creative energies, the self-effacing self, the cosmogonic infinity.

The morning vibrations were low frequency, loose, elongated curves. They undulated their flat waves through sunshine to the gates of Golden Gate Park where Haight Street ends. The gates are not gates but two stone columns; on top of each would be a young man, stretched out naked to the waist, taking in the warm rays. Beyond them in the center of a small, grassy incline—a natural amphitheater—would be Ashleigh Brilliant. He would be standing on a wire milk-bottle container. Next to him he'd have a shopping cart with the amplifier and loudspeaker for his power megaphone. A twinkly-eyed man with a beard and a frowzy head of hair, this was his place in the park and he'd be there every day, entertaining, selling his song book and the long-playing record of himself performing.

He was supposed to have a Ph.D. Everybody in the Haight has credentials, academic, military, or genealogical. Astounding numbers of the kids visiting for the summer were the children of chairmen of the boards of the largest corporations, the most successful lawyers, the richest stockbrokers. The same myth used to circulate about the down-and-outers on skid row; they were *must* material for every Sunday supplement around Christmastime.

Ashleigh had to put up with a degree of heckling from his indolent morning audience: a girl with an ocelot, seven or eight black winos, a girl with a police dog, fifteen or twenty dozing hippies who had probably been up all night because they couldn't find a place to crash, a girl with a Russian wolfhound, twenty-five or thirty tourists with cameras, a girl with a Spanish water spaniel, a miscellany of lawn-frolicking children, a girl with a weimaraner, two teen-age boys with one kitten, and a gossip of scandalized and aging Irish ladies on a more distant bench.

"Do you know what happened to the hippy who crossed IBM with LSD?" Ashleigh asked, and then paused to let it sink in before he answered. "He went on a business trip."

The winos booed; the tourists took pictures; the ocelot clawed the ground; the children laughed and the dogs sniffed. "All right, all right, I'll sing a song," Ashleigh said, and he did:

### IT'S A NARK
(To the tune of the Lone Ranger theme from the William Tell Overture)

*"It's a nark, it's a nark, it's a nasty nark,*
*If you've got any pot, better keep it dark;*
*To and fro let him go up the wrong tree bark;*
*It's a nark, it's a nasty nark."*

The black winos booed some more and some of the hippies woke up to groan. "What can I do to make you part of the group?" Ashleigh asked them, and they shouted back at him, "Turn us on, turn us on."

"I'll read my poetry," the entertainer responded. "I call them unpoems. Each line is a separate poem:

*"Congratulate me, I don't love you anymore.*
*A man could grow old waiting for his life to end.*

**15**

*Why don't you take this life home for a few days*
*and see how you like it?*
*How can I possibly respect anyone who respects me?"*

Beyond Ashleigh was a small pool where children splashed; on good days the community-minded hips would come with nets and shovels to clean its bottom of beer cans and refuse. Beyond the pool was a field where on this day five Catholic priests in mufti played touch football against five long-haired hips. Looking down on them from Hippy Hill several hundred people lay on the grass, catching the last of the sun, playing bongos, and smoking pot. A happy morning scene.

Most of the hip population slept the mornings out, but the straights in the neighborhood arose to the harmonics of the good morning vibrations and did their straight things, like going to work, cleaning house, and playing ball in the park. Probably more than four-fifths of the thirty thousand people making up the Haight-Ashbury were straights, half Negro and the rest whites, too old and too rooted to move to the suburbs. There were also a few bohemians and university intellectuals who had gotten there before the young people called hippies.

Miles away in Oakland, the phone was off the hook in Papa Al's pad. He usually slept until noon. He wouldn't drive his big Chrysler back across the Bay for hours yet. Then he'd make his first appearance of the day at Benches or Tracy's or the Free Medical Clinic. In the mornings there would be a sign on the clinic's door: BUM TRIPPERS AND EMERGENCIES ONLY. NO DOCTORS TILL 4 P.M.

Some hip people were up and working early. Peggy went to her store, and this morning Damien was behind the counter at the God's Eye Ice Cream and Pizza Parlor. The sun picked up colors of the mural on the wall opposite him and changed the magic mushrooms and psychotic cacti in the picture into benign, polka-dotted flora, the precious technicolor background of children's movie cartoons. Damien was a Jesuit boy who liked to talk of moral decay and the decline and fall of the Roman Empire.

16

"Tonight's when they're going to do it. They're over in their pad right now, rapping about it, I'll bet . . . waiting for his plane to come in. The moral sickness of our times," Damien pronounced. "I've seen sick hippy scenes before, but these people are burnt out. Oh, weird! Oh, wow! They're capable of any sick, sexual act. Ugh, burnt out, the darkness under their eyes. They're burnt out enough to do something like kill him," Damien declared. The "him" referred to was a New York underground moviemaker who was supposed to be landing at the San Francisco airport that night.

"It was not a typical Haight-Ashbury pad. I mean, it didn't belong in our thing. I'll tell you what it was like; it was sort of like a faggot scene. The majority of them had short hair and they were sitting around mumbling to themselves. Then this guy came in and said that it was definite, the moviemaker would definitely be on the plane tonight. They all brightened up when they heard that. I think they're from New York. They had the New York sickness —leather and torture, smack and people tied down on beds while they stick pins in their nipples. It's the Roman Empire, the decline and fall of. Oh, weirdly, weirdly, and they're so used up. Degenerate. You can tell they're not from the Coast. See, they can't get back into New York. This chick who took me there explained it. I only went there for free acid, but once I'd dug that scene, I got outa there before the acid came on. Ohhhhhh," Damien said softly, sucking in his breath like somebody who had barely averted serious danger, "that scene was too bizarre to take on acid, sitting around talking about killing people."

Howard, one of the co-proprietors of the God's Eye, observed, "People on acid are very suggestible. Maybe they mean it."

"The chick explained it to me," Damien said. "The moviemaker *used* them. Shot 'em full of speed and other junk and then took pictures of them. I guess they were doing all kinds of sex for the movie, which they didn't mind because he was taking them around New York and making all the better scenes with them; but then, when he was finished, he dropped them. They didn't know till then that it was only him, the moviemaker, that got them in; once he was finished with them, they couldn't make the good scenes

17

anymore. They were finished, destroyed. That's why they have this plot of meeting him at the airport. See, he still thinks he's good friends with them. He doesn't know how they hate him. They were sitting there in their pad talking about it, an' what they were going to do to him. They're gonna get and give 'im a lot of stuff—I mean make him take it—and then *they're* going to make a movie of *him*. An' after that they're going to kill him by cutting his balls off—castration! I call that the decline and fall of the Roman Empire. America's finished. The only thing that can save a society which does things like that is plowing up the airfields and growing vegetables on them."

"Well, if they're stoned, they might forget to go to the airport. They could be sitting in their place talking about it for a week. And if they do it to him, he deserves it. He destroys people, that man. Let them cut his balls off."

"Oh, I got outa there," Damien said. "I walked all the way back from the Fillmore, jus' saying to myself, 'Wow, those cats!' "

In the back of a storefront almost next door to the God's Eye, Melanie was cooking lunch in the Radha Krishna Temple of the International Society for Krishna Consciousness. Melanie was a thin girl who always wore a sari, which, with the flower behind her ear, gave her an air of maidenish docility. "Swami said Sam and I had to get married. The red dot between my eyes is the sign of a married woman," she said, working at the Hindu vegetarian dishes she and the other girls prepared when there was enough food.

She once was a Presbyterian girl from the bland and lush northwest, Washington and Oregon, where there are apples and prosperous routine. "Swami says you're not your body," she said, pouring a huge bowl of carefully chopped onions into a frying pan. "Swami says people are foolish to worry about paddy wagons and jails, because they hold your body for a few hours or days even. Swami says we are consciousness," Melanie recited, working on the food that would serve the Temple devotees and the free-loaders who turned up for lunch. The Temple wasn't on Haight Street; it was hidden at the edge of the community near Kezar

18

Stadium in a section most of the young people didn't know about.

While she cooked, she talked about how Swami says we shouldn't take drugs and Swami says we shouldn't smoke and Swami says we shouldn't eat the flesh of any living thing.

Sam, her husband, a purposeful, lanky boy, was at Peggy's store, putting in a new door. He would not go back to the Temple for lunch. "I'm fasting," he said. Sam fasted a lot, for whole days at a time. He was a good carpenter, a Reed College boy, and a Temple devotee who occasionally smoked behind Melanie's back. Sam said he was an ex-speed freak, and that may have been why he gave the impression of spiritual fragility. He acted the way some people do after psychoanalysis, as though if they do anything untoward, their neuroses will come rushing back into them. For an ex-speed freak, he looked healthy and muscular, even if he was thin. In the Haight they say, "There are no ex-speed freaks. Speed is a brain burner."

"Yeah," said Sam, alive and working on Peggy's door, "speed can burn you out, but when I was on it Melanie took care of me. I told her she had to feed me good food. She did. She fed me a lot of meat, protein. You need that if you're on speed. She made me eat too."

Peggy was chattering away at Sam. She got down to the store early because, she said, "I'm on a money trip." But she also liked it in the morning when the street was free of the crowds that were going to make her "rich, rich, rich, I tell you! But did you know I used to skateboard up and down in front of this store on that sidewalk not two years ago? There were so few people then."

It was noon. The vibrations were beginning to tighten. The dope dealers were starting to move about, pushing their old ladies off the mattresses to make them get up and make coffee, the first upper of the day. Those that had the price were making their way to Tracy's, Benches, or the House of Do-Nuts for coffee and a sweet roll. Those without money were thinking up a hustle or going on the street to catch the first heavy tide of tourists and panhandle them.

Several time zones away Useless, as Papa Al called him, probably slept on in Hawaii. There's supposed to be a big scene on Maui. People have come back to the Haight from the islands telling about beautiful people sitting on the bottom of extinct volcano cones, turning on and watching the petrified lava return to its liquid state. Useless was remembered by the dealers for an epic $11,000 burn that paid for the trip to Maui.

"HARE KRISHNA, HARE KRISHNA, KRISHNA KRISHNA, HARE HARE, HARE RAMA, HARE RAMA, RAMA RAMA, HARE HARE," came the chant from the storefront Temple. Little brass thumb cymbals kept the tempo. There were thirty or more people seated on the floor and out the door onto the sidewalk. They sat on small pillows and had paper plates high with food in front of them. Those who came only to eat sat upright, while the devotees bowed forward in piety and listened to the chant on the low-fidelity record imported from India. It was Melanie, seated behind the secondhand record player, who served the food and, in her weak-smiling way, appeared to direct everything. Every noon that the visitors to the Temple could be fed was a satisfaction to her, because "Swami says the Hare Krishna chant has the power to make sure you have enough food to eat and a place to crash. You have to chant it, of course, and must believe."

John Burrell, the young Englishman who was working in a small experimental theater nearby, glanced through the Temple windows on his way to a cup of coffee at the God's Eye. He saw them on the floor, holding the plates up to their chins and putting the food in their mouths with their fingers, young Presbyterians discovering the tactile senses.

"Rice Hinduism, that's what I call it," John pronounced. "Around here it's either a rock dance or a pagan ritual. You know, really—these laughable attempts to reach the cosmos. My God, they're so superstitious. If the stars aren't right you can't walk down the street. When you meet, they don't ask you your name. They want to know what sign you were born under. Libra, Cancer, Sagittarius! It's like ancient times. You need an augur to get anything done around here. It's like Thailand, no business can be

20

transacted until an astrologer's been consulted. I don't know if any good can come of this. America may have gone too far this time."

Damien bent over the counter to listen to the Englishman's analysis: "I'll admit I've taken acid a few times. I feel it's sort of, well, indicative, you know. I've seen a few things, but the people here turn on all the time. They're lethargic; they lack incentive, and if they have any, it's all askew. I'm as concerned as anyone else about learning what can be done toward realizing one's self, but through the theater, using sound and film and light to blow people's minds, not some damn chemical."

"It's too late, too late," Damien announced. "Either we destroy the structure quickly or it will destroy us as it comes down. Take the air bases, plow them up, and grow food on them."

"What the hell are you talking about?" John asked.

Damien blinked.

"See, they talk like damn soothsayers."

"You would too if you knew what I know," said Damien. "It so happens a special plane is coming in from New York tonight, and when it arrives a horrible, degenerate, revolting, disgusting crime is going to be committed."

"Oh, repent yourself," John retorted.

The first fog appeared in the blue. It was so dark, so separated from the washed sky, it might have come from a fire on the other side of the mountain. It had not yet blocked the sun from the God's Eye, but it cast its shadow over the house on Ashbury Street where Pigpen and Captain Trips looked out the window at the foreshortening day. The two most famous members of The Grateful Dead, the Haight's best-loved rock band, withdrew from sight, but one of their managers, Rock Scully, went out to catch the sun and caught the quickening vibrations.

Rock and the Dead were there at the beginning of the Haight, the memoried first months of the dope movement, Ken Kesey's Acid Tests, the Trips Festival, and the great Human Be-In, when, they say, thousands and thousands came. It was only three years ago and already people bragged about it like old Bolsheviks must brag of having been at the Winter Palace; and already people were lamenting that something had gone wrong with this revolution too.

But before Rock had been in the Haight, he'd had to go to many other places. He had to go to Earlham College, spend two years with the Student Nonviolent Coordinating Committee (Snick), had to study philosophy in Switzerland, and get arrested for taking part in the civil rights demonstrations against the Sheraton Palace Hotel and the franchise holders on auto row along Van Ness Avenue. "I served no real purpose in those demonstrations," he has decided. "I spent a good part of the summer of 1966 in jail, and I didn't serve any real purpose there, either, except I could listen to the colored prisoners talk about Malcolm X. I was in jail with one very militant young cat who's opened the Black Man's Free Store. I can remember the judge telling him he was a black son of a bitch."

Rock was up in the morning. He and the band, The Grateful Dead, would be leaving soon, not to return till the fall. Until they went, Rock emerged on the streets in the morning during the hours of the friendly vibrations. Then he could half walk, half skip down the hill to Haight Street, walking along it without bumping into people, hailing his friends, stopping to chat with the ones who were there before the place became an international byword.

"Actually," he said in a cheery tone that never deserts him, even when he talks about his disillusionments, "the band is a partnership, five musicians and two managers, and we've been in the neighborhood four or five years. About three years ago a bunch of us discovered LSD and the psychedelics [at least one member of the band doesn't use dope] and we learned what it was like to feel community and take care of our brothers. At that time there were about fifteen houses in the Haight with young people living without parental supervision. A lot of them were on hard drugs, but then something happened and we found what we called 'getting together.' Ding! Everybody was really excited then. San Francisco was a party town then. Everybody was going to parties in these big old three-story apartment buildings and the big band was the

Charlatans. They were the originals. They played the first dances at the Longshoreman's Hall. Then we threw some dances at the California Hall with the Jefferson Airplane, and it was about then that Ken Kesey came to town with the Acid Test. Ding! Do I remember those days. Ding! Going from the Fillmore Auditorium and back to the California Hall. Ding! It was crazy. Sometimes I really thought the floor was going to fall through with two-thirds of the people high on LSD.

"But we just can't keep up with these kids now. We were pioneers in LSD. We took it very sparingly. These kids coming in here now drop it two and three times a week and go a little crazy. When we started, we read about it, talked it over, and tried to get into each other's heads. We didn't just take it anywhere but in the surroundings we were most comfortable in. Even with the Acid Test, when you had lights and drums and bells and paints, you did it so you could work and play together all night long. Right now I can't imagine taking acid and going to one of those shows. The Grateful Dead used to play high on acid, but under the present circumstances we couldn't get in contact with each other.

"Ding! I remember. Ding, ding! The event that pulled a lot of us together was the Trips Festival [October 1966]. A thousand people were there for three days, all the rock bands, all the light shows, the San Francisco Mime Troop, the Committee Theatre. They were there to interact and grow together. It isn't true that people like Timothy Leary were listened to. They weren't . . . ever. We went back to the neighborhood here bound and determined to make it a better place. After that we started our friendship with the Diggers and helped them take care of people and people began to pour in. Ding! Just a few weeks ago it looked like there was going to be a riot—so many new kids, not knowing themselves or anybody else—so we quickly got a truck and put the band on top of it. Then we drove down Haight Street, right where the people and the cops were. We drove and the people followed until we led them into the park, where we had a dance. We went to New York. Ding! We played in Tompkins Square, where they'd had a riot the night before; but this time the Puerto Rican kids jumped up on the stage and started dancing instead of throwing rocks.

"The Grateful Dead went from being an acid band to being a community band. We just refused to go the route of the Jefferson Airplane. [After the Airplane took off from San Francisco it became so successful that it's now doing singing commercials for network advertising.] We held out for a long time before we signed a contract with a recording company, a whole year we held out. Finally we signed with Warner Brothers, but only after we got artistic control, and that's something San Francisco groups don't do. They sign. Ding! Money. Ding, ding!

"Then our band started falling apart. We'd been working all the time for free, and bands like ours that compose so much of their own music and style have to spend of lot of time alone together. Anyway, we've been driven out of our community. At the beginning of the summer we thought we could stick it out, but here it's just started to be July and the place is full of dope pushers. They have a cover charge at the Drogstore! Imagine! Fifty cents for a cup of coffee here in our community! Tourists all over. We used to be able to walk down the street and see our friends. We could be concerned about the neighborhood, help keep it clean and try and improve it, but now the sidewalks are full of these Tenderloin types. The only thing I can see to save it from its collective head is for us to withdraw for a while.

"We have to get out of here to keep our heads. Since the summer began our doorstep has been littered—there's no other way to describe it—with every kind of freak. I can't use the word hippy. I was a hippy, but I don't have anything to do with what's going on here. We used to have one cardinal rule: Do not impose your trip on anyone else. Well, that's what these people are doing, and we don't want to go on their trip. Our neighborhood worked until the newspapers shot it up, and then the kids and the tourists came and imposed their trip on us, a sidewalk freak show. If it were a festival it would be great, but it's just another form of cruising up and down in your car, putting on a show bumper to bumper.

24

"Ding!" Rock said in a voice that, for him, sounded woebegone. "We were happy and we were making other people happy, and as we saw it we were building an alternative society, a little one, here. We'll come back in the fall and start all over again. Maybe we'll have another big powwow like the Trips Festival, but, I don't know, the city's no place to take drugs."

But the nation thought the Haight was a festival:

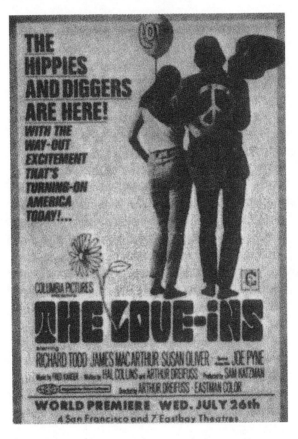

If the Love Generation, platonic, sexual, or political, was easy to announce on the billboard, it was harder to find in fact, though God knows there were enough reporters sent looking for it. *Look, Cosmopolitan,* the *Saturday Evening Post,* the *Atlantic Monthly,*

25

the *Nation, Playboy,* the *New York Times,* and the *Washington Post* had their people searching and sending back the word, and every word was different. Arnold Toynbee and the International Boy Scout Jamboree, Senator Charles Percy of Illinois and Governor George Romney of Michigan, Dame Judith Anderson and the Beatle George Harrison, and nuns and radicals and conservatives and tourists in cars and tourists in campers stuffed with Coleman lamps, refrigerators, and canasta sets for life in the woodsy wild, came to watch, to pass judgment, and go away. It was, they said, the salvation of the Western world, the ruin of the Western world, a conspiracy, the incarnation of the gospel or its profanation, the degraded degeneracy of youth—no, it was an ascension to a higher plane. They announced it was the same old thing, youth in rebellion, youth going through its phase of alienation; they proclaimed it was utterly new, the first epiphany of the leisure society.

Every day there came new, fresh, and famous faces. One Saturday afternoon it was James Goddard, head of the Food and Drug Administration in Washington. The rumor was out that the next drug to be introduced to the psychedelic market would be named FDA. His presence brought more than the regular group of doctors to the Free Clinic, new physicians who wanted to shake an important official's hand and others sniffing out the grounds for research grants. The corridor and the little rooms of the apartment which was the clinic were crowded with them, with kids looking for treatment, and with paperozzi of the mass media, reporters asking questions and cameramen backing up into people, squinting into their viewfinders and making their Nikons go click-whizz, click-whizz. The clinic's young director, Dr. David Smith, was this week's psychopharmacological news out of the Haight-Ashbury. Assignment editors all over the country had him down on their clipboard schedules.

"No, I'm not disturbed by the lack of tile and chrome," the important visiting doctor from Washington said, responding to proud apologies for the make-do equipment, the scarred and nicked proofs that the clinic was a front-line dressing station in

26

the youth war. "I've practiced in small towns of five hundred people and made deliveries under worse conditions," Goddard said.

They guided him into a back room, where one of the doctors told Goddard, "I'm amazed to meet you on Haight Street."

"That's where the action is." He had mastered the idiom, but it wouldn't do to sound too hip, so he added, "This is a major problem in our society."

Everybody nodded. Even White Rabbit and Kelly, who had slid into the room because they had business with Goddard too.

"Does this business of acid imprinting itself on RNA mean passing it on to your children?" Kelly asked the man the doctors were treating as the last word and highest authority.

"Well, it could happen. It's only a hypothesis at this point, of course, but there are indications, very definite ones."

"You mean people might be born stoned?"

"That's one way of putting it."

"Hey, that would be a great title for a movie. BORN STONED, starring who?" Kelly wanted to know.

The doctors who had come a-courting looked annoyed at the two young hips. "Another area of investigation that might be done is the effect on children whose mothers took LSD *during* pregnancy," a psychiatrist shot in.

Kelly didn't want to sabotage—he never did—his weapons being his looks and his charm, so he said, "If the kids find out you're doing studies like these they'd cooperate. I think we could even get them to take special doses . . . for science."

"Run some tests on the aftereffect of Acapulco Red, eh?" Goddard said, trying to swing with it.

"Gold. It's Acapulco Gold," White Rabbit corrected the doctor, who was mixing up the slang names for different kinds of marijuana.

"I mean Panama Red," Goddard corrected himself, as he worked, a little ill at ease, to fill his pipe. "I gave up cigarettes four weeks ago and I haven't gotten the hang of the pipe yet."

"Everybody's got some kind of dope," Kelly and White Rabbit said nearly in unison.

27

"You're nearly right. There were ten billion amphetamine and barbiturate pills manufactured last year, and though we don't know how large a percentage has been diverted into illegal channels, it's a lot. Perhaps as much as half. One of our major jobs is to stop it."

"Wow! Outa sight," White Rabbit exulted. "The whole country must be stoned."

Kelly immediately asked, "Doctor, did you know there's marijuana growing around the Golden Gate Park police station right now?"

"No, I didn't, but abuse isn't confined to Haight-Ashbury hippy groups. We find middle-class women, mothers, introduced to these drugs through weight-reducing programs."

"Have you ever tried marijuana?" White Rabbit wanted to know.

"No, I haven't."

"Well, why are you knocking it?"

"I'm not knocking it."

"Have you ever tried acid?" This last from Kelly.

"No, I haven't."

"Then how do you know it's no good? How can you tell?"

"There have been a great many studies on it, and there's not much to make us believe it has any therapeutic use."

"Well, don't you think you, somebody in your position, I mean the man in charge of all the dope in America, ought to try it?"

Goddard was puffing on his pipe, enjoying White Rabbit and Kelly more than the doctors. "No," he answered. "I wouldn't take it. I wouldn't try it because there have been many bad trips with people my age. You see, as you grow older your character, your personality settles. A drug like this one, which seems to affect personality, can have very adverse effects. But that doesn't mean I can't know about LSD. I've never been an alcoholic but I've treated them, though I concede I might have a far different understanding as far as its intensity is concerned if I had taken LSD."

One of the doctors inserted himself in the conversation to say, "I'm an internist with a middle-class practice in Los Angeles. I've started asking my patients about their drug consumption and I'd say about one out of six tell me they've taken at least one of these exotics."

"There!" White Rabbit let out. "Do you really think you can shut down LSD?"

"No, it's too diverse. We can't shut it down completely," Goddard replied. "As a society we're becoming rather hedonistic, and I think we'll continue that way for the next three decades, so there will be more and more use of chemical agents for pleasure. I think we all recognize that."

The fog destroys the afternoons and turns them into a protracted, blackening dusk. The street turns dismal. The tourists in the Gray Line buses have gray-lined faces. They're nervous. They paid to look, not participate, but they're being involved: the hippies hold up mirrors in front of the bus windows so the people must see themselves. It got so bad the guided tours were stopped, because, as the young lady in the office said, "The natives were getting too restless." But the national surrogates of personal tourism, the photographers, stayed. They picked their shots and cut them carefully to present a picture of Haight Street that was a tumultuous fauvism of color and free form for the magazine covers and the television tubes.

Haight Street was a gray, foggy street, which made the brightly costumed people stand out because they were so rare. White Rabbit stood out. He selected the material and designed his clothes; sometimes he sewed them himself, sometimes he got a girl to do it for him, so he looked like a singing pirate in an old MGM flick. Mike went through a period when he stood out. That was when he dyed his hair a startling blond and walked the street clad in the vestments of a Catholic priest, triangular, folding, rich cloth of gold and white, emblematic of double feast days of rejoicing, beneath which he kept his grass. When Apache wore his wedding clothes he looked colorful enough, in his tan and tassled, high-topped soft moccasins, blue corduroy pants, and lacy white blouse, over which was a wide necklace of Indian beads. But most

29

of Haight Street lived in secondhand blankets, cast-off army coats, jeans, thick sweaters with pulled-out loops; a refugee camp in which the long hair on the males is only picturesque if you live in the land of the crew cut. There was jewelry, cheap bibelots good enough to flash on when you're stoned and colors glow with luminous intensities straight nervous systems can't register. The Haight was a show, but not a light show of colors like the ones at the rock dances. The Haight show was emotion and mood, the invisible and varying frequencies between people.

The phone was back on the hook in Oakland. Papa Al was in the Haight, standing in front of Benches talking to Big Tiny and Joe Morningstar, the handsome Hell's Angel. "Joe, you're not very smart, but you can make a living some way besides rolling queers."

"Why would I roll a queer?"

"Yeah, why would ya? I hear you an' Big Tiny rolled that queer you stomped the other night."

"He hit me. He hit me three times before I stomped 'im. I told the queer he shouldn'ta hit me. After the third time, I stomped 'im."

"Didn't he hit ya because ya rolled him up in the Jeffery-Haight?"

"I didn't roll 'im."

"Figured he owed ya, 'cause ya let 'im blow ya? That it, Joe? You're a great boy, Joe, a credit to all of us."

"I want to buy a dirty book," Joe said, and the three of them moved a few feet into a store that sold them on a rack. Joe busied himself looking at the dirty pictures while Big Tiny, the bikeless street commando who sniffed and fetched for the Angels, complained, "I don't know what to do, Papa Al. My old lady doesn't ball; she doesn't have sex with men or women."

"Why don'tcha ask Joe if he wants to be your old lady?" Papa Al suggested, and then, zipping up the little waist-length jacket he usually wore, walked back out onto the street to catch a kid he'd seen moving by the door.

"What's up?" Papa Al asked. "Selling anything good?"

"Just these," the kid answered, and showed a fistful of large white tablets daubed with splotches of red vegetable dye.

"How many mikes?" Papa Al wanted to know.

"Ahh, I dunno. They'll get ya off, I guess. I don't know how far. Haven't had any complaints. They're not a burn."

"No, I know. You wouldn't burn anybody. What are ya selling 'em for?"

"I'm asking two-fifty."

"What are ya getting?"

"There're people around here who'll pay two-fifty."

"Gimme a sample, will ya?"

"Sure, Al," the kid said. Papa Al took the tablet and dropped it inside a little transparent plastic bag, which always contained a selection of other samples in a variety of different-colored tablets and capsules.

Larry Burton caught up with Papa Al on the street. He'd come over from the other side of the Bay where he worked as a computer programmer. Since he was busted for dealing, Larry had cut his hair, taken off his beads, and gone to work. Everybody in the Haight does it. When you see a guy with a haircut, that's the first thing you ask him. "When d'ya get busted?" Larry wasn't dealing anymore, but he couldn't leave the life alone.

The two walk together, the fast-frequency vibes of night beginning to skip and dart on the street. Around them tambourines chunk, quick and metallic, a steely sitar hums. There are offers to sell dope, paper flowers, bits of jewelry—and the young beggars: "Got any spare change? Any spare change, mister? Gimme a quarter to support my habit. Gimme a quarter to get a haircut. Ruin the economy, demonetize it, give your money away to me." The traffic is bumper to bumper. It takes an hour to drive the six main blocks on Haight from Masonic to Stanyon, so the underground newspaper vendors can go out into the street to coax the tourists to roll down their windows and buy.

"Get your *Berkeley Barb*. Soaked in opium. After you read it, roll it up and smoke it."

Papa Al and Larry pass recessed stairway entrances to the flats above the stores. There are newly installed aluminum grilles on many of them to keep off the lounging street hippies, who sit wherever they can and pass time without demarcation, looking without focus at the ambling crowd. They sit barefooted on the sidewalks with thin sticks of smoking incense stuck in the crack between their upper incisors, or they toke on joints or exchange grapes and french fries. The tourists aim their cameras and filthy Beast jumps at them, making his animal noises. Drop acid, and then take a walk and look at them; they'll melt and turn into birdlings, enormous pink mouths, straining young maws out of which grow trembling, sharp tongues. Give them anything, feed them, they'll put it in their mouths.

At the God's Eye, Damien has news: "They're going ahead with it. The chick who knows them phoned. She's with them now."

"It's a terrible thing," said Charles, an older man who seemed straight but was wearing hippy beads. During the day he is a salesman; but now he was making a God's eye design while talking to a very young-looking chick and throwing an occasional comment back to Damien.

"I turned on my mother," the chick told Charles. "I sat her down, put a joint in her mouth, and said, 'Mother, you'll never know where I'm at till you smoke this.' So she got stoned."

"That's like me," Charles agreed. "I got loaded so I could communicate with my daughter—fourteen years old. I don't know which world I'm in. I'm in a schizophrenic position. During the day I'm a hotshot salesman, then I come here after work and put on these clothes. I've taken everything they all take so I can understand them, but this is degeneracy."

"That's right, America's over," Damien chipped in. "We're in a breakdown situation. This is the decline and fall of the American Empire."

"I don't know what's going to become of us. There's no communication between parents and children. Occasionally, I can put in a word with her, because I've done it. So she listens to me a little. Well, she's still just on grass—I hope. I allow her two reefers a day until school starts, then she's gotta cut it out," Charles said, and, taking up his partially completed God's eye, walked out the back.

"Dirty old man!" hissed Damien, squinting through the black hair that almost covered his eyes. "What bullshit. He just likes those young chicks, that's why he's here."

Night and the armed private guard arrived at Benches, the cavernous pizza parlor, at the same time. The Angels hang at Benches, and the guard is supposed to keep order. Some nights the Angels don't show, but the street commandos are always there waiting for them. The commandos brag to each other how close they are with Chocolate George, or how Hank always asks their advice and St. Louis wants them to help break down his bike, and Joe Morningstar has promised they can make the next big run with the Angels down to San Diego—if they can get a bike.

Tonight they stood in front of Benches as always, waiting. The gunning acceleration of a bike could be heard in the stalled traffic. A biker made S's around the cars, drawing abreast of the commandos, but it was a Gypsy Joker. The Jokers don't hang at Benches. The Angels are supposed to have driven them out. The Jokers hang at Compton's, down in the Tenderloin. At Compton's there are guards too, who watch the Jokers move from table to table, coffee mug in hand, and make sure the drag queens don't occupy space without buying.

Another bike went by, but it was just a bike. Its rider wasn't wearing cutaways and didn't have a club insignia. He had a nice bike, though. The commandos told each other they knew who the guy was and how they could burn the bike, that it was okay to burn a bike that belongs to somebody who isn't in a club.

The Angels came. First one alone, then two more and a space, and then a flock of them, seven or eight. The commandos surrounded each as he dismounted. They were like soft, quivering blood cells engulfing an enemy germ. Joe Morningstar shrugged; St. Louis joked with them; Hank was courtly, but Chocolate George was friendly. Chocolate was everybody's favorite.

33

After the Angels had gone inside, the lesser commandos shaped a circle around the bikes, admiring their grotesquely high handlebars and the A-shaped chrome frames, called pussy holders, that angle up obtusely from behind the leather saddles. The commandos didn't touch anything.

The waves of the night vibes oscillate sharply. At the God's Eye, Damien said, "It's eleven o'clock. The plane's landing now."

Night vibes are high frequency and short. Their waves break into particles. They beep a warning violence. The gentle ones vanish. Now the Haight is a freak show, a street of poisoners, killers, geezers, burn artists, sadists, beggars, and thieves.

> **"Man has the capacity to be more than a flower-picking primate."—Dr. Sidney Cohen, psychologist.**
>
> —*San Francisco Chronicle,* August 27
>
> ### HIPPY PUSHER IS DEATH TARGET
>
> **San Francisco, Sept. 5 (Chronicle)—Police raided a Haight-Ashbury hippy pad last night on a tip that a juvenile pill-peddler had been marked for murder there.**

The random air of lunacy. There is Ashleigh Brilliant, standing in a Haight Street doorway, telling passersby, "I'm a human jukebox, put a quarter in me and I'll play." Someone does, and he sings to the tune of "Cielito Lindo":

*Folks are free in Haight-Ashbury;*
*They can live and be what they wanna;*
*Wedding cake gives you stomach ache*
*So the hippies take marijuana.*
*High, high, high, high,*
*It's no dishonor —*
*Phony matrimony's a lousy life;*
*If you need a wife, marry Juana!*

A cop comes along in the passing crowd and cautions Ashleigh, "Ugh, ugh, ugh! Remember you believe in free, free, free. No soliciting." The gesture is lost in the disorder of the street. The bongo players on the steps of the United California Bank carry on. The notes of a lutist mingle with the throaty evocative call of a shofar, the ram's horn sounding the remembrance of atonements which a Jesus-Saves preaching couple are demanding here and now of the sluggish, exuding jell of passersby.

The chthonic madness of the place, the shouts, the chasing, the gunning bikes, the chaotic, occasional screams of girls running drive people into thinking that the Haight is a rare species of insane disorganization, or into finding a ruling philosophy to explicate the zigzaggery of the human water bugs they see at rest and in flashing motion.

The Haight offers plenty of elucidating philosophy: Zen, anarchism, nihilism, Taoism, Jesus, astrology, visions of new social rectitudes. Many of the people who came to write and broadcast picked up these themes and used them to explain why thousands of mostly young people make their endless circular perambulations up and down the six blocks from Stanyon to Masonic. These ideas are important, but they don't encompass what the people on the street do.

What they do, regardless of philosophy and world-view, is deal dope. (Dope, not drugs, is the preferred word.) In fact, they deal so much dope and take so much dope that the Haight-Ashbury could be studied as a unique social experiment: a community in which, de facto, all narcotics laws have been repealed or held in suspension. The Haight is a market in the formal sense of the word, as it is used by professional economists; that is, a place where buyers and sellers come to transact business in a reasonably orderly or institutionalized way. The contacts between buyer and seller aren't haphazard. The buyers know the sellers will be there and vice versa.

Although the business is illegal, it's a publicly recognized fact in the community. Places like the Free Medical Clinic that are not in the trade and don't want to be busted by the police put up

35

signs which read, NO DEALING. NO HOLDING. (No buying and selling, and no having merchandise on your person.)

This truth is reflected in the language of the Haight. Hip people —hippies—are people who know, who cut in, who are in. The rest of the world is straight, a word used by criminals and homosexuals to make the same kind of them/us distinction which exists in every occupation that is especially absorbing and formative of a collective identity: soldier/civilian, politician/voter, doctor/layman. Straight, by extension, can be the dope equivalent to alcoholic sobriety, as in "I'm straight. I'm not stoned on anything." There are conservative and liberal hippies; there are hippies who hate the establishment and are indifferent to it; there are hippies who love money and there are hippies who love love, love free food, free rent, free everything; but if the word means anything, it means a hippy is a dope dealer. It has been applied to so many radically different kinds of young people it no longer has much precise meaning left. Dealing dope is the one thing most of them have in common. An estimate would be that seven out of ten hippies making the Haight scene for six months or longer have dealt professionally—been involved in deals where the ultimate consumer isn't a friend.

The products traded include every kind of dope there is. There are the exotics, like woodrow nuts, magic mushrooms, and opium, but these are quite rare; the uppers and downers, amphetamines and barbiturates, are traded too. ("I want to buy pep peels. You know where I buy pep peels?" the Mexican laborer says, inquiring of the coffee-sipping dealers in the House of Do-Nuts on Stanyon Street.) But the three staples of the market are methamphetamine (usually called crystal, speed, or by the trade name Methedrine), marijuana (pot), and acid, as LSD is always referred to.

The Haight is the acid center of the world, the place where it was first mass-marketed and where it is cheapest and most plentiful. The trade in the other drugs has grown up around it. Without acid San Francisco would be simply another urban drug center, not a national marketplace. Even now, smack (heroin) is cheaper in

New York, and the grass (marijuana) trade in Los Angeles is certainly bigger. Not that it's small in the Haight, where grass is available in five-hundred-kilogram lots (2.2 pounds per kilo, or "key" as they say in the trade).

Business on this scale begins to demand warehousing. There is almost certainly a big storage place across the Bay in Sausalito, and probably three others in San Francisco. They say that private garages are hard to rent because so many of them are being used to store grass. Most of this merchandise is not consumed in the Haight-Ashbury, but by short-haired, straight Americans who turn on for pleasure. (Last year the Customs Service seized 26,313 pounds of grass, probably a fraction of what came over the border.) The curb market in grass on Haight Street is like the Chicago commodity exchange. It fluctuates daily according to supply. Early in the summer of 1967, when two border guards were murdered, presumably by people bringing pot across the Rio Grande River, the price zoomed out of sight and the San Francisco market collapsed. Pot virtually couldn't be bought; but by mid-August stocks were replenished and you could buy it at prices which varied with the quantity of the order and the quality of the grass. For very large orders, decent grass can be bought for as little as $20 a key. This is "uninsured" grass, which the shipper guarantees only to try and get across the border. If it is captured by customs agents, the buyer is out of pocket. Forty to fifty dollars is about the lowest price per key for guaranteed delivery.

The acid market is huge too. People come to cop (buy) from New York, Washington, D.C., Seattle, Minneapolis, Dallas—from all over America. These are local dealers who journey out to buy and then retail back home. Thus the organization of the national LSD market resembles the New York fashion market, the Chicago furniture market, the electrical appliance business, or any business where local dealers come together to make their purchases.

While acid manufacturers appear to want to advertise their product—and have with unqualified success—their illegal status makes them less assertive about themselves. After putting together scraps of information from perhaps two dozen dealers, a certain amount of street skivvy, and a few hints from police sources, you can guess there were probably three to five chemists active in the San Francisco area in the summer of 1967. One was most likely in Berkeley, another in Palo Alto, and a third somewhere farther south. These chemists operated intermittently, or at least products said to come from their labs were put on the market in batches.

In the acid wholesale business, the basic unit of manufacture is the gram. This almost microscopic amount of pure LSD (.035 of an ounce) will sell for around $2,000. Two hundred and fifty micrograms (a "mike" is one-millionth of a gram) is a full dose. Thus this tiny amount, a gram, will make up into something like thirty-five hundred to four thousand acid doses, and a lab turning out enough acid for twenty thousand doses a week is still producing, by bulk, a substance that weighs less than an ounce. From the police point of view, looking for a needle in a haystack must be better. The needle is bigger, heavier, and easier to see.

The equipment for making acid isn't so hard to find, but chemists only sell to one, two, or possibly three trustworthy people. These in turn are just as careful about the two or three people they allow to cop from them, and these people, big dealers in pure acid, aren't seen doing casual business on Haight Street, where it's easy to get a crack at them.

Apparently not all the acid sold in the Haight market is made in the Bay area. One large shipment was referred to as "MIT" acid. It seems reasonable that chemists from other parts of the country sell in the Haight, not only because there is an organized market but also because, in the confusion of buyers, sellers, and dealers, tracing the stuff back to its source is much harder. The lowest figure consistent with the most reliable information would show the monthly acid market in the Haight to be 200,000 doses selling at not less than fifty cents apiece, and there aren't that many hippies in the world.

## LSD "KING,"
## FOUR OTHERS ARRESTED

**Orinda, Calif., Dec. 21 (UPI) — Federal agents raided a suburban home today and arrested Augustus Owsley Stanley III, 32, reputed to be the millionaire mystery man of the LSD industry.**

## A WEED GROWS IN BERKELEY

**San Francisco, Oct. 24 (Chronicle)—University of California police began a search yesterday for the person who planted marijuana in the chancellor's front yard.**

Jerry is an eye bulger. It's not a metaphor. When he talks he purses his lips into a small tulip and pops his eyes out in an expression of awe, intimidation, and aghast astonishment. A year ago Jerry was a salesman for a big soap manufacturing company. "That's where my head was at," he will say, leaning up toward you, laying a delicate index finger across the tulip in a straight line with the cleft of his chin and the point of the goatee growing on it. "Oh, I was straight. Was I straight! Once I slapped my cousin when I heard she was going out with a boy who smoked a joint. That's where my head was at. I was a very good soap salesman. They were going to transfer me to Cincinnati . . . headquarters."

Jerry is still a salesman, but he's switched lines. Now he sells dope. He cops here and sometimes sells retail on the street, or sometimes goes to New York where the mark-up on acid is higher. He uses the same skills in the dope business that he applied to soap. He has enthusiasm and he knows the market: "Pot is selling for $50 a key in L.A., $65 here, $95 or thereabouts in Portland, and you know what it is in Anchorage? *One hundred and sixty-five dollars.*" He doesn't shout when he emphasizes. He drops his voice into a whisper, makes his tulip more distinct, and pops his eyes

39

out further, an effective sales technique. It always seems important, what he has to say: ". . . and it's cool there. They're so straight in Anchorage, if you go up to a cop and say, 'Hey, where can I buy some pot?' he'll direct you to a hardware store."

Like everybody else who's in business in America, Jerry is brand-name conscious: "Once, once, I had a white Sandoz. Oh, oh, I can't tell you. Such acid! So fine! I will never forget that trip. It was the most beautiful trip of my life . . . of course, you can't get them anymore." Sandoz, a Swiss pharmaceutical company, stopped making acid available when it became illegal, but another brand has taken its place, and today Owsley acid is considered the best available. It is so named after Augustus Owsley Stanley, a young man in his early thirties who either may make it himself or supervise its distribution and merchandising. Owsley, despite the Haight's universal faith in him as the world's No. 1 acid manufacturer, has never been convicted in a court of law, and it is possible that the brand bearing his name is actually made by other people.

Owsley makes himself invisible most of the time, but Owsley-brand business techniques aren't. Owsley acid tablets are smaller than most, slightly larger than saccharine. They have been manufactured in three colors: white, purple, and, most recently, orange, if the street consensus is correct. Dr. Smith at the Free Clinic says, "The acid manufacturers do the same thing that the legal drug houses do. They vary the product ever so slightly so they can claim they're putting something new on the market."

Like Westinghouse and Buick, the Owsley brand is out after repeat business by marketing a product that people have learned to have confidence in. Owsley tabs, enthusiastic customers aver, are always pure and always potent. Squibb or Lilly couldn't get more sincere testimonials.

This isn't true of all acid. People have been seen parading around the Haight with signs reading, SYNDICATE ACID STINKS. Gangster, or Mafia, acid is reputed to come from Italy and is believed to be of poorer quality. It, or at least somebody's acid, is sometimes cut with Methedrine, a combination many dealers disapprove of; but tastes in dope range as much as tastes in everything else. There are people who prefer the combination. "It gets you off faster," they say, sounding like the cowboy from Marlboro country.

The Owsleys are also given away as free samples. The stories that pop up in the papers from time to time of thousands of acid tabs being given away to the crowds at free rock concerts are true. Maybe not as much is given away as is claimed—five thousand pills worth twice that figure in retail dollars—but a lot does get handed out. A new dope product is introduced to the market via the same methods used for skin cream, toothpaste, and washing machine detergents.

Most chemists don't tab their own acid. They sell it in crystal or liquid form to wholesale distributors. The wholesalers usually dissolve it in vodka, then color it with vegetable dye and drop it on some relatively inert tablet. Vitamin C tablets are preferred because they are big enough to work with and take the substance well. There are many Haight-Ashbury stories about the surprised looks on the faces of check-out counter clerks who are ringing up a sale of ten or twenty thousand Vitamin C tablets for some cheery young customer. There are other stories about "tabbing parties," the long sessions when the vodka-acid mix is put, a drop at a time, on each of the thousands of pills. By the time the party's over, everybody, owing to the touching of fingers to lips, is stoned. He who's lucky enough to get to lick the bowl is most stoned of all.

Free dope is the customary compensation for tabbing acid. It's one of many instances of secondary business enterprises growing up around the major industry—hardly unique in America where automobile specialty companies cluster in Detroit, steel fabricators in Pittsburgh, and research labs surround Washington. Ancillary, dope-related businesses are growing as fast as, if not faster than, dope itself. You can make a living manufacturing dope pipes, which come in every price range, design, and all colors. (They're used for marijuana, hashish, and, if you know how to get it, opium.) Coming along *pari passu* are dope jewelry (roach clips, mandalas, God's eyes, and so on), special lighting equipment, posters, music, and publications.

Many words have been written asserting that hippies are shaking off the mass-production consumer economy. The better-publicized hippies make statements about their belief in a free world without money. They have started free stores, free places to live; they give away free food. Andrew Carnegie started free libraries and gave away free educations, but he sold steel. Without the profits from the dope trade, few hip institutions could exist.

A national high school grass market of a million is quite possible with a yet larger collegiate and older customer pool. Not bad for an industry which three years ago had no capital, no mass-production equipment, no distribution system, and a product which nobody had heard of. Acid started off even further back, since it was defined as dope—immoral, unhealthy, dangerous, and criminal.

The advertising campaign which sold acid has to be among the great feats of American merchandising—on a par with the building of Sears, Roebuck or the early sloganeering of Lucky Strike. By comparison, look at the history of drugs like marijuana and heroin, both of which have been around for years. With all their money and distributive organization, the gangsters, the chief purveyors of smack, could never get it out of the ghettos and the working class. The same holds true of pot, which remained the dope for musicians, Negroes, Mexican farm hands, and semi-criminal whites until it was incorporated into the acid trade.

The country's advertising agencies have recognized genius by imitating the dope industry's techniques. Dope slogans like "tuned in," "switched on," "where it's at" have been used so much they've lost their freshness. Dope photography, not only psychedelic color arrangements but things like the use of the fisheye lens, is as common. Those silent TV commercials with the distorted, bug-eyed heads coming out at you are doped up too. The art nouveau hand lettering is as distinct a dope trademark as the trapezoid-like Chevrolet symbol.

The dope style is more than empty, inventive facility—the

creativity of the account executive. It carries meaning at many levels. The most obvious has been using it to connect the product, as do automobile manufacturers, with youth and modernity; but like Avis, except more successfully, the dope industry identifies its merchandise with deeper emotions. Avis uses the underdog theme. The dope pushers connect their stuff with nothing less than God, infinity, eternal truth, morality, every soteriological value the society has. They get *Time* magazine to write: ". . . in their independence of material possessions and their emphasis on peacefulness and honesty, hippies lead considerably more virtuous lives than the great majority of their fellow citizens."

There is Jerry late at night, drinking his coffee in the House of Do-Nuts. In the booths and at the counter, all around him are chattering speed freaks and dealers gabbling of money. While he drinks his coffee, his bulging eyes swing back and forth in frightened arcs, trying to pick up the blips of danger. "Man," he says, doing the tulip with his mouth, "I'm a walking dope warehouse an' I've got a thousand dollars on me. I'm afraid to go to my pad, 'cause I think some of these cats in here know what I'm holding . . . Oh, oh, oh, it's a heavy scene all over. There are three cats in a room at the Jeffery-Haight, right now, with three guns. They're passing the word they have dope to sell. They're getting the dealers up there so they can see their faces; then later, they're sending somebody around to them to tell the dealers, 'You're out of the dope business.' Those cats want to take over. They want a monopoly. Heavy scene, man, and did you know there was a $3,000 burn in the Fillmore last night? They burned that guy for his life too. I was in on that deal—that guy went down there to cop for some of us—but I caught the bad vibes and asked for my money back. I've never been burned. That's as close as I've come."

**COUPON GOOD FOR FREE LSD TRIP**

**Copenhagen, Denmark, Aug. 15 (Reuters)— A left-wing magazine claiming to contain a coupon impregnated with the hallucinatory drug LSD went on sale here recently.**

The mass media, in their internal organization and in the types of people they tend to recruit, are ill-adapted to picking up and describing complex social phenomena. This is one reason they became the unknowing means of dope advertising. The dope industry grew up entwined in an important segment of American youth culture, an area of life the media have a very hard time reporting.

Dope was associated with ideas which have no necessary connection with the dope business: the sharing, the search for community, the looking for an alternate way of life, the love and flower-power themes. All of these ancient ideas were revived and revised for present conditions in the early sixties by the radical youth wing of what was then still being called the civil rights movement. The Snick platform of 1963–64, with its idea of building "parallel structures" and forming "the loving community," became the foundation rhetoric for the hippy subculture four years later. Snick, under attack as leprously antiwhite and pro-Communist, went off in a different direction, but people like Rock Scully were profoundly and permanently moved by this social vision. It was they, with musicians, painters, writers, and actors who had had similar social experiences, who first began playing with psychedelics as something other than an obscurantist, mystical sacrament.

This group never dropped out. Its members removed themselves from laws, governments, and social practices they detested; but that was also their method in the South, particularly in the "Mississippi Summer of '64," when they tried to erect a whole parallel society of free people. They failed, but the underlying ideas remained a moving force in the more militant, creative, and free-booting part of the youth culture. When they surfaced the next time, the music had changed from folk to folk rock, and there was acid to go along with the pot. It's worth noting that pot was smoked by some civil rights workers in the South four or five years ago, probably brought there by black kids from the Northern ghettos. It was no big thing, however, and at that time it had none of the social meanings it was subsequently given.

44

The civil rights movement never became a dope scene, and even the early Haight-Ashbury could hardly be considered one. Dope was something you experimented with in connection with doing other things. That's why somebody like Rock was appalled at what happened. "I don't know when or if I'll take LSD again. I'm still learning from the last time I took it, which was quite a while ago. That's why I'm against this machine-gun taking of acid; you can't learn anything like that. It just makes you crazy."

The love and flower-power themes have the same origins. The love ethic—this intense, secular Christianity—was revived and taken over by the civil rights radicals. But there is another side to love. For impotent people without guns or social power, love may be used as an engine of aggression. Martin Luther King proved that, leading his columns in front of the courthouses of the South while they sang, "I love Bull Connor in my heart; I love George Wallace in my heart." It's terrifying to be loved that way.

In time Snick opted for the undisguised tools of power, but the white kids never forgot the devastated confusion you can bring about through the appropriate use of hateful love. It was natural that they should go back North and toss flowers at cops. Cop-loving spread from peace demonstrations to the narcotics squad and farther. The expression of anger with affection—"love through clenched teeth," somebody has called it—was taken up by kids who had no political interests but who seemed to have a lot of difficulty articulating hostility to parents, teachers, or anyone. These middle-class youngsters found a way of letting out their angry emotions—they could say it with flowers. Coincidentally, it happens that these passive-aggressive types, suffering from emotional constipation, are especially attracted to psychedelic chemicals.

Love and acid fused in muzzy associations through these non-political youngsters. They began running around with fluorescent pansies painted on their cheeks, giving the impression that these were intrinsically connected with the dope they were taking. In fact, it was the circumstances under which they were taking the dope that formed their reactions. Before they took acid, they were told they would see the oneness of life, nature's beautiful infinities, and that they would feel a love so great they'd want to worship it. They were told these things in the context of a social philosophy that evolved out of the civil rights movement, and as the first mass wave of acid droppers they reacted just as they were told to.

This reaction relates to one of the properties of the drug: it makes people very vulnerable to suggestion. The dope world knows this, and that's why one of its favorite amusements is programming trips, that is, providing suggestions and stimuli for people who are going to take it. Larry Burton has what some heads call a "trip kit," a selection of music, liqueurs, religious readings, and all sorts of other things used in guiding people's acid experiences.

Acid may make the taker so vulnerable to stimuli that it creates a problem. The brain and the nervous system are overloaded; too much is going in too fast to be sorted out, appreciated, and used. This is one reason why thoughtful acid droppers will often say things like, "It takes me three or four weeks to get all I can out of a trip," or "I never take acid more than once a month." Some users who want to go on a "head trip"—that is, spend the time they're high thinking about themselves—go to great pains to isolate themselves from any stimulus. They will seal up a room to make it sound- and lightproof, and then they'll take their clothes off to reduce the sense of touch from the fabric and lie motionless on a bed.

The first large groups to play with acid had the social philosophy of the pioneers (Rock's group) programmed into them. But by this time the meanings attached to the drug were both proliferating and vitiating. Leary and others had been experimenting with it long before there was anybody in the Haight or the East Village, and they had given the drug its Eastern religious and more mystic meanings. These meanings hung on too, serving to confuse all the more. It was Rock's generation, the artists, the musicians, who truly popularized the psychedelics; but their own genius for manipulating the mass media and dominating the youth culture undid them. The taste and demand for pot and acid increased

46

exponentially; the programming diminished. People didn't prepare themselves for dropping it; they didn't take it within the bounds of the little millenarian communities of the Haight or select university campuses; they just swallowed pills anywhere, everywhere, because they wanted to get stoned and see the colors. They overran the Haight and turned the small, ignored, urban nook of a community into an international "scene." They changed its internal organization from a friendly, fraternal barter into a social system based on the cash nexus that regulates any growth industry.

> **There are comets**
> **connected to chemicals**
> **that telescope**
> **down our tongues**
> **to burn out against**
> **the air.**
>
> —From *All Watched Over by Machines of*
> *Loving Grace* by Richard Brautigan

There are two places you can find Bill for sure. You may run into him in a doorway up on Waller Street standing with Sarah, who will have a shawl around her head, peering out of granny glasses, wizened in her early twenties. Sarah says, "Bill doesn't care for anybody. He wants people to worry about him and take care of him. If he cares for anybody, it's probably me."

But the better way to find Bill is at the corner of Haight and Ashbury. He'll be leaning against a light post, one foot on the ground, one foot drawn up under his bottom, flat against the pole. He'll be rapping, always rapping with two or three chicks, dumb little chirpers who are waiting for him to put something in their mouths, little hippy girls passing through, wanting to be stoned. He'll be smiling and moving his head sideways to get his long dyed hair back over his right ear.

Late at night you can find Bill at his place up the hill. Bang on the door and wait. If Jonathan, the carefree dealer boy in the room next to Bill, comes to the door, you can go right in. Jonathan is a heedless one who doesn't believe in narks. If one of the speed freaks in the other room comes, hold up two fingers in the V sign, whisper, "Maintain," say it's cool, tell him you're no nark—he won't believe you, but it may reassure the crazy paranoid while he gets Bill.

Bill takes you down the blueish corridor by the kitchen, where the speed freaks are shooting up, into his room. A couch, a dresser, a mattress, and a TV set. "I could be the only dealer in the Haight who has a TV set—I like to watch the news. I like to watch when I'm stoned. TV's a very fortunate thing, even though it's very plastic, but there's something real about it . . . It's real plastic," he says, searching for a lapel button so he can take the pin out of it to clean his water pipe.

He paws through the wreckage on the floor: butts, bits of paper, pots. Sometimes there's a girl on the mattress and sometimes he remembers her name. He apologizes for the mess. Sometimes he says, "I'm sorry. I haven't had any motherly types in here to clean up," and sometimes he says, "I can't let the chicks clean up because then they kinda get to thinking you belong to them." Sometimes he cleans up and then he's pleased with himself and talks of going to school and living differently. He finds a button over by a book—Kierkegaard's *Ethics*. The button reads, MAY THE BABY JESUS SHUT YOUR MOUTH AND OPEN YOUR MIND. He starts to clean the water pipe. He likes grass better that way.

"I'm twenty-two but I feel old," he says as he works. "Pretty soon I'm going to be twenty-five, then twenty-seven, then you're almost middle-aged. It's easier for me when I'm young with the chicks and the fellows, whichever you prefer." Is it death he fears? Or is he afraid age will end his strange, numbed, anaclitic relationships? "I make money by having sex with men. It's not repulsive. I'm not against it. I don't think I'm gay. I'm not attracted to their bodies but what they can do for me. They can give me an orgasm, which I always enjoy. I would prefer to be bisexual so that I could really dig everybody. I don't think I have a homosexual hang-up. I used to hustle down on Market Street [the San Francisco Tenderloin] when I first got started. I'd turn as many tricks as I could, but then it was my sole source of income. I've slipped off a lot since I've gotten into dope. Now I have three steady customers. One's a professor of psychology at Berkeley who pays me $40 to $60 to go on an acid trip with him and have sex."

Bill enjoys his professor; he talks about him a lot. They rap about intellectual subjects and Bill, with his B.A. from Berkeley (a philosophy major), dies for a chance at serious conversation, living as he does among the mindless teeni-boppers he beds down with. "I haven't read a whole lot in the last year. Reading is hard when you're taking dope for some reason, but man, I like to rap. Philosophy is where it's at for me. I think after a while the Haight-Ashbury isn't going to be enough. What I'm doing now isn't really worthwhile. If I had an M.A. or a Ph.D.—I can see myself teaching, growing old like Mr. Chips."

In the interim, he says, "What I'd like to do is get higher up in the dope business, where there's more money so I'm not dealing on the streets, but even that's better than panhandling. I don't understand that, but people give them money, like the people are almost like suckers." But Bill, with all the trouble he has copping dope to sell, still isn't at the bottom of the business. You can be sitting in his place, rapping, when there will be a knock on his door and a stiffening in the room. In the back of every dealer's mind there is a nark following him.

"Come in."

It's Nick. Pink-cheeked little burn artist. Says he's nineteen, but he's probably three years younger.

"I'm looking to cop acid. They said on the street you had some. Is it righteous?"

"Yeah."

"What color?"

"It's the pink caps. They're good, man," Bill says, and then adds, "But I don't have many left."

"How much?"

"Two-fifty apiece."

"Too much. Look, I've got blue dots I'm selling for $1.75. I know they're not as good as the pink caps, but two-fifty . . ."

"I don't really want to sell. I mean, I don't want to sell all of them."

Nick is trying to cop acid on the side. He's from Daly City and he's in town waiting around for a pot shipment to take back there, where he sells lids at high prices to the high school kids. They talk for a while, but the only deal is that Sarah buys a blue dot to split with a friend. "It's not the best stuff in the world," Nick concedes as he takes the money. The two girls split the pill and drop it, but it's a burn job. There isn't enough acid in it to get a cockroach off.

Then Nick's gone. You don't see him on the streets for a few weeks. After a while he's back in front of the Drogstore on the corner of Masonic and Haight, mewling and carrying on like a frightened dervish. He's burnt somebody else and they're out to beat hell out of him, but he can't leave town because he's waiting to cop again. He is begging Papa Al to protect him. "Go back to Daly City. Do your thing there. What is your thing, Nick? Oh, yeah, selling high school kids joints in the malt shop. Well, whatever's right."

"I can't go back for a few hours, Papa Al. I'm waiting to cop."

"I hope it's a burn, so you know what it feels like."

"I didn't burn anybody."

"Well, who was it? Who'd ya burn?"

"I didn't burn anybody. Chester says I did, but I didn't. He's a liar."

"Aww, go do your thing. Nobody's gonna bother to beat you up."

Dealing dope on Haight Street wasn't dangerous during the summer. Money and merchandise passed openly back and forth and almost nobody was busted, but it was wasteful of time and energy, as it is in all industries where there are too many low-volume independent businessmen. Prices fluctuated wildly, and the cheating among the dealers themselves and with their customers was so pandemic that each transaction had a wild, furtive uncertainty about it.

50

There was always the dream of stabilizing the market, administering prices the way big corporations do. One communal apartment of acid dealers was working to establish a kind of LSD federal reserve, a bank in which seven or eight grams would be stored and released on the market when the price per tab went above $3. There were other schemes too, but every try failed. By the autumn Teddybear was admitting it. "You're asking me why we don't combine. Don't you think we haven't tried? Guess how many times we've tried, but we can't. Too many dishonest, crooked, bad-shit peddlers. There always will be. They gotta legalize it so we can get government regulation."

Teddybear walks through the foggy night toward his pad on Haight Street. It's a famous house, a dealer in almost every apartment. You could get any drug by going door to door knocking, weird junk like ibogaine and nightshade. Teddybear doesn't believe in stuff like that. Like a lot of the dealers he only deals the dope he takes. He likes to ball chicks and stick to grass and acid. He and his partner keep the grass in a guitar case. Teddybear dresses in sandals, wide-wale corduroy pants, and a thick oatmeal sweater, which he gets into like a coat and wraps around his belly. He has a big face and a goatee and bells on a leather thong, which ring as he marches along, rapping about what lovers the hippies are. "Why do I wear the bells? There's three reasons I wear the bells. One, Buddha says they warn living creatures you're coming; two, I like to hear them; and three, they tell me where I am so I don't get lost," Teddybear says, but finally he lost the bells at Chocolate George's funeral.

Teddybear's pad is carpeted with mattresses, and the light is stroboscopic blue with dull white specks scintillating in the air. Everybody's stoned. Some girl's already crashed sound asleep, but one of the guys won't leave her alone. He keeps adjusting her foot so he can paint luminescent flowers on the boot she's wearing. There's another girl, a wan, blonde thing who's putting the glowing paint on a piece of paper while she talks about getting a job as an artist. There are other guys talking away.

51

Loud knocking from without. Enter three angry hips. They've been burned and they want money and vengeance, but the culprit isn't there.

"We'll let a contract out on him," Teddybear says. (The Haight thinks gangsters talk this way.)

"Give us a gun."

"I'm not giving you no gun," says Teddybear, implying he has one, which he doesn't. "We'll take care of this. I'll get the Hell's Angels to take care of this. I'll call Chocolate George. He's a brother of mine. We're all brothers. We're closer than we are to our real brothers, members of the same tribe, true love of man for man. We'll let a contract out on him."

The burned hips leave and Teddybear turns back to lecture: "See, that's why we're forming a brotherhood. This'll be a brotherhood of all the righteous dealers who sell only righteous stuff. We're gonna arrange it so nobody who isn't in the brotherhood can cop, so you'll know when you buy that you're going to get good dope. The Angels have already agreed to help. See, we have our hippy ways, which you don't understand. You think we're gonna kill this burn artist, but, you see, that's where you're wrong. I jus' told 'em that. We do it with love. That's what we did with Lucky. He gave out bad shit. We warned him he wasn't to burn people with more of the bad shit; well, he did, and there was four contracts out to kill him. That's a proven fact. But me and the Angels, we got to him first. We didn't hurt him or nuthin'. We made him take sixty thousand mikes in the three STP capsules, and he doesn't burn anybody anymore. He came out of that trip a beautiful human who only sells good shit now. Ask on the street about Lucky now. Everyone'll tell you Lucky only deals righteous shit. See, that's how we hippy people do it with love. See, that's where society is all fucked up. If they gave acid to people who committed a crime, we wouldn't need penitentiaries."

At Bill's the scene is never like this. It's quiet, the chick on the mattress never talking, the philosophy books unread but remembered, and Bill quietly rapping or casually examining the dreck on the floor. There is a Meher Baba pamphlet near his hand, a picture of the stringy-haired Indian mystic printed on gray paper and something about his being "the avatar of the age," followed by the words, "If God can be found through the medium of any drug, God is not worthy of being God."

### NEWPORT IS HIS
### JUST FOR A SONG

**By John S. Wilson**
**Special to the New York Times**

**Newport, R.I., July 17—The most unlikely song hit since "Yes, We Have No Bananas" swept triumphantly through the Newport Folk Festival yesterday. The song, "Alice's Restaurant," was composed and sung by Arlo Guthrie. For an audience of 9,500 "Alice's Restaurant" provided a climax to the festival.**

There are dope scenes in every city of any size. Through the underground press, through cross-campus contacts, through youth's endless coming and going, the news spreads about what the scene is like.

"Where've you been?" a boy will ask an acquaintance he hasn't seen for a while.

"Maui."

"I hear that's a great scene. Volcanos, palms, and lots of pot."

"It's nothing. There's no grass, only some burn artists hiding out. I came back. I couldn't stand it. I'm going to Denver. I hear it's a very good scene there. Not much heat, beautiful people, no speed freaks, and righteous dope."

In the summer of 1967 the scene was San Francisco, the Haight-Ashbury; in 1968 it may be Denver, although there's talk now of making it London. The acid industry will probably stay rooted in its headquarters, but the thousands of young people who gave the city new fame may create a scene elsewhere.

For there is more to a scene than dope. There is mobility, the adolescent need for locomotion, and this generation is traveling as no other. The automobile of the twenties and thirties gave youth a city-wide range, but the federal highways system, the half-fare youth plans, and cheap bus transportation have increased the range to cover a continent. The proof of the ease with which they can swoop down and congregate any place was the New York Peace Demonstration in April 1967, when more than 200,000 young assembled to march.

The word went out, and those who wanted to came. A second change which made both the New York and the San Francisco scene possible is that the word *can* get out. The segregation of youth in America is now so complete that youth has its own organizations, its own communications system, which can be monitored but not controlled by the adult world. George Gallup reports that American distaste for the Vietnam War may have reached the same level it did for Korea, but the thought of 35,000 collegians laying the Pentagon under siege in 1952 is inconceivable. Youth institutions weren't sufficiently wealthy, independent, or elaborate.

In San Francisco the scene has developed to the point of having its own radio station. KMPX, which all the heads listen to, is Radio Free Hashbury, the only station in the world where you'll see hips frozen in the lotus position in the lobby. The Haight comes there every evening to chat, to ask for announcements to be put on the air, or listen to the music and use the crayons and paper supplied by the management for itinerant speed freaks who have to do something with their hands. Most of all, the Haight comes to watch Tom Donahue, the 350-pound program director and disc jockey who broke with the Top Forty idea to play albums, mostly dope music.

This huge, bearded man with a strand of beads, a sinister face, and a tiny old lady named Rachel, who rolls his joints and takes care of his correspondence, has made a seeming success out of the FM station. The company, he explains while he talks about going to India to sign Mrs. Ravi Shankar to a recording contract,

54

has hit it so big they've bought another station in L.A. Donahue expects the same format of institutionalized dope music and service to the drug community will be used there.

KMPX doesn't yak-yak about dope. None of this "Hello out there, all you dieters," the way Top Forty deejays do. "One thing some of the Top Forty stations do is drug talk, but we don't do it. It's usually alcoholic deejays who do. We don't even use slang. They do because they're looking for the youth audience," says Donahue.

For KMPX's audience, mass-media institutionalization has advanced past cute "in" remarks; it's enough to play the drug music and provide the public service announcements to the hip world. "Listen, if you want to print what's going on here, just print the lyrics of Country Joe and the Fish's song, 'Bass Strings,' " Donahue says, as he plays it on the air. Very acidic, soft and reverberating, a many-chambered path out, out far away:

> *Hey pardner*
> *Won't you put me around*
> *My world is spinnin', yeaaaa*
> *Floatin' all around*
> *Yeaa, you know I've sure*
> *Got this moment down*
> *It's so high this time*
> *That I know I'll never come down*
> *Ahhhh . . . ohhhhhh . . . never come down.*

The big scene is possible because prosperity enables more of youth to live a leisured life and to feel, when they can free themselves of their parents' ambitions for them, a diminishing pressure to complete schooling and get a job. Chronically worried about unemployment, the country is always postponing the time of entry into the job market by keeping youth in school longer and devising more formidable licensing procedures to be a plumber or a microbiologist. These practices favor the creation of scenes. The kids have to be dumped somewhere. They are, as youth calls itself, "surplus personnel," and apparently the nation would prefer them to spend their time in psychedelic playpens if the alternative is upsetting the job market. Another proposal is school all year round; this would confirm what social critics like Edgar Z. Friedenberg are saying, namely that schools are places of incarceration administered like jails.

Both San Francisco and the New York demonstration show a growing complexity, competence, and worldliness in the youth scenes that are being created now. For a long time only juvenile delinquents and affluent playboys on college campuses had scenes. By today's standards they were simple, very local affairs that seldom progressed beyond panty raids and rumbles. The 1950's saw more complicated scenes that were a little less temporary, a little more institutionalized—the surfing scene, the Fort Lauderdale bacchanalia, the jazz and folk festivals with their growing undertow of political and social meaning.

In the late fifties the civil rights movement brought to life the first national, semi-permanent youth organizations that adults could not control. (Organizations like the National Student Association are older, but they've had a good deal of adult guidance and manipulation, of which the CIA episode is the best-known example.) Snick and Students for a Democratic Society both owe their origins to breaking away from adult sponsoring organizations.

Our working definition of youth now includes superlatively well-educated people who have all the skills needed to build or destroy on an impressive scale. People were shocked at the students' ability to outthink and outmaneuver the university's officials at Berkeley in 1964–65; people are astonished that youth could build the Haight scene into a new industry; people are outraged that youth fake out the military and penetrate the Pentagon itself in the face of five thousand soldiers who were, presumably, under the command of practiced Army tacticians. They shouldn't be. A twenty-four- or twenty-five-year-old "youth" with several years' political experience in mass movements, who may also be a candidate for a doctor's degree in chemistry or history, can be a skillful and resourceful opponent.

Other nations have watched their socially segregated youth combine to become a political force, if not a kind of non-Marxist social class. This seems to be a universal tendency in every society as it moves away from regulation by folk tradition. America has managed the change with relatively little friction. Most youth scenes here are mild, centering more on music, dance, dress, and fun than political controversies. Only in the last few years have American youth begun to act like the politicized youth of many European countries or Japan.

"The adolescent was invented at the same time as the steam engine. The principal architect of the latter was Watt in 1765, of the former Rousseau in 1762."* That may be overstating it, but the underlying point is the nut of the matter. The psycho-social creature who is half child and half man is an idea and social fact of datable origin. Once there weren't any adolescents, then they were created; once adolescence was a short period, now it may stretch on to age thirty. The youth culture has been called into existence by glacial social change over at least two centuries. The chances of reversing the direction of things are as good as those of reversing any other kind of glacier. If older people are reconciled to that idea, they can view today's scenes as intense and specialized expressions of the youth culture, serving a variety of purposes.†

It has been suggested that one of the purposes youth culture serves is to give kids a variety of models of social roles and attitudes, which they will need in life but which most families cannot provide because they are too small and the people in them too much alike. Traditionalistic families may inculcate handicaps in their children that membership in the youth culture can eliminate. The favorite American example of this is the child from the immigrant home who does battle against his parents' peasant folkways. But children from families that are too strictly religious, too graspingly materialistic, too culturally square may face the same kinds of conflicts in less obvious forms. Dope pushing aside, the

*F. Musgrove, *Youth and the Social Order*, Bloomington, Ind., 1964, p. 33.
†See S. N. Eisenstadt, *From Generation to Generation*, Chicago, 1956.

Haight scene lasted long enough and became complex enough to teach a young person how to be a model American of a certain stripe.

"We've got our own everything here. We don't need anybody else. We have ourselves, our tribes, and our families and we live in love and brotherhood. We have our free hippy medical clinic. We have our own employment agency. We have our newspapers and we're getting our own farms, where pretty soon we'll be growing our own food. Why, we even have our own police force . . . The Hell's Angels, that's right, they're our police force. You don't believe me? Well, it's true. They've all dropped acid an' they're different now."

It's Teddybear talking. Teddybear, the street loudmouth, frightened petty dope pusher. He's a short fat fellow, always on the street putting his hands around the young chicks, squeezing them up against himself and talking like a floorwalker in a department store: "See how she kisses me back? Heh, heh, I'm a dirty old man, only I'm not, though," he declares in a voice that mixes squeaks and low tones in a way that makes your ears itch.

"I'm thirty-three but I'm young because I'm a hippy an' I'm not afraid to say it. You may not believe me, but I love this little chick," he says, and kisses the little chick. She responds with an oscular gesture that reminds you of a baby's automatic reaction to having his lips touched. "Sure, I want to ball her—you want to ball with me? You want to be my old lady? Yes you do, yes you do—but even if I didn't want to ball her, I'd love her anyway. That's the way we are here, brothers and sisters. She's closer to me than my real family. She knows I'd do anything in the world for her."

He lets go of the girl and starts down the street looking for some particular people who might want to cop acid. He's trying to play middleman for eight grams, which on that day would have been worth about $25,000. But most of Teddybear's deals are fiction, bragging talk, or ridiculous fiascoes, like the time he and a pal were supposed to have been busted in San Diego, when they were asleep in a hearse with $11,000 and a truck full of dope. Half the time Teddybear's out of cigarette money.

"This's my last deal. After I've done this, I'm not dealing anymore. I'm going to devote myself to helping people. I wanta see these poor kids who come here have something to eat and a place to crash. If we don't help them, who will? You know what the straight world thinks about hippies," says Teddybear, continuing to expatiate on the sacrifices he's already made for the common Haight-Ashbury good. "I'm gonna work for Papa Al. He's gonna get some bread an' I'll help him with the kids. I'm changing. The Haight did that for me. The Teddybear you see is only a façade. There's another me whose name is Harold. Right now Harold is a very tiny person inside of me, but he's still there. When you come to the Haight, everybody chooses a name and builds a personality to fit it. I built Teddybear; but now I'm starting to lose Teddybear—thank God!—and some day Teddybear will be dead. I want to keep the good parts of Teddybear. You come here to change, and I think the ultimate change you come here to find is the 'you' that you imagine and the real 'you' merging into one. I don't know, maybe it's all the acid I've dropped, but there're still definite changes that I've been going through since I came here, and maybe the biggest change is Papa Al. He made me stand up and showed me what loyalty and friendship is. That's why I want to help other people now. I really do believe that's my true thing."

In his way Teddybear has sketched the public, institutional face of the first community in America to be founded on making, taking, and selling dope. His Rotarian's gabbling about civic pride and doing good is as self-serving as all chamber of commerce yak-yak, but at the same time there is no reason not to take him at his word when he says he's been able to use the scene to learn and change. The formation of personality in his childhood certainly had not worked favorably for him. He grew up in the blue-collar world of Jewish Brooklyn, but it gave him none of the emotional and cultural satisfactions that ethnic urban neighborhoods gave many people. For Teddybear it was a drab, low-level technical employment, a marriage that didn't work, and a child he wasn't capable of sustaining as a father. The best he could think of to say about his old life was, "I have an aunt who's really flamboyant. She used to hang with hoods left over from prohibition and do 'em favors, like keep their heat under the mattress of my baby carriage."

It was no place and no life to be other than Harold. The strong part of him that wanted to be the flamboyant Teddybear didn't know how to operate in Brooklyn, where he could never be more than the clown at the gang's weekend pill-popping parties.

So he made the scene in the Haight. There he found a jerry-built but temporarily operative social structure. This structure, manned by perhaps no more than two thousand people, was the frame for the changing street tableaux of tourists, itinerant youths, cops, deviants, small-time entrepreneurial criminals, reporters, government officials, parents in search of lost children, soldiers in pursuit of hippy girls, and toughs out after peaceniks to beat up. Teddybear joined the parade on the boardwalk and recapitulated a familiar American theme: the unwanted and the unhappy, the cramped and restricted moving on to find themselves by building new communities. But the Haight was different. It was built where a community existed already, so it sits like one of the cities of Troy, which were erected one on top of the other.

The community's language—dropping out as opposed to climbing up—suggests vertical movement, but the real motion is lateral. The Haight has hierarchies of prestige outside the dope business, but they were not universally recognized and, even where people were aware of them, the distance between top and bottom wasn't great. The major figures—The Dead and Janis Joplin in music, Wes Wilson and Mouse in posters, the better-known Diggers— were more like celebrities or TV stars than commanding personages. They didn't lead, and their very success switched them out of the Haight onto the ordinary prestige ladders of the straight world.

People didn't come to the Haight to learn how to handle the pressures for going up and against falling down. Hierarchical ascent seems to be less and less important. Although much of the place looked like skid row and the people talked about going on the skids and dropping out, their preoccupation was lateral, the problem of fitting in. The predominant movement of people was coming and going in and out. Many more people might have been destroyed by the Haight if they'd come to climb and conquer it. The scene seemed to teach them other kinds of qualities the society needs in its human digits. Some of this comes across quite strongly in Peggy's autobiography. She was one of the first to open a hip store on the street. She expresses the lateral theme, the feeling of luck and hard work, the admixture of poor and rich, the drifting, the impression that the Haight is a mining camp which may stabilize into permanence or disappear:

"I come from a little town in the South. I won't say which because I don't want my parents to see what you write. I've lived all over. I've lived on Coconut Grove in Miami, the French Quarter in New Orleans, and in Greenwich Village. We starved the first year with the store but it was my trip. I worked fourteen hours a day and two jobs to keep it going. This year the store will do over $100,000, and I'm opening another one in Seattle. I can't believe it. I don't really know anything about money except I'm making a lot of it. I turn my inventory over twelve times a year and they tell me that's good. Businessmen get with me like I'm some kind of child genius. I can't give them answers. I just sell clothes.

"I'm not lucky and I'm not smart. I just happened to be on the most famous corner in America. I put my store on a dying street because I knew the Haight-Ashbury would be the next happening in this country. The store was an acid trip. The LSD made me realize I was young, reasonably intelligent, and energetic, and that I should do it because I hated five out of the seven days where I was working as an airline clerk."

The sense of impermanence and striking it rich and maybe losing it just as fast is fortified by the illegal nature of the community's largest industry. Everybody knows people who have been busted and more who are in jeopardy. Even the legal businesses like Peggy's depend on a public taste that can change in a few months. At any time the vein's gold may play out, and this too serves to structure the Haight into a place of coming and going, sideways motion. Thus the community which won for itself an international reputation as rebellious and anti-establishmentarian serves the greater society. America demands portable people, unrooted individuals who can move as technology and economic organization require. The country needs human replaceable parts who may be used in Boston this year and Tacoma, Washington, the next, and the institutional life of the Haight strongly reinforces a life of lateral motion.

Peggy, for instance, is married. Her husband lives and works in New York and sees her perhaps twice a year. It would be unprofitable for either to move. On a larger scale, it could be said that personal freedom, emancipation from the customs of home, hearth, and family, make people more useful in a nation where technological considerations come first. From this point of view, the sexual practices of the Haight have a utilitarian function. They teach the young people they don't need the companionship of the same mates, that people, like tools, can be had and used with about equal satisfaction. In this light, much that is said and done looks less bizarre. The hippy girl is revealing something when she says, "I've decided that from now on I'm not going to sleep with any boy unless I know his name." This is called love, but in effect it just carries the trends in the lives of their parents several steps further. There are no figures, but you can't spend time in the Haight without observing a high proportion of people who come from fractionated backgrounds. The children of servicemen who have spent their lives going from one base to another (for a full generation, America has had millions under arms), the children of itinerant executives and wandering academics, children from divorced homes and children from narrow-waisted modern families that consist of a younger brother and two parents in an undistinguished, air-conditioned high-rise in Queens.

The Haight was a large enough scene, with such a variety of overlapping sub-scenes that it could be used in different ways by different people. Young people came there for things other than dope and sometimes refused it even when in communes where there was social pressure to take it. There was Bernie, in his early twenties, who was like that: "I wouldn't want people to know it, but I don't use dope. I'm afraid of it, afraid of what it might do to me. I came here because my head's pretty badly fucked over by life in general. I want to be here quietly and think things out, and not get my head fucked over some new way with acid."

At a distance, Bernie looks like a kid who took too much dope, lost his incentive for any other kind of living, and then dropped out, but a closer look shows him to be someone in need of a period of withdrawal. He is having a "moratorium" to collect himself, as psychologist Erik Erikson might say. There appear to have been a lot of young people who used the Haight as a place to sit out their moratoriums. A few of them were like Bernie in being total abstainers from dope; but many seemed to think that psychedelic chemicals would help them find themselves. It's a doubtful proposition, just as a scene as exploitive and cruel as the Haight is a dubious place for people with great internal pain and confusion. But there aren't many places for youth to go. The Haight might be considered a social experiment which may be superseded by a better and gentler one.

The Haight was also a runaway scene. Bruno Bettelheim has said that in this era, when offspring are not an economic asset or a form of social security, some parents have an emotional need only for small children and don't want the costly, sticky-to-handle adolescents they grow up to be. Some of these unwanted kids clear out, but their alternatives are usually limited to being dishwashers or joining the Marines; elaborate youth scenes are a different alternative, just as they are for those youngsters who are born out of kilter with their surroundings, who have lived their childhoods with an inner knowledge that they are different, like this young runaway girl talking at the God's Eye: "If I went home, I'd have food and fine clothes, but I'd be lowering myself. I'd have to give up and be somebody I'm not. When I grew up there wasn't a name for it. The word 'hippy' didn't exist, but I knew I wasn't the same as the kids of the other officers on the Air Force base. Oh, wow! You talk about a plastic community. Everything you do reflects on your father—how you dress, anything you say . . . and all the rules and regulations! I knew when I grew up I'd go away and find people like me somewhere. I was what you call a problem child. They sent me to a psychiatrist. When I was thirteen I was considered a hood, even though I didn't hang out with any hoodish people. There weren't any hoodish people around the air base. Even then I felt I was right. I didn't feel it, I knew it. I knew there was something wrong with the society I was living in, but I couldn't put my finger on it. I only found out when I got here."

This girl appeared to have her inner gyroscope in good working order. She had chosen not to adjust; she consciously and deliberately decided the life of Air Force officer's wife or daughter was not for her; at the earliest moment she left home to find the life that was. But some people came to the Haight with the bloodiest, the ugliest wounds of the soul. Tom was like that, suffering from what he knew not, except that it hurt.

He sat in the park one day waiting for the awful free food the Diggers were still giving out. That was in the early part of the summer, before the killings and the great grass shortage, when everything went so badly to hell nobody could deny it. Tom had a crayon picture he'd done which he was interpreting. He drew pictures and dropped acid like a vomiting cat will search the lawn for the leaves of medicinal weed. "The sun here, that represents true life and warmth—the purple and the yellow is the fabric of life. This middle line, I'm not sure about it, but I think it divides clean from dirty. Clean is wholesomeness and dirty is lack of health. The grass there shows that God created the devil, and there in it is a black penis—man and his cannon ever penetrating the circle of human viciousness. That's everything this picture means, I guess."

He was dressed very vaguely like an Indian. He had the headband and beads, and he wore tight-fitting pants like an Indian in the movies. He had a bell and on his feet were sandals. He was loathsomely dirty. It was hard to believe that even in a city he could have gotten so dirty in three weeks. The dirt was on him like the finish of good furniture, applied, sanded down, rubbed, and applied again. You could see how it had caked up, then partially cracked off from the movement of skin, then another layer of dirt. He stank.

There was three weeks' worth of blond beard on his cheeks, but the hair on top of his head told of his origins. The crew cut of his immediate past life hadn't had time to grow out. His father had died when he was very young and his mother had married a Navy man in 1945. He'd grown up in the good, healthy living of the West Coast and the American Pacific: Portland, San Diego, Hawaii, Chula Vista, Alameda, and Seattle. He had that ageless naiveté that some West Coast people have. Sometimes it appears as an irritating, childish blandness, a deficiency of moral understanding, the assumption that everything will work out right and everybody is doing right. In its ageless, sun-browned body, the West Coast mind can't catch hold of the fact of fat-gutted, out-of-condition Chicago avarice, or of a mean, crazy-eyed New York scag-shooter. It made Tom's affliction the worse because he was trained in circumstances where people don't feel what he felt. It confused him, made him silent, suffering those old woes in his new-age body.

He enlisted in the Navy when he was seventeen, got married the next year, and was discharged the year after. "It was a discharge for unsuitability and immaturity, but it was honorable. I was in the Mediterranean on a six months' tour of duty when some things got to bugging me so bad I wasn't taking orders. So they shipped me off to a hospital in Germany, where the doc said, 'You are immature or you're not. If you're not we've got to court-martial you.' Half an hour later he came back and said, 'You're immature.' " Tom's troubles in the Navy coincided with his wife Bonnie's giving birth to a brain-damaged baby, whom "my ex-mother-in-law keeps inside the house all the time because she doesn't want the neighbors to know."

After he got out of the Navy, Tom went to live in West Frankfort, Illinois, Bonnie's hometown. "It was a bad winter. We had a very up-tight financial situation. I did some TV repair work, but then I got picked up by the local police because Bonnie was outside running around in the nude and I was trying to catch her. At the time, I doubted that she loved me. For instance, when the baby was born she could have contacted the Red Cross to get me leave to come home. The police charge against me was dropped. I went to Alton to get a job in the steel plant there, but I didn't. The only job I could get was in a TV shop for five days. They had me there to fix the dogs. It was a bad winter. There were some periods of near-starvation. Once we lived for a week on five pounds of potatoes. It was much worse than anything you've seen, Sharon."

Sharon was sitting next to him on the ground. She was his present wife, a year younger than he, a pleasant-looking young woman with a good figure, who appeared to be badly miscast. Everything about her bespoke the steady wife, living in a slab-foundation bungalow bought with a Veterans Administration loan. There was nothing wild or experimental about her. She must have been with him because she had no other instincts but those of a faithful wife. Maybe at a Saturday night party she'd let the guy next door give her a quick, intoxicated feel, but what her husband was going through had to be incomprehensible to her. She had on a black, buttonless topcoat against the San Francisco weather. It was held together by two safety pins, but she was much cleaner than he. Tom didn't believe in covering up. He said one of the things he'd learned from acid was that coldness was a state of mind.

Sharon was stoned on STP. "She's been up about forty hours now," Tom said. "I think she's beginning to come down. I gave it to her. She has to learn about herself, the way I did. She has to change with me or I'm going to have to get rid of her. I don't think she's learning."

Sharon was very quiet. After Tom had said what he'd fed her, you could see something was with her, a misty preoccupation with notes and harmonies inaudible to the ears of the people around her. But she wasn't in a trance. Every so often, she'd say,

"Where's Linda, where did Linda go?" And then, if Tom wouldn't, she'd get up, acting like any mother in the park, and get their daughter, a two-and-a-half-year-old blonde puffball. The family was broke, but it must have been better than the winter in Illinois. When they'd come down from Hayward, California, three weeks before, Tom had spent the last of their money on the rent for a month's living in a Market Street flophouse. Every day they'd walked or hitchhiked to the Haight, save the one or two times Sharon had complained that she and Linda weren't going to be able to make it; then Tom had given them bus money, which he'd earned selling underground newspapers. For food they scrounged, and came to the park every afternoon at four to wait for the Diggers or someone else to show up and feed them. Some days there would be a hundred or more making that little scene. Despite the verdure of the grass and the grandness of the flaky-barked eucalyptus trees, it looked like a picture of a Pennsylvania coal town during the depression.

"That winter," he continued, "the winter of the potatoes, our second child died. It only lived two or three hours. It was fourteen ounces at birth. That's when I made the decision to go back West. I thought I could get a good job at Boeing, but there wasn't anything but gas station attendant for a dollar an hour. I took it and held on to it and started doing light repairs and tune-up work. I pulled about five raises and worked up to $2 an hour, which is good in the area for that type of job classification. In 1961 Donald was born. He was premature too, only three and a half pounds, but he seemed to be progressing. My hopes for a healthy child were pinned on Donald. I got a new job doing repair work in a garage for $2.75 an hour, then Donald stopped making progress and the doctors started talking about water on the brain. He looked okay to me, and it was going pretty good for us. Seemed like this was a job I could stick with. Then I ran into a small snag about tools and things like that. On June 12, 1963, they were stolen out of my car while we were visiting friends. It was there that the call came that Donald was dead. Bonnie and I sort of looked at each other. The next day she asked me for a bus ticket to go back to Illinois. She left with Viola [the only living child], and that was the last time I was to see them in two years.

"It was another bad time for me. I got an ulcer soon after Bonnie left. I collapsed at work—there's a groove. I don't remember how I got to the doctor's office that time. I was feeling bad and I was financially $3,000 in the red for Donald. Then I got thoroughly drunk, more than once, and I got rid of my ulcer. I know that sounds funny, but it's true. The first night I got drunk I met Sharon in a tavern. There was something about her being quiet that got to me. She was different from Bonnie in that way, but they were both dependent or repressed types, call it what you will.

"Sharon and I got married in '64, and then we had Linda. I was hoping for a boy, but Linda was very healthy. She weighed nine pounds, ten ounces. After that we started having squabbles because Sharon's needs had been fulfilled . . . mine too, I guess; maybe it was my needs that had been fulfilled. She filled the vacuum Bonnie left and I proved I could have a healthy child. I should have been happy. I don't know why I wasn't, but I started to be more of a heavy drinker. I'd drink two weeks at a time. Then Bonnie wrote and asked me to come back. I did, just to see her, and I ended up divorcing Sharon. As soon as I did, Bonnie said to me, 'Get lost, sucker.'

"That showed my capacity for making some pretty drastic goof-ups. After Bonnie told me to get lost, I came back to Seattle, where I got a job as a truck driver. That's how I met this girl in Kansas City. She came out to Seattle and we got married on Valentine's Day. She was nineteen and about half hip. It was another of my goof-ups. We hassled and hassled and hassled and one day the key was on the table and she was gone. When she left in May—was it May? Yeah, May—Sharon and I got together again. We went to Hayward, where I have a buddy from Seattle. He told me about acid when we went to San Francisco one night. I used to feel like most straight types do about drugs and drug addicts. John and I were up all night debating it. Then we went over to the Haight-Ashbury for the first time and sat around and talked some more till about five o'clock in the morning. After that night, I told John I would come back and drop [acid], but I didn't. I kept spending all night in the Haight-Ashbury and taking the eight-o'clock bus home. The next Friday night I went with John and a friend to the Haight-Ashbury. Then we went to a small coffeehouse in the Fillmore, where John met somebody he knew and bought a tab of acid. John told me to head out for home and, when I got about halfway, to drop it and then stop and have a couple of beers. I did and the beer hit me hard, but nothing much happened with the acid. I felt a little color, that was about all, went to bed, got up the next morning and went to work and did a brake job. The boss said it was a good brake job. I decided I'd been burned, but it was really that the effect on me was very serene. I didn't realize it was good acid, but, anyway, the next night I went back and told John I'd been burned. We went back to the coffeehouse and he got me another acid tab, which he said was guaranteed good to get me off. Then he left and this Negro fellow said he could make love to me so I'd like it. Man, when he said that, I needed to motate out of there. There was probably speed in the acid, which didn't do me any good. I found John and told him I was hung-up badly because this guy wanted to blow me. John asked me, 'What do you want to do?' I said I didn't want it and John said, 'Then it's his hang-up, not yours.' Just then, when he said that, I felt the biggest relief of my life, because I knew it really *wasn't* my hang-up, and I'd been scared it might be for fifteen years. Now I knew it was no sweat about that.

"That was a little more than a month ago, the first time I dropped. Before I dropped acid, I could remember back to when I was about five years old. After acid, I can go back to the walls of conception. I've thought if I can search back carefully I can find the reasons for the irrational fears that cause my problems.

"The first memory I have after birth is of a brightness. I don't think it's light. I think it's an emotional memory. Then I have a memory of my real father. He was a kind of a rapper—loud, you know—and I have the impression he was balding. My mom hated him pretty badly. I can remember her having a hate thing about him. Maybe it was because he'd been married two or three times. Funny, I have a memory of wanting to take up for him but not knowing how. [Tom has two brothers and a sister. According to him, his only full sibling, his twenty-four-year-old brother Michael, was in the Kansas State penitentiary serving a term for burglary.] I was close to my stepdad until I dropped, and then I recognized some of his true feelings about my brother and me. He resented Mike and me because we came first and were getting an equal share.

"You want to know about my mom? I grew up to be something of a perfectionist. Mom fed us meals just at certain hours, and you couldn't be late. She didn't allow us to pick up anything on the streets, and she had me into a kind of super-orderly thing. Then she criticized me for being too fussy, and I was doing it to please her in the first place! I connect her in some way with my latent homo thing. Growing up with that wasn't just bad, it was horrifying. You know you're a man and you don't know how to prove it. My mom did something, by the way, when I was four. I remembered this under acid. It was punishment. She set me out on the porch with a dress on and no underwear in front of all the neighborhood kids. My mom was one of the most violent people I think I've ever known. You know, I think she had some kind of sexual thing going with me when I was two. Then she started going out with lots of men. My stepdad was pretty much in the background. He never took a stand or said anything. I haven't been able to connect everything yet, but I think most of my sexual thing has been to prove to someone, or to myself, that I was interested in sex. What do you think? Do you think I'm better now?"

Tom is not typical of the people in the Haight. Even using the idea of typicality or representativeness in connection with people making the scene serves to disguise more than it explains. There are some things about Tom, however, that recur often with several types of acid takers.

Tom has picked up some psychological ideas. Some of them

70

probably come from his brushes with psychiatrists in the Navy, but they are also in the air. In spite of his occupation, Tom is only partly a blue-collar type. He's an example of how far middle-class, or white-collar, training and ideas have percolated down and taken hold of what used to be working-class types. One of these ideas is that somebody who feels as he does is sick in the head and has got to get straightened out. The therapeutic goal is implanted in him, and the method of approach is certainly American middle class. Health will come from knowing yourself. These notions are endemic in the Haight and in the hip world generally, as is Tom's method, which is analogous to psychoanalysis. He decided he could make himself whole by taking acid, which would do for him chemically what an analyst does person to person: bring up bucketfuls of suppressed primary matter.

But the psychoanalyst strives to have the patient bring the material up and discuss it in a way that is progressively more ordered for understanding. In Tom's case it comes up chaotically, and the patches of understanding that appear only induce new fears. Often nothing comes up because Tom is going backward to act out childhood and infancy without the rewards of self-knowledge. He goes back in his acting out when he's not stoned on acid and also, apparently, when he is. The only difference is that on acid he regresses back before conception into the aboriginal, biological stewpot—nothing, the blessed time of nonbeing. Whether acting out this way is therapeutic is a question for medicine, as is the question of the curative efficacy of the drug itself; but the acting-out, regressional drama is common among a certain type of acidhead. Tom is one of a class in this respect. Sometimes the going back is slow and stops at a particular phase of infancy, maybe the phase where that person's troubles began. Others rush backward, as though they could outrun themselves into a state of liberated unconsciousness.

One of the reasons Tom is so filthy is that he has reversed the running of the reels of his life: now he can play with the Freudian bowel movement his Mom wouldn't let him touch. In the hip world, there is great crying out against not only the plastic but the hygienic. Asepsis is condemned as artificiality. But some of the young people called hippies are dirty because they're traveling around the country with very little money and showers aren't always easy to come by; others have a little money and are as clean as anyone else.

Tom describes his mother as being a violent woman. Among his type of acid taker, this is unusual. These kids rarely describe either of their parents as being violent, but then most are more truly middle class than Tom, who certainly has parts of the older wham-bang, shut-up-kid, working-class culture in his background. What he does say that is very frequently said by others is that his mother, not his father, was the vivid person in his childhood. This is not necessarily the father who is too busy making money to be bothered by his children. This kind of father may spend time and attention on his kids, but he's a washed-out figure.*

Tom displays a horrible uncertainty about who he is. He becomes a Navy man like his stepfather and enjoys periods of relative tranquility, but something always happens to make the role he tries to cast himself in more than he can bear. He gets along well enough in the Navy at first, but the marriage and Bonnie's telling him she's pregnant are more than he can handle. His whole psychic house comes down; his career as a sailor is ruined; his marriage is unendurable; he can't hold a minimum job and almost starves. His problem is not that he is pitting himself against an identity that is being forced on him; quite the contrary, he is stumbling around looking for any suit of clothes that will fit. He is willing to take any role that will take him out of his misery. He even suggests that he'd take the homosexual role, abhorrent as it is to him, if it would work, if he could sigh and say to himself, "Okay, that's me. I know now and I can live with it."

This is not rebellion. This is confusion. The people who won't see the difference and chalk off the youngsters making the scene as "rebellious kids, rebelling the way kids always have," are wrong. There *is* a type of acidhead who is rebelling against a strong parent

*Erik Erikson gives something of an outline of this kind of father and his family in Chapter Eight of *Childhood and Society*, New York, 1950.

or set of parents; he or she often seems to be the oldest child,* subject to strong pressures to pursue some kind of high-status way of life. This sort of person is in rebellion, knows it, and can express it unmistakably. He will, characteristically, call his parents "irrelevant idiots"; Tom's type, who are more numerous, ask, "Am *I* an irrelevant idiot?"

The kid in rebellion may have pain, but he also seems to have an outward-going passion that may fasten onto politics or making money, some activity that helps him come to terms with himself. Kids like Tom have pain enough to spare, but they give you the impression of not being capable of passion. They're like zombies, people with deadened nervous systems, people who see themselves as skeletons festooned with flesh. They're like people who never had anybody to love or hate.

So many acidheads give the impression of having been reared by parents who read the Freudian books carefully and tried to see that baby could be anal and oral and genital and gooey; but they tricked themselves and their children. They permissively inhibited their children's senses. The result is a young person who has barbed-wire guts, to use a phrase suggested by Erikson. He's not neurotic, as the word is usually used, he's a zombie; he feels dead; he labors under a compulsive belief that he is a toad child who must hop across the immense, black-topped flatnesses of shopping center parking lots until he is kissed by the life princess. Such a mania is not the same as the classic search for "real life" that youth pursues; this is more like a condition of hysteria, a frozen obsession that one's senses are deadened even to the nerve endings of the fingertips.

For such people, taking dope may be a form of acting out— like getting dirty. Some kids call all dope "shit" or "junk," terms that were once synonyms for heroin. When one boy named Supersex stole poison pills of copper sulphate and caustic soda from the Free Clinic and passed them out on the street without even claiming they were dope, sure enough there were kids who stuffed them into their mouths. The same line of speculation applies to

*There are no statistics to back up any of these fallible personal observations.

their penchant for having so many animals around. The animals may be identity fragments akin to taking names from the world of J. R. R. Tolkien's dear little hobbits; but the way the animals are cuddled, stroked, and felt suggests their owners use them to keep in contact with life—if only at the simplest, tactile level.

Acid must be everything it's claimed to be for these adolescent zombies. The drug's incredible power to hypo every kind of stimulus must make it appear that for the first time they can touch, they can taste, they can feel, they can awaken their sluggish organs of sight and sound. Expressions like "turn on" and "switch on" must exactly describe how they feel, and for people in their straits the risk of playing with such a powerful and dangerous chemical must seem worth it . . . if they think in terms of risk. Their deadness affects their sense of fear. Whether they're dropping acid or selling it on the street corner, they act as though they don't know how to be frightened.

A couple of days before his month's rent was up at the flophouse, Tom decided it was time to go to the country. The three of them packed such rags as were left from times of relative prosperity. They took them and bedrolls and a few tabs of acid and bummed a ride north into the mountains of the Russian River country of Sonoma County. There it would be warm, with no fog, and Tom already had what sounded like bronchitis. "Bronchitis is a cop out, but if it gets worse, like pneumonia, then I'll really have to think of what to do."

Their destination was the most famous of the hippy rural communes, Morningstar Ranch, a beautifully wild place of twenty-three hilltop acres owned by Lou Gottlieb, a man who'd made a lot of money with a folk-singing group in the early sixties, and then chucked it. He lived in a cabin on his place in the company of a valuable piano, a Bösendorfer. "It's a helluva piano. The upper strings are individually tied. Not even a Steinway has that. It's the best piano in the world . . . A Steinway or a Beckstein? Well, it shows them up."

He threw his place open to those young people he described as "the children of Alamogordo. By that I mean their personalities were formed in an environment which is chemically different from that in which mine was formed. Nuclear fission created new elements, strontium 90, cesium 137, and carbon 14. It radically altered the message of the chemicals at the cellular level of conciousness in the children of Alamogordo. It tells them any hour may be their last."

Some children came to chance their hours with him, grow a few vegetables, and live in tree houses and shacks of their own construction. He played the piano, practicing for the night of his debut as a concert pianist, and spoke obiter dicta that sounded more sensible each day the summer lengthened: "By disconnecting the TV, radio, newspapers, and all other media, the Average American has at least one functional counterirritant to the daily dose of impotent outrage inspired by the news. Impotent outrage is lethal, and a man ought to do everything he can to avoid having to endure it. That's why living up here alone without communication is an oppositional political act. It is really no longer possible to be truly alone, but certain tribes of us Americans are refusing to be 'informed' on an up-to-the-minute basis of Washington's latest steps in the march toward nuclear extinction. What else is there? Political action is the opium of the people. Thirty-five thousand citizens get irate at the butchery in Vietnam and march down Market Street, so the next day the State Department announces new raids on Hanoi. It's much better to declare peace wherever you are, and we're here on this mountaintop. I've tried the other way, but it's evidently impossible to convince people of their own nation's savageries in an age of the disk jockey."

That was Gottlieb, but if he wouldn't pay attention to the mass media, they would find him. First *Time,* then the television people advertised the place and turned it into a tourist trap. The new people who overran Morningstar were a wormy lot who prospered like bad microbes in the yeasty festering of their own discharge. Gottlieb continued to welcome one and all, but the county authorities went into court to get an injunction against him for running an "organized camp" in violation of the sanitary regulations. "If they find any evidence of organization here, I wish they would

75

show it to me," Gottlieb said, but the place finally was invaded by health officers, deputy sheriffs, and snooping narks.

Not all rural communes were run like Morningstar. Farther north, the commune at Top of the World Ranch was run by an ex–rock band manager named Ambrose. Ambrose said he was the dictator of the commune, which ran a small school of the occult. It had a permanent staff of nine or ten, which included the position of "lover of children." Some of the staff members had plump, organically fed children with Hindu names like Ananda. The school taught astrology and agriculture à l'indienne. None of the staff seemed to know much about the nature lore they instructed their students in, but the rules of the place were posted on the door and apparently closely enforced: "We Welcome the Weary and the Sick FOR ONE NIGHT. There is a purpose here and a plan. Some are offended by the fact, others are embarrassed. Some go for it. To accomplish our purpose none may stay other than one night—no exceptions, no special friends, no burn trips, no personal deals."

Top of the World was germicidally clean.

Tom, Sharon, and Linda got to Morningstar at night. The place was arranged so that the parking lot was a long, dark walk below where most of the people lived. They arrived in time to be scared by a group of drunken townies beating the bejabbers out of three or four hippy boys they'd caught in the lot. "Fuckin', peace-loving, Communist bastards," they chanted in tempo with their blows. Mother, carrying daughter, and father bypassed the violence on up to the top of the hill, where there was a low campfire and flickering, moving lights. As they approached, macrobiotic shades came at them from the darkness and rasped, "Got any grass? D'ja bring any grass? No grass here for a day and a half."

Tom scraped out a level place on a hillside for the three of them to sleep. Tom's fever was higher. He didn't sleep well and the next morning he looked worse. A good-hearted girl with a fire and a skillet fried up some flaked oatmeal in peanut oil and gave it to them. Then Tom went fruit picking. He was in very bad shape when he got back, but Sharon was down from her STP trip so it was easier for her to help. Seeing her down only discouraged Tom. "There isn't very much change in her. The STP didn't do anything. I think I'll have to get rid of her, but maybe we'll go on the best we can."

He made it to his little hole in the ground, where he covered himself up in the bedroll and shivered. Linda, a piece of fruit in her hand, followed, looked at him, and stuck it against his lips. "Here, Daddy, apple, bite," the little girl said.

### PIKE'S CASE
### FOR LIFE
### AFTER DEATH

#### By Charles Raudebaugh

**Bishop James A. Pike detailed to The Chronicle yesterday the strange sequence of events that led him to the public declaration that he believes he has had communication with his dead son.**
—*San Francisco Chronicle*, September 29

At the beginning of the Summer of Love there was a pleasantness about the Haight. The ratio of frightening people to nice ones was favorable, and the nice ones, like Al Rinker and George Darling, were doing low-keyed, relaxed things. They'd opened what they called the Switchboard, which was more like a telephonic bulletin board. You could call there any hour of the day and night to leave a message or get one; the Switchboard would also supply you with the best and newest rumors, and sometimes it was able to steer you toward a crash pad or even a free lawyer. Late at night, if you didn't feel up to the madmen in the House of Do-Nuts, you could go over to the Switchboard, sit in the kitchen, and listen to Al discuss acid. He was an amateur acid scientist and he loved to discuss his findings:

"Two years ago I had a friend who took acid and he kept taking more acid, forty or fifty trips. I had the idea if you took a lot of acid in a short period of time it would deteriorate your personality, so I began to study this thing. I pre- and post-tested people on acid, not in a clinical situation but in the Haight-Ashbury. Then I checked out my first twenty-five cases. I was really surprised. I found there was a *positive* change equivalent to about three years of effective therapy. But I got another impression from my data. My impression is that people who have taken thirty or forty trips and never had a bummer aren't in as good shape as those who have. I also believe that no person who has really let go can avoid having a bummer. The person who's had a few good trips and thinks he's learned something is deluding himself. He only has it on a conceptual, not an experiential, level. He may be the type who thinks, as a result of his acid, he's living like a saint, and then, bang! he gets a glimpse of himself . . . I know of one case—a professor at San Francisco State—who had four or five good trips, then he took one and went through hell. He got a look at all the evil inside himself. They had to bring him down with thorazine after six hours.* His trip was the worst trip ever recorded. He saw the male and female personification of evil in himself. He called the one Prince and the other Becky. After the trip, he always had a fear he'd see them whenever the phone rang or somebody knocked on the door. Finally, he made a simple act of faith, that it would be all right even if he met them, and that seemed to work. Actually, what he was getting was an acid recurrence—sometimes they call it a flash. Now I believe an acid recurrence is the spirit trying to work through an incomplete trip.

"It's a very complicated subject and it keeps changing. For example, when they first had acid in the Haight-Ashbury, some people singled themselves out by having religious experiences. Do you know, there was one guy at 1090 Page who actually had a throne and people were waiting on him just like he was—you

*This is one of a number of preparations that will bring you down if you're bad-tripping, but the lore of the dope world is against it. It's felt that a chemically induced come-down is like premature termination of pregnancy. You get an unpleasant, residual effect for a while. The favored method is "talking" people down. For some dope, like STP, there is no known antidote. About the best they can do for you, if you're having a bummer on it, is shoot you full of tranquilizers and wait till the stuff wears off.

know. But now lots of people have religious experiences. Enough people have taken acid and had them so they're not impressed by your religious trip anymore. I know a commune where they all picked up and moved out, all but two meth freaks, because this one guy would sit there with that religious smile on his face all day, but he'd never do the dishes."

The Switchboard people were hipped on the notion that they were the best interpreters of the Haight to the straight world, so they sailed out on evangelizing missions. George and his girl, Joan, in the company of several others, were invited to talk to a Montgomery Street businessmen's group. "As the word goes," said George, who would never have made a public speaker, "we're there in the Haight trying to do our thing. We were doing it too, until people were told by *Time* and *Life* the housing was free. Now there're hoards of them walking around being pinched by the police. Perhaps if we can get them housing, they'll be able to do their thing."

"In other words, they're a bunch of freeloaders," said one of the men in the luncheon audience.

"Well, some of them who come to our community are amazing," said one of George's colleagues. "I've seen them drive in and park their $7,000 Mercedes-Benz sports cars, change their expensive clothes and put on rags, and then go sit on the curb on Haight Street and panhandle."

"Another thing, why do they get so dirty?"

"We don't know about that. I'm clean. I take baths all the time," George told them. "See, we're not here to talk about the kids who come to smoke a little dope and go home. We're trying to build a community with stores and institutions. You should be in favor of that."

"Yeah?" said one guy, who wasn't exactly agreeing, "What I want to know is at what age do you change from being a hippy into being a bum?"

His fellows thought that was pretty funny. George replied, "Maybe the guy sitting next to you is a hippy." They thought that was funnier. The message wasn't getting across. George and his friends put their heads together to discuss inviting these obtuse men out to the community. They couldn't agree, and at length one of them said to the businessmen, "If you have any sons and daughters who escape and drop out, you'd better be thankful that there are people like us in the Haight-Ashbury who aren't like that Mission Street crowd, who destroy everybody with needles and VD."

At that point the toastmaster said, "I think we should commend them for the way they conducted themselves here." Some applause followed.

### WE ARE THE PEOPLE OUR PARENTS WARNED US AGAINST
—Graffito, coffeehouse wall, Summer 1967

Every day the scene got a little heavier, a little crazier. Pot was getting harder to find. There was plenty of acid, but you can only take acid every other day or so; more often than that and you won't get off. The body builds an absolute tolerance to it very rapidly. More alcohol, more speed, and more freaky people appeared on the streets. Like Chancellor. Chancellor was a white boy whose curly, uncut hair made him look like a fuzzy-wuzzy. His real name was unknown. He was called Chancellor because of the discarded, orange-red doorman's coat he wore. On the coat were stitched the words, "Hotel Chancellor." Chancellor didn't walk; he rotated in order to achieve locomotion. He would gyrate in unexpected directions, sometimes whirling out into the traffic. As he did this, he emitted a buzzing-humming noise, and when going at top speed he would bounce off automobile fenders like an incredible, haired-over, distended top.

Papa Al was spending more and more time in the neighborhood, getting there a little earlier, leaving a little later. "There are no undercover agents from the narcotics squad in the Haight as of yesterday. The last one had his cover blown. It will be a month before another group can come in. It's getting to be a very heavy scene," he said one afternoon, while taking a private walk in the park, which he did occasionally. "But don't think about it. Just do your thing, whatever's right."

He began spending more time at the Free Clinic. Next, he unaccountably was being called the clinic's "senior supervisor." It changed the tone of the place, because Papa Al's street commandos and dealers followed him. Kurt Feibusch and Shalom objected to their hanging out, but they were always coming in and looking for him: Big Tiny, Hutch, Apache, Cowboy, Iron Man, White Preacher, Spider, the lot of them. They had an unsettling effect on White Rabbit, who seemed to be riding out his identity crisis quietly while doing voluntary chores of an unclassifiable nature for the clinic.

White Rabbit liked to say things that would blow your mind: "I can turn on radios by feeling waves through the back of my neck. I just recently put a clamp on it because I was going around turning on people's radios and TV sets, and it was beginning to bug them." After he'd say something like that, he'd twinkle at you, twitch the end of his long nose, and be disappointed if you changed the subject. His Princeton father and his Vassar mother combined to make a well-to-do, upstate New York family, where White Rabbit, the oldest of four children, grew up in the better private boarding schools until he reached an age (twenty) when he could say, "Even before I was accepted at Berkeley, I was having psychological problems which I couldn't straighten out with the psychiatrist at prep school. I had a nervous breakdown two weeks before school ended."

On the whole, White Rabbit's childhood must have been quietly pleasant. One of his earliest memories is of an electric Santa Claus bowing mechanically from the living room fireplace. His father, he remembered, slapped him once, but it was never traumatic; usually he was sent to his room or had his allowance cut or couldn't watch TV. He had diagnosed himself: "I have a sexual identity problem. Many people have it but they repress it. Everybody has almost equal parts maleness and femaleness, but they don't know it.

Acid helps to break down these barriers. After acid, I was able to think about it and talk about it."

Papa Al took one look at White Rabbit and came to a different understanding. "Hippies like fuzzy rabbit here were lost before they ever came to the Haight," Papa Al said. "To them acid is instant psychiatry, a way to find out where your head's at . . . Of course, it's on their neck, where it's always been, but White Rabbit doesn't know that. He's a typical product of a permissive society, so he's suffering from what most of them are suffering from, a massive Peter Pan complex. There's a tremendous amount of regression among these kids, like this large rodent here next to me with the white fur. Look at them up on Hippy Hill every day, smoking pot, flying kites, and blowing soap bubbles. Regression."

Papa Al could talk that way when he wanted to. He was supposed to have a master's degree in psychology; he was also supposed to be an ex–social worker who'd gotten rich in the stock market. It was true that almost every afternoon he bought a paper and said, "I want to see how I'm doing," as he turned to the final market quotations.

It changed day to day with White Rabbit. Sometimes he used the scene as a backdrop for costumes. Then he appeared to be capitalizing on the social weightlessness of the Haight, the strange place where you could assume any role you chose, make up any kind of personal history you wanted. At other times, White Rabbit had no personality of his own; what he had was derived from the scene; the backdrop, the set made him into a person. On those days he was especially susceptible to Papa Al's group. He'd appear and ask, "Know where I can hide out?"

"Why do you want to hide out, White Rabbit?"

"There's a contract let out on me!"

"You mean somebody wants to kill you?"

"That's right, there's one, maybe two contracts out on me. I've gotta hide out for a while. I may have to split the scene completely."

"White Rabbit, you're bragging. You've never done anything

important enough to merit somebody murdering you, or even short-sheeting your bed."

"It isn't anything I've done."

"I'm sure of that."

"No, this is serious. It's something I've heard. I was with a chick and she took me to this house where there were some very heavy cats, and they said some things in front of me . . . Well, if it ever got out—I can't tell you any more, except it concerns a lot of important people, like Papa Al."

"White Rabbit, can you get the DT's from acid?"

"They didn't realize this chick had brought me, and, oh, wow! I wish she hadn't!"

Other days he'd come on square-shouldered and talk out of the side of his mouth: "Goin' over to the islands."

"Yeah?" you were supposed to answer, just as tough as he. "Some action over there?"

"I might tell ya, but ya can't come. Let ya in on it, 'cause you've been righteous. Only reporter around here that writes the truth."

"How would you know? You've never read a word I've written, not even a postcard."

"We know. Doncha think we check you guys out? We have a line on everybody who stays around here for more than two days, but you can't write about this. There's a bunch of us going over to the islands to make a hit on Useless."

"Useless? What's Useless done now?"

"Nothing, but he pulled an $11,000 burn, and we're not going to let him get away with that."

"Look, Walter Mitty White Rabbit, Useless didn't burn you. You've never even met Useless."

"He burnt my friends."

Each day grass got tighter and the scene got freakier. Dr. Smith, the director of the clinic, kept on an even keel, saying the same things to the reporters. They'd come around of an evening and catch him in the room in the clinic that had FCREW YOU painted on

83

the wall above the filing cabinet: "I was three-fourths of my way to a Ph.D. when the Haight-Ashbury struck. There was a void created and somebody had to respond. There still is a void in many ways because this society doesn't treat drug abuse as a health problem but as a police problem . . . The Haight-Ashbury has tremendous energy. It's broken with the past, but it hasn't found a new way yet, so it symbolizes what I call a 'generation at risk' . . . My biggest criticism of the straight community is that they don't try to understand why the kids do it, and it's not just a few kids. Do you know that in the month of July we treated over two thousand of them?"

As the grass shortage continued, the doctor's talk became less visionary and more stridently concerned: "I still think of this as a movement, but the rebellion is crumbling at the edges. They're hung up on drugs, too many of them; they're not moving on to something else. I am appalled at the number of teeni-boppers who've taken LSD three hundred and four hundred times. They stay stoned all the time. What are we going to do with them? Drag them back by the hair? They think they know better . . . I don't know, I don't know, I guess you could go down Haight Street tonight and arrest half the boys as draft dodgers . . . It's getting frightening. One day the Hell's Angels stormed in here, demanding to know if we'd called the police. I don't know what they might have done if we had . . . We don't tell the police anything but what the law says a doctor has to; a rumor got around that we were reporting to the fuzz, and I was worried for a while. I thought everybody might just decide we were all a big come-down, but the underground papers helped us. They put out the word that we were cool . . . I've never seen such paranoia."

The clinic kitchen was run by John. When he was sober, he tried hard to give the place a certain institutional class. He wasn't a snob; he was a forty-six-year-old Irishman from New York, and that meant he was always braced, waiting for some mark of condescension. His tactic was to strike first. "These children's English! . . . It's such a pleasure to talk to someone who can speak the language correctly, who knows how to make his meaning clear. A hippy—this I do believe is the real definition of a hippy—well, a hippy is a person who persists in committing grammatical mistakes even after he's been corrected. I thank God I went to Cathedral College, but then I had the benefit of a classical education. I studied for the priesthood but I realized in time that my vocation wasn't celibate. I thank God for that or I would never have married Shirley. We'd been married fourteen years when she died of a massive stroke. I took up the bottle the day Shirley died . . . could you contribute, well, let's say $10, or call it a loan until tomorrow? . . . some sisters and priests are coming for lunch, and, as usual, this establishment is bereft of funds . . . The religious want to see our work and I think we should offer them some food. I have a very nice luncheon menu."

"John, if I give you this will you drink up tomorrow's lunch? I can't afford to make two contributions."

"Oh, gracious no. You know, it's such a pleasure talking to you. Your English—you do speak exceptionally well. I wish you'd known Shirley. She had a doctorate—in English. I never drank until the day she died. You know, I've sat in Park Avenue apartments where there were bigger hippies than there are here. I've never cared for that kind of life. I could have done it if I'd wanted, but I didn't. I've made a success in two business careers. Oh yes, I was an assistant buyer at Macy's. I left Macy's when they told me they were going to promote me to buyer but they had to 'sell' me upstairs first. I didn't have the Harvard or the Yale background, you see. They were going to sell me upstairs. I told them they needn't bother. After fourteen years of working in their store, I didn't care to be sold upstairs, so I went home after fourteen years and I told my wife I had quit. I'm square, buddy boy. That's what I did. Then I went into the printing business and I was very successful, but one day I told my partner, 'Here, you can have it,' and I walked out to come to San Francisco. I can go back any time I want. I don't have to be here. These children think they're revolutionaries! I've known Dorothy Day. We had Peter Maurin speak at Our Lady of Lourdes Holy Name Society. They were revolutionaries. I know. I was with the *Catholic Worker*. Oh, these children aren't doing anything I don't know about. I studied for the priesthood. Oh, don't tell me. *Introibo ad altare Dei. Ad Deum qui laetificat juventutem meam* . . . Don't tell me."

John made an excellent hash, a hunky, meaty hash with crusty potatoes. It gave the clinic a solid, institutional continuity. Then one day he was gone. Nobody ever explained why anybody was gone from the clinic. They became nonpeople, and the staff looked as though you'd done something in bad taste if you mentioned them. John was replaced by George, who was less critical and had the enthusiasm of a coolie, always running and offering to get things; but he couldn't cook.

It got freakier. The room with the FCREW YOU on the wall was the theater for strange dialogues and dramas in which the characters would push their way in, say their lines, and leave.

### FREAK NIGHT IN THE FCREW YOU ROOM

WHITE RABBIT: Aldous Huxley died high on acid . . . died high and happy, just tripped out of life into death.

SHRINK: Yes, but have you ever thought of the possibilities of chromosomal damage? You kids never think of the side effects. You can't play fast and loose with nature. It makes you pay.

WHITE RABBIT: He was dying of cancer.

SHRINK: Why are you so angry with me?

WALLY *(an aging fag):* I tell you, Teddybear, I used to hate the hippies. I hated the hippies. I hated the hippies 'cause I am what you call an entrepreneur. I buy and sell property. But now I work twenty-four hours a day for them. Before, when I'd see these people on the street corner, I'd say that it was abominable. They were doing nothing. Oh, but I changed. I dropped acid. Then I saw them panhandling an' I saw that they give to each other.

TEDDYBEAR: You can't o-d on acid. I took four white Owsleys on the Fourth of July. *(exit* SHRINK; WHITE RABBIT *stands in front of the filing cabinet and eats potato chips)*

WALLY: When I take acid, I know why I like the hippies. I'm

86

a homosexual. I'm a persecuted minority too. So now, every night, I take off the business suit; I put on the beads; I'm a happy, hippy homo.

TEDDYBEAR: We're the most hated minority in America. We have no rights. We're lower than the spades and the spics. Our hippy women are raped, and we go to the police station and they don't even write it down.

SPEED FREAK (*entering as he holds a bleeding hand*): I need somebody to fix this.

SHALOM: The only doctor we got right now is a shrink, and this shrink won't bandage people. Says he's forgotten how. You got to come back tomorrow or go to a hospital.

SPEED FREAK: If a fuckin' psychiatrist comes in here I'm gonna kill 'im. (*plucks at his tufty beard*)

SHALOM: I know what kind of a trip you're on. I know your trip.

SPEED FREAK: I know yours too.

SHALOM: You can leave. I tried to talk to you reasonably.

WALLY: Well, I tell you honestly, Teddybear, the hippies run down property values.

SPEED FREAK: I thought this was a place ya come for help.

SHALOM: Don't put your bum trip on me.

SPEED FREAK (*exiting*): I won't be back.

WHITE RABBIT: Speed freak.

SHALOM: Speed freak.

TEDDYBEAR: We don't run down values. We build values. People copy from us—styles, music, everything.

WALLY: You do, you do, Teddybear. I can tell you. By day I'm establishment. The savings and loan associations have drawn a line against you. That means you drop property values. I wouldn't rent to you. Maybe that means I'm hypocritical.

WHITE RABBIT: I'm on librium. Very low high. (*re-enter* SHRINK, *followed by* PLEADING GIRL, *followed by* PAPA AL *and* BIG TINY, *who are doing their own thing*)

PLEADING GIRL: Aren't you going to help my friend? She's old. She must be nearly fifty an' she's bum-tripping bad.

SHRINK: She's been bum-tripping for thirty years.

PLEADING GIRL: It's the universe that's been on a bad trip.

SHRINK: I'm sorry. I shouldn't have said that.

BIG TINY: I want the Angels so bad, I don't want anything fuckin' else, Papa Al.

WHITE RABBIT: Talk about bad trips! Kelly's back from Fresno. He looks awful. Been on a series of death-ego trips. Wow!

SHRINK (*picking up the phone*): I need an ambulance . . . yes . . . yes . . . for a forty-eight-year-old woman with multiple cuts and abrasions, malnutrition, and occasional hallucinations.

PLEADING GIRL: Where're you going to send her? I'll take care of her. What she needs is macrobiotic food and serenity.

SHRINK: Why the hell are you bothering me if you don't want me to take care of your friend?

PLEADING GIRL: There's a lot of shit happening around this city.

SHRINK: Agreed.

WHITE RABBIT: You're feeling the tug of the tribal imperative, doctor, and you're resisting. Flow with it.

SHRINK: White Rabbit, will you—oh, never mind. I've been here too long tonight.

PLEADING GIRL: I almost died last Sunday of sensitivity . . . and a few mind poisoners, doctor. I'm going.

SHRINK: In peace, in peace. (*exit* SHRINK *and girl, who is almost knocked over by* COWBOY *entering*)

COWBOY: Papa Al, Papa Al, I gotta talk to you. I need your thirty-eight. I gotta have it now.

PAPA AL: Well, well, well, if it isn't Cowboy.

BIG TINY: I'm talkin' to Papa Al.

PAPA AL: Cowboy's upset. He's having his monthlies . . . Tsk, tsk, you missed the most interesting part of the evening, Cowboy. A nine-year-old boy was up here earlier freaking out on acid. Maybe you sold it to him. It was quite interesting. The kid's tongue was hanging out of his mouth and he couldn't get it back in . . . hung over his teeth dripping spit.

COWBOY: There's too many fuckin' people around here.

PAPA AL: Well, you split, Cowboy. Big Tiny and me are doing

our thing and we don't need you.

COWBOY: Papa Al, I gotta have a gun. I gotta have a gun fast.

PAPA AL: Cowboy, you can't make it as a biker, you can't make it as a dealer, you can't make it as a hippy, you can't make it as a human being.

COWBOY: Don't call me "Cowboy." That's not my name.

BIG TINY: Me an' Al are talking.

COWBOY: Gee, wow! I'm stoned. I'm behind everything, grass, acid, STP, speed, alcohol. I'm behind everything. Stoned outta my brain. Papa Al, I gotta have a gun.

BIG TINY: Me an' Papa Al are talkin'.

COWBOY: *Me* an' Papa Al are talkin'.

BIG TINY: Don't hassle me, Cowboy. You're comin' down on me.

PAPA AL: Okay, son, you got what you wanted. You're the center of attention.

COWBOY: I'm not your son.

PAPA AL: Okay, Cowboy, then.

BIG TINY: Papa Al, if he don't get outta here, I'm gonna cold-cock him.

COWBOY: My name's Mike an' there're too many fuckin' people around here. *(exit COWBOY)*

VOICE FROM DOWN THE HALL: Panic button! Panic button! I'm pushing the panic button! There's a boy in here who's all sliced up. The Angels or the spades got 'im. He can't talk. Who wants to drive him to the hospital?

COWBOY *(sticking his head back in for an instant):* It was the syndicate. An' they're going to get me too, Papa Al, 'cause you won't give me your gun.

BIG TINY: I'll cold-cock the son of a bitch.

PAPA AL: So Tiny, you want to be an Angel, do you? Well, well, well, an' all the time I thought you were the only 315-pound woman's hairdresser in the world. But, seriously, son, if you want to be an Angel, you better watch yourself. You keep jumping in on their fights, you're going to be in trouble. You're not going about it right.

BIG TINY: I'm always helping 'em. I always jump in on their side. St. Louis said I could go on the next run if I can get a bike, but Papa Al, where am I going to get a bike?

PAPA AL: You be careful, Tiny. You could get stomped, you know.

WHITE RABBIT: Fcrew you all. *(titters at himself and trips out making a silent, laughing face)*

PAPA AL: Whatever's right.

### HELP!!

**Big Sur community starving. At close of Gorda Ranch, groups split into the mountains and running out of food. If you can help call Joseph at 387-4552.**
—Want ad in *Haight-Ashbury Tribune*

### DENVER BOY, 2, FOUND WITH HEART CUT OUT

**Denver, Nov. 21 (AP)—The body of a two-year-old boy—his heart cut out and a soft drink bottle inserted in the cavity—was found in an east Denver hippy house today, police reported.**

As the grass was burnt up and not replaced, the mood of the street turned paranoid and fearful. Everybody reported huge increases in speed shooting. The old-time psychedelic heads inveighed against crystal and put up signs warning people that SPEED KILLS. In the clinic, the doctors told speed jokes: "I had a hippy in here who couldn't understand how he got serum hepatitis. He told me he only let his closest friends use his needle."

Nothing bothered Beast. He leaped and jingled along the sidewalks, scaring the tourists as always. Coyote showed no signs of concern; he continued projects like his peace petition. It took him seven hours to type it on the clinic machine. Only people he trusted were allowed to sign it, because "I'm going to give it to, ah . . .

who am I going to give it to? . . . Oh, I know, either the United Nations or God, whichever is interested." Others, who were more sensitive or less reckless, began getting off the streets earlier. Brian and Mike could now be found on the mattresses in their room by eleven.

Mike said he was dying of cancer of the brain—no more than six months to live. There were at least four other such tragedies in the Haight. The girls, however, favored diseases of the lungs, except for Ginger, who said she had cancer of the stomach and only five months to live. The coincidence of names was also very high. There couldn't have been fewer than eight Candys, ten White Rabbits, five Cowboys, seventeen Loves, and nine Frodos. Mike also said he'd been in a Connecticut prison for the criminally insane because he'd killed his father with a shotgun. Patricide, though, wasn't especially popular; tastes ran more to being a hit man for the syndicate or something along those lines; but even bank robbery or hints that you were really an undercover nark enjoyed a degree of popularity.

Brian suffered from a real disease. His legs were nearly useless and without his aluminum crutches he'd never have been able to get around. Brian was a June graduate of Queens College and enough of a New Left radical to have stopped at the Students for a Democratic Society national convention in Ann Arbor, Michigan, on his way to the Haight. He looked exactly like the scarecrow in the *Wizard of Oz* and said he had been planning to go to Oxford and study English in the fall. "But I don't know now. This experience here really opened me up. Wow! All of a sudden things really locked in one beautiful circle. Wow! I've really found myself! Wow! I've met so many beautiful people. I may change my field to the communication arts or the ministry . . . I think the ministry."

The two got on well, except when they talked politics and the war. "You're a communist," Mike would say. "Don't you realize if we pulled out of Vietnam the communists would be on the way to world domination? You don't know it but communism is a sickness. Who do you think was behind all that radical shit in Detroit and Los Angeles?"

"Oh, wow! You're wrong there," Brian would say. "See, what this is is the same as between people . . . on a man-to-man basis you get paranoia, and on a world scale you get war. We're afraid of them and they're afraid of us, so it's kill, kill, kill. Oh, wow! War's a downer. It's a bum trip for everybody, Mike."

In another apartment building, a boy who thought like Brian was holding the end of an arm tourniquet in his teeth, while his thumb pushed up and down against the small of his arm to raise a vein. "I'd rather shoot myself up with meth than be shot down by the Viet Cong," he said through his teeth as the blue vein swelled up. It was in good condition. The boy had just started shooting speed.

The grass shortage was becoming acute. The dealers were rushing around talking about monumental cops—two, three, five hundred, a thousand keys. Shipments were being predicted and expected at every hour . . . tomorrow . . . eight o'clock in the morning . . . no later than eleven . . . sometime this afternoon . . . it's definite, it'll be here tonight . . . I can't figure out what happened . . . we haven't heard anything from them. The quality of the grass around for sale was miserable, twigs and stalks; or you could buy sugar-cured grass, which was soaked in sugar water to up its weight.

The burns were ferocious and getting worse. Hawaiian Chuck was handing out hepatitis-infected points to friends who'd burned him. A freaky story blew down the street about a boy who shot Drano. It was supposed to have been a burn substituted on him when he bought speed. At the clinic, the doctors debated. "Taking Drano I-V? Terribly painful, quite possibly fatal . . . Naaa, it's ridiculous. If you add water to Drano, it vaporizes. You can't shoot it." Over at Benches, Papa Al said, "Of course it was Drano. I could tell when he flushed himself. He had the cleanest pipes in town. Drano's a good trip. All you fine young men should take it."

Speed adulteration and poisoning grew so much that the community was crisscrossed with vengeful youths. Speed was mixed with baking soda, tooth powder, talcum powder, and even such substances as battery acid. "What they do is grab anything, put it in the packet, and sell it," said one speed merchant named Rod. "They'll run into the street, get liquid out of the car battery, put it on a saucer, evaporate it, and what's left looks just like real crystal."

Whimpering kids were brought into the clinic, their arms psychedelically colored from the junk they'd shot into their veins. "When I get hold of a burn artist, he's going to have pain," said Rod, a big twenty-two-year-old who looked like he could inflict it. "I make 'em take their own stuff, overamp [overdose] till they scream. I put 'em in the hospital, not for a couple of days either. I put 'em in the hospital for six or eight months because I don't break their bones, I break their joints and that snaps their tendons and rips their muscles."

Walking the street was like being caught outdoors in a flat field with the enemy in the bushes. There were fewer places to go or hide, unless you had money like Barthol. Barthol said he was broke, but he drove to The Grateful Dead's house in a Cadillac and he had an embossed business card that said he was the president of a record company. Two girls, who'd just gotten out of jail, were on the steps looking at him with wide-eyed suspicion. They'd fled for refuge to the house of the Dead, but things were getting so bad that Rock was repelling boarders the last days before they went to New Mexico. "I wanted $10 million to retire on before I was thirty. I was a business wizard, but I went broke, took LSD, and found out I'd retired already," Barthol said, waiting in his fine car to take a portion of the Dead off for a spin. "But I was a wizard. I knew how to overextend myself no matter how much the resources. The end was fun, though. I had a whole hippy night staff helping me forge collateral. It was one of those things. I needed instant money, but nobody got hurt. I bought it all back. Now I'm a photographer who regards himself as a historian. I want to record this country going down." His passengers got in, and the last words that the frightened girls on the step could hear were him saying, "The Haight-Ashbury scene is the last hope of this country."

The girls watched. They were ugly things, the sort who convinced the visitors the neighborhood was populated with kids who couldn't hack it back home. Susan, the one with horrible buck teeth and high-topped rubber boots over her jeans, said, "You can't walk down the street stoned anymore. I don't know where I'm going to go, but jail was a bummer, the spade chicks in there for prostitution getting down on the hippies. And the matron was too much, man. These two spade chicks were fighting and tearing their hair out, and the matron didn't do anything but yell at them. I think she was grooving on it."

Her friend Phyllis nodded and advised, "The best thing is to bang your head against the wall or talk backward or push bread up your nostrils. Then they'll take you to a psycho ward where they have groovy chicks who aren't gay."

"Guess what about this chick they put me in jail with?" Susan answered. "She's a social worker and they busted her for about $157 worth of traffic tickets. She turned on to grass an' acid, a

94

really groovy chick, but, no, no, no TV, no magazines, you just sit there and they don't even give you any milk."

"Don't tell me. My parents put me in jail. It was my fault. I was living with Timothy and I liked it so much I wanted my parents to see it, so I invited them to dinner. We had a good time, they kissed me and split. The next morning the heat came and arrested Timothy for statutory rape and me for being a wayward minor. My head was so scrambled, when they took me away I signed a paper. In court Timothy whispered, 'You didn't sign anything, did you?' I said, 'Yes,' and he said, 'You bitch! They'll put me away for years now!' That was the last time I saw him. I can't find out what jail he's in or anything. What am I going to do? I'm afraid here after dark."

"Yeah," agreed Susan. "What's a street for if you can't stand on a corner safely waiting for no one?"

The street was becoming so mean it was getting to be like war in Saigon via satellite transmission, people sticking arms out of doorways to pull the helpless off the street and out of the sniper fire. Bernie and Kate, two calm ones from one of the few well-ordered apartment communes, fished Candy out of the I/Thou Coffee House. She was one of the infinite number of Candys, but a beautiful one. She was from Louisiana, nothing like the loud, paranoid Illinois Candy, who was always roaring around saying the syndicate was after her and that she had a new organization with a chemist all their own. The Louisiana Candy first turned up in the clinic, bum-tripping and hallucinating. "I killed somebody. I can't tell anybody who I killed or they'll lock me up. They'll make me alone—Daddy, Daddy, I'm a big girl now. I can stand on my feet without you." She thought every older man in the place was her father. They got her calmed down and her head fairly well straightened out, but she had to go drop more acid.

Next she was in the I/Thou, sitting on a chair weeping, saying, "My Daddy's just back from Saigon. He kills people for a living." (In fact, her father was a retired military officer with a half-interest in a firm that did a lot of business with the United States government in Saigon, but it had to do with freighting supplies, not shooting.) The others sat her down at a table, got her a cup of coffee and a sandwich, and tried to soothe her. "Everybody else is stoned. I'm not . . . I was so scared growing up, I wanted to die . . . I think I'm going to go out and get arrested so I can find out if this is for real."

"I have a friend who goes to jail just to test reality," Bernie told her.

Candy nodded and continued her monologue: "I think I'll hitch-hike down and see the straight world. The straight world doesn't exist, not in San Francisco. It does in L.A. The man is still there . . . I wish I could tell how this lettuce tastes. What a weird trip. I can't taste the lettuce but I can hear two thousand sounds. Some-body's breaking a potato chip in here. It's tickling my eardrums . . . Who's doing it? . . . Oh, it's that little spade boy in the cowboy suit . . . He's stoned too. I wonder what kind of a trip he's on. Hmmmm, he's part of my trip. I don't have to say a word; he knows exactly what my brain is saying. ESP is real, man. Anyone have a joint? ANY DOPE IN THE HOUSE? . . . Know what I'm flashing on? My family back in Louisiana . . . Oh, I feel like I want a nice, secure bed, warm and safe. I want a mother. I need a mother. That's from bumming around so much. They shouldn't let me do it. I need a fucking mother. Oh, none of us are real . . . Oh, wow! Look what's with this green pepper. Whoever sliced this poor thing up is a murderer. I'm going to be one too. I'm going to tear it apart and see what it's made of. I don't know which to eat, the green pepper, the sandwich, or the plate. I'm flashing on when I used to live at home, on our maid, our dogs, and my aunt always screaming at me."

Bernie and Kate took her to the commune and bedded her down for the night. In the morning she was gone. No one knew where.

## JAPANESE VERSION OF THE HIPPY

Tokyo, Aug. 29 (New York Times Service) —Japanese call them futenzoku, which means "crazy tribe." Americans, if judging by outward appearance and personal habits only, might identify them as hippies. "Some call them beggars, drug addicts or screwballs. Others say they are prophets or saints," observed the popular Japanese magazine, Shukan Asahi.

The kids on the street put their blankets over their heads like monks' cowls and moved closer together on the shadowy stairways where they sat looking out at the tourists. The sun was gone in the fog. The street hippies cuddled their kittens, gently pushed them under the blankets, felt their fur, and smoked dope, if they were lucky enough to have any.

"It's a hassle," they agreed. "Hassles, gee, wow, are a bummer, and you shouldn't think about it or you'll spoil your own trip." They didn't think about Chob. They hadn't known him. They were the passers through, the plastics.

There's a story that Chob's body was found by someone looking for his cat. It could be. There are so many of these Egyptian animals, members of the Haight's mystical menagerie of scarabs, owls, toads, and phoenixes who live in the high mushroom forest. Chob was found dead by a cat, by somebody, stabbed in the heart, his right arm cut off and stolen with his money, $3,000 of it. Chob was a dope dealer and maybe he burned somebody with his right arm. Across the Bay in Marin County, where the acid bands practiced their music, a girl in one of the rehearsal halls remarked, "He had to be a speed freak who killed Chob. They caught the guy, didn't they, in Chob's car with the arm sewed up in a velvet bag, grooving on it?"

The boy's lawyer said his client had made himself crazy on acid. It was not to be believed that it was acid. The Haight concluded that it was speed, or that the Mafia had done it, for the Haight could not think that one of the beloved community would murder. Then Superspade was turned up in a sleeping bag over in Marin with a bullet in his head. Proof convincing that the syndicate was moving in, but on the street the drifting kids repeated to each other, "Don't hassle yourself." They hadn't known Superspade, though they may have flashed on a Negro wearing a button that said, SUPERSPADE, FASTER THAN A SPEEDING MIND. So they petted their cats and panhandled for dog food and howled for dope and chanted for dope and didn't understand that with Superspade dead there'd be no dope for a while.

The dealers were running out of the city.

Jerry bulged his eyes and disappeared, evaporating into Los Angeles, Topanga Canyon. Frodo took his nonchalant, barefooted self off Haight Street, traveling the less used, parallel routes till he could clear town. "I'm going to New York. The trouble hasn't gotten to me yet, but I'm not waiting. I still don't think they'll be able to take over the Haight." Teddybear cooled it. Even Papa Al's boys walked with caution. Others left for Mendocino, the Santa Cruz Mountains, and Indian reservations in Arizona. Chob's murder could be explained, but this killing was a sign the vibrations were at an evil confluence. Only people like Howard at the God's Eye could shake their heads and smirk with superior knowledge. He'd been in the dope business in L.A., where he was the only one of the seventeen in the ring who hadn't been arrested. When they got out of jail, they'd come looking for him, and he'd split for the north. "I don't do that anymore," he said comfortably. "I had myself declared insane. I have 100 per cent disability and live on a pension from the Social Security Administration."

Superspade was one of the rare Negroes who cared to integrate themselves into the Haight. There were some others, Uncle Toms in paisleys, but no matter. Superspade was loved. Even Peggy shook her head, full of frightened eyes, and declared, "You know how I feel about spades—they come in here and steal the leather jackets. They won't steal anything inexpensive, but Superspade was different. He was a real, beautiful person, but I know somebody else who's going to get killed. Shhhh! Lemme tell you . . . Roman's missing. He's a good friend of ours, and I'm sure some speed freaks found out about him and killed him, or maybe it's the Mafia. Don't you think the Mafia killed Superspade? Who else'd do it?"

Peggy was in four simultaneous dithers. Kimmie, her best friend and co-conspirator in every form of girlishness, was hours overdue driving up from Monterey with a Volkswagen full of pot. "I'm scared out of my wits. She doesn't have a driver's license . . . Well, I don't know why she does it. We have enough in our dope stash for ourselves. It's the excitement. She's doing it for a friend. My God, I can't call up the police and ask them, 'Have you arrested anybody with ten keys of grass in a blue-gray Volkswagen?' "

She was also in a dither because her accountant was negotiating for a country house she'd fallen in love with and it was dragging on for days and days while he got the price down for her. "He says if he can't get it down more, I can't afford it. I don't see why. I'm going to be rich. Did I tell you I'm going to buy a Jaguar? I dare those goddam cops to give *it* a parking ticket. I hear they don't ticket Jaguars and Rolls Royces, do you think that's true? Oh, God, I'm so worried. Who's going to get killed next? I know those people; they're my friends."

Peggy was also in a milder dither about Sam. She had some work for him to do, and he was spending some of his time getting letters of recommendation to show the judge when he came up for sentencing on an old crystal charge. Somehow, this involved Melanie's coming up to watch the shop.

Melanie grated on Peggy with her talk about Swami's food edicts. So the owner swept her out of the store to go down the street to Connie's Restaurant where they serve curries. "Oh, she's all right," Peggy declared, "an' Sam's good, but the rest of them are dirty Hindu beggars. There's one I call Das Gruber Peas who's always stoned and lying on the sidewalk next to Peter. Oh, Peter, he came in and got the most beautiful brocade shirt this morning. He said, 'Charge it,' and I know he'll never pay me. Seventeen dollars . . . no, that's the retail price. Well, it wouldn't have mattered, but Beast was in before and I outfitted him. I couldn't stand it any longer. I told him, I said, 'Oh, Beast, you're so dirty and filthy and disgusting. I'm going to give you a new set of clothes.' He looked very nice in them and he made animal sounds for me, which I guess meant he was grateful. God, what's going to happen? Who's going to be killed next?"

As much as it could, the community broke off from its preoccupation with dealing dope, hooking tourists, and getting stoned to react against a sense of being invaded. Iron Man, the bearded, one-armed pusher who kept his merchandise in the hollow of his prosthetic limb, raced the streets crying out softly to his friends, "Stop!" And when they did, he extended his good hand, palm out, and then slowly wiggled his fingers as he asked, "Do you feel it? Do you feel the good vibrations?" "Iron Man will bring love back to the Haight," he'd cry, and run off.

In the window of the arcade where Grant was opening a knick-knackery to sell tourists the same stuff they could buy downtown for half the price, they talked about doing something. "I've been on a three-day speed trip. I didn't sleep all that time," Grant, an elegant blond who popped his pills from a silver case, announced, like somebody returning from a far place. "It's a socially destructive trip, speed is. I walked till my feet were bloody, but I'm going to walk over to the meeting on Hippy Hill this afternoon. It's a meeting of the energy movers of the community to discuss the spiritual state of the Haight, which, I must say, is abominably low. Hmmmm," said Grant, interrupting himself, "do you think it would be a good idea to put a drag queen in the shop window? We don't have anything in there now, and she could dance. We'd be busted, of course. And it *is* a circus trip, but we'd get publicity and that *would* help business."

There were about three hundred on Hippy Hill as the gong from the Psychedelic Shop reverberated and the sitting people expelled their breath to make the slow sound of the god-centering ommmmmmm. At the summit was Felicia, dressed in silky magentas that moved with the wind as it blew her red hair. She had her staff, on which was mounted the upside down Y of the peace symbol. She made her living dancing topless on North Beach and had probably had too much acid, but on the day of the meeting she resembled a girl king in a Lost Atlantis amazon movie. Hippy Doc was there too, away from the center of the crowd with Foxy, his old lady, smoking dope and declaring foursquare, "I'm for war, war that will stop the man." Tall Peter, who ran the Hip Job Coop, was present in the new brocade shirt from Peggy's, but not Peggy. Father Grosjean, the long-haired Episcopalian minister who was really straight, hung on the outside of the crowd. A thin, middle-aged Negro named Jimmy—police intelligence suspected him of wanting to start a riot—spoke first and long about "winged infinity . . . In this earth time of 1967, we're stretched out in cosmic consciousness. We have the center point and it's traveling at cosmic speeds out there at the perimeters."

"Jimmy, you're lousing up the whole meeting," cried Tobacco, and the gong sounded. Tobacco was a Digger, one of the angry, politically slanted group that started the Free Store and used to do the free feeding in the Park. "Jimmy, you're trying to be a swami," announced Tobacco as he got up and stood next to Jimmy, the gong player, and Felicia, who'd come down from the hilltop.

"Everything was okay when the Diggers were doing their thing," he continued. "We had our crash pads busted and nobody helped us feed, so we lost the whole thing. We gotta get started again. In one month we'll have the entire Haight-Ashbury changed. See, what it was when the Diggers were doing their thing was a house of natural-state anarchy. It was always the dream of the white man to live in a natural state, and that's what we got to do. The Polynesians, the black man, every race has done it but the white man, except for seventeenth-century England. It's a free frame of experience, that's what it is."

"Groups! Forces!" another voice called out. "Give your attention to the fly that appears when your eyes are closed, for it is a spiritual light which is but the manifestation of your concentration. We are all one God! As you see light, become one with that light, flow with it, so I will ask you to be silent for ten minutes. We must save this planet, and it's us, if anybody's going to. We must become more self-sufficient. The role of karma yoga is also very important."

A girl shrieked, "I thought we were going to talk about the murders. There's supposed to be another one and several people are missing. All my friends who aren't dead are hiding."

Ned was carrying his pack of tarot cards in a leather box attached to his belt. He was a misty algebraic, given to making final

101

clarifying statements that nobody could understand. "Two good friends of mine were murdered," he declared. "They were murdered because they were paranoid. They carried knives and guns. If you don't want to be murdered, don't be paranoid and don't carry weapons."

The girl shrieked again: "It's like a whore man coming at you from New York, Chicago, New Orleans. You know what I'm talking about. You know, and I'm scared. Two of my friends have been killed."

"It's bigger than paranoia," a voice shouted, as another yelled, "Let's don't buy or sell dope anymore. Then they won't kill us."

"We're in a society that still takes money, man. How're we gonna live if we don't sell dope?" came a hollering retort, but the question went unanswered for still another voice was commanding attention: "I just came from Detroit. I saw a lotta people get the crap kicked out of 'em and a lot get killed. This country is over, man, it's over. What you gotta do is get the people out of the cities. Get together everybody who has a skill; let's go to the country."

"Dichotomies! Dichotomies," Ned reproved them. "Total up everything you have here today and divide it."

"No, no," called out Pan, the hippy dope-pipe maker. "The country is a good scene, man. Build your own tepee, man, your own hogan. Do it for yourself, man."

"Christ almighty, we haven't dropped out of society," a protesting voice shouted. "We're still part of society if we like it or not."

Tobacco disagreed: "No. I've been living for free for years, doing my thing. I was wrote about in the *Wall Street Journal* doing my thing, so let's all get together and unitize. We'll get flyers out and announcements on the radio."

The voices began to come from all parts of the crowd:

—"No sir, man, what I want to know is when're we going to be self-sufficient and not keep on begging from the establishment."

—"We gotta beg or sell dope. We need the tourists even if they may have mucked up the Haight, but they're people, so if they roll up their windows and won't buy newspapers from you, don't say 'Fuck you' to them. Say 'Thank you.'

—"What're we going to do about tonight?"

—"What're we going to do about the syndicate?"

—"Two of my friends have been murdered!"

—"All this world needs is love, love, love. Ya gotta have love, love, love."

—"I need dope. Anybody who's got grass, break it out."

—"Purple Owsleys!!"

A chant started: "WE WANT DOPE! WE WANT DOPE! WE WANT DOPE!" The ringer began to hit the gong, its brassy reverberations catching up with each other in fused and fuzzy circles of sound, but the chant was still audible. "WE WANT DOPE, DOPE, DOPE!"

### THE GRASS LOOKED GREENER IN IOWA

**Guthrie City, Iowa, Oct. 5 (AP)—Four young men were charged with illegal possession of marijuana yesterday after they allegedly were caught picking it wild on a farm.**

### COUPLE GUILTY IN SMUGGLING POT INTO JAIL

**San Francisco, July 26—A Marin county jail inmate and his common-law wife were found guilty yesterday of conspiracy to smuggle marijuana into the jail.**

"As a matter of fact, I grew my beard long before there was a Haight-Ashbury," said Professor Leonard Wolf of San Francisco State College. On him the gray-black beard looked old-fashioned. "When I was growing up in Cleveland as a young YCLer, what I wanted for myself and for others was the neat, secure bungalows with lawns that we have now; but experience modifies your ideas. The Haight-Ashbury is, nevertheless, stunning, if you grew up as

103

I did, a Marxist. This is a community that wants to discover the landscape of madness the way people in the sixteenth century used to visit the madhouse on a Sunday . . . Hieronymus Bosch . . . I will say loud and clear I took marijuana years ago, but I'm not a user. I got nothing from it. I'm no drug taker and I know they are. I wish they would go where they're going without drugs, but it's irrelevant for me to tell them. I myself am old enough to value my consciousness. I'm not morally superior, but I just can't risk drugs. Too big a risk."

The professor was the Haight's best-known square. Everybody in the socially aware hip establishment knew him as the guiding personality of Happening House, a yet-to-be-born settlement house fitted to the community's unusual needs. It was hard to tell if the professor was only tolerated or actually liked, but he was there in a room at All Saints Church, conducting a Happening House meeting and acting like a man who didn't know that two people had been murdered, that there was a grass drought or a crisis. It would probably come to him, for he was not a hardhearted man, only a professor of English, a dope abstainer, and a fellow who, in his youth, had mistaken the split-level ranch house for the withering away of the state.

"Well, it seems everybody in the room is new this week," he said, looking around, "except you, of course, Father Harris." It was the Episcopalian Father Harris' church. The others in the room included Tobacco, tall Peter from the Hip Job Coop, a surly young peacenik who was badly cast for his politics, George from the Switchboard, and an older man who introduced himself as Swami. He wasn't Melanie's Swami, however, who was last reported either ailing or short of funds in Calcutta.

The professor opened by announcing that Happening House would soon have a place where the weekly psychodrama and a pottery class could bed down. He outlined some other possibilities while the younger people looked increasingly less interested. The professor sensed the lack of response, so he said, "The big thing in the community is being open and spontaneous, but there is something to be said for planning and structure. If there's too much . . . well, the fear is that the helping agencies will take over and the hippies will sneak off to Sausalito."

Father Harris spoke next: "We seem to have run into a bit of a misunderstanding with some of the young people. Perhaps you've seen the posters we've had tacked up here and there? The ones which read, GET THE FEELING YOU'RE MISSING SOMETHING? EAT RIGHT FOR A CHANGE. TURN ON TO FOOD AT ALL SAINTS CHURCH. Lots of them have been showing up thinking there'd be free food. They were very disappointed when they learned we were advertising our cooking class."

Another young man said there would be a new organization, which was really an old commune; but it would have a triangular blue-and-white pennant with a phoenix stenciled on it as its symbol. People flying the phoenix would be in the park, on the street, everywhere, "ready to rap with whoever wants to rap, so that if an Athenian idea does happen here, you might bring a phoenix flag home with you and start rapping in your city."

"I think the phoenix is a beautiful idea," the professor admired, "but I wanted to say a little bit more about the pottery class. With all the abrasion in the last six months, I'm still interested in pottery classes and things like that."

There was a murmuring among the young that if pottery classes were the professor's thing it was cool with them.

"I just put the idea in the air, because I find that things that aren't put in the air, well, sometimes their vibrations don't happen," the professor said, acting defensive and having a little trouble with the argot. "Ah, but here's Peter, come with some pressing anxieties, I think."

Tall Peter answered, "No, I like the phoenix flag trip. I'm going to make that trip, but the Hip Job Coop is in trouble. The place looks like a pigpen and we owe an awful lot of money. Also, there are people at the Coop who are drones at the end of a honey trip. We need $208 for rent. We're going on a survive or perish trip." The meeting adjourned inconclusively with tall Peter going on a back-to-the-Coop trip.

His storefront office was as he described it at the meeting. In

105

the piles of debris on which people lolled, nothing was clean, nothing was intact except the poster of Timothy Leary on the wall and the mandala above the Hindu altar, on which the flowers had wilted. "I used to say Leary has a guru complex, but is there anything wrong with a guru complex? Leary's a heavy cat," said Peter, the son of a professor of botany. His Coop was supposed to find kids jobs, but outside of lining them up to sell underground newspapers, it hadn't been very successful and it was short of money. They were living on nothing more than the distant hope of a benefit and the more immediate one of a big dope cop. Peter and his friends talked about the big shipment to come, but they were too disorganized to deal big.

The place, the back rooms, the shambly kitchen, everywhere was glutted with people and their bedrolls. It had become a crash pad, a macrobiotic baggage room.

Ego enjoyed the mess. The diapered toddler ran around climbing over people and caved-in furniture till he came to a stop on his mother's lap. Raena Love patted her son on the head and gave him a toke from her joint. "If a kid's around somebody who's giving off good vibrations, the kid'll get a total high. Like Ego here. He doesn't need grass. He's a great kid. If I'm talking about him and he's asleep, he stirs. He's a Leo. He's a Leo since the day he's born, and nobody fucks with a Leo."

A bunch of them were talking: Raena, her friend and stablemate, Tracy, a girl with hair two inches long; another girl, Irene, who said she was sixteen and might have been younger; and Brooks, a grave-sounding young man who had dropped out of his last year at the University of Texas law school. Brooks had been saying that he'd never had a good trip, and this had prompted Raena to reply, "I've never had a bad one and I've taken at least two hundred doses. I'm better when I'm high. Being high is my way of life and it works." Raena always saw the bright side, even about her own life, even about her nightmares: "Last night I freaked out in my sleep. I dreamt I was running through Golden Gate Park looking for a lost girl who was screaming somewhere in the fog and the leaves of bushes. The girl was screaming, 'Help!

Somebody come help me!' " Raena said cheerfully. It didn't strike her that she might be the girl, although, as she told her own life story, you'd think it would: "I was raised in Chicago, but I did my folding out in New York. I used to be a madam in a Manhattan penthouse, $50 a night and two or three girls there all the time. I was lesbian for four years. Every man I slept with I almost castrated, when I was a hooker. I was almost a butch drag, but I got straight when I dropped acid. I still sleep with women but my attitude is different; my consciousness is different. I used to sleep with men I could dominate, because my head was messed up, but acid is a soul-straightener. Now I can see the energy coming out of me when I walk down the street. You take acid and you can see maybe you really want to be a Seventh Day Adventist or a communist. I don't know what beauty the communists can offer. On acid you see the colors, you have a visual experience; you see the universe breathing."

"On acid," tall Peter interjected, "you can hear the ommmm all the time. Ommmm means peace in Sanskrit. All sounds, all music comes from it. On acid you can hear it from the mandala, the infinite that will go on after the other energy forms have congealed; it will go on, and on acid you will hear the cosmos breathe . . . it breathes in and out every eleven billion years."

"I'm not so religious," said Brooks. "I like to study the scene, and the man who fascinates me is Owsley. Why hasn't he been busted?"

"I've heard he's too big for the government," said Tracy, but Raena had another theory: "He may have gone into another dimension."

Brooks pondered that for a minute. "Well, they can't find him. I'm in the middle of the scene and I can't find him."

Since Raena had told her life story, Irene wanted the chance too. "I first dropped when I was fourteen, which I'll never forget. My mother drops acid too. She divorced my father because he didn't drop. Mother's mind was liberal and his was straight; he disapproves of acid dropping, but he *is* trying to understand it. That's why he doesn't hassle me. I think if someone's under eighteen, they should tell their parents if they're dropping. If you don't and they come into the room, you can freak trying to act straight. Acid's truth serum and it's hard to act against it. My mother planned my first trip. Really we planned it together. She went out the day we were going to do it and I dropped before she came back. She was angry I did it and she made me freak out. That's when I dropped out and left home. Since then we've gotten closer and closer so that I know when she's going on a trip, even though we are three thousand miles apart. But even still, I feel my mother's part of the straight world. I can't really go back to school and play her game."

"Don't be hard on our parents," tall Peter intoned. "They've been through some ugly, ugly karma."

The community's energy movers, as tall Peter liked to say, met again a few days later to dispel the ugly karma in the Haight. This meeting was in the Psychedelic Shop's calm room. The same principals were there as were at the Hippy Hill meeting, plus Allen Cohen, the editor of the *San Francisco Oracle,* and the professor. The grass shortage was worse, but now, along with murder, there was also a spade crisis. Bad vibes were coming out of the Fillmore and there was no pot.

"The spades attacked this cat and his chick in front of the *Oracle* office, and the other hippies just stood around and watched," somebody complained.

"They stand around and watch when the Angels beat up a spade in front of Benches."

"It's a drag, but being passive is part of our culture."

"We have to say the ommmm sound. Every day there should be a procession down Haight Street to bring the good vibes back. We'll have the gong and we'll go into the park at five o'clock and make the ommmm sound and chant mantras. We need a symbol, though."

"The phoenix flag."

"I think it would be a good idea to open a cathouse, because there're lots of straight guys on the street who're always asking where they can get laid. They have wine in them, and when they can't get laid their energy gets very negative."

"We could get outside help to get it started. There are so many foundations and philanthropists who love young people and want to do their thing. Their thing is helping us to help ourselves."

Tobacco objected again: "I feel this meeting is like all the other meetings. We've got to get rid of the bullshit. All these people on power trips and ego trips! What makes me sick is all the shit that's been poured into people's heads—the Diggers didn't really get going until I opened the first crash pad."

"You weren't the only one who worked there, Tobacco," another old resident corrected him. "Besides, it wasn't that groovy. The bikers took it over and destroyed it."

"Well, I agree with Ron Thelin. We should do the ommmm. Right at dusk today. It would be a good idea to carry flowers and chant because of these tensions."

"Like Tobacco says," the editor of the *Oracle* put in, "he doesn't want to be a Digger always doing things for the people here."

"Yeah," said Tobacco, "I feel like quitting, like saying, 'Man, fuck it.' All these people away on power trips and ego trips. I'm almost to the point of being sick of it, sick of being a Digger."

He'd gone too far for an audience with a passive culture. "Look at your own ego," somebody told him, while someone else said, "We'll pin a medal on you, Tobacco."

But the editor of the *Oracle* cut it short by continuing his anti-communitarian line: "Sometimes I think we get too hung up on geography. It's not the Haight-Ashbury; it's the whole thing we're doing that's important. I think it might be a good idea for us to get a pocketful of acid and go to Topeka, Kansas, and begin the work of turning people on. There's a lot of turned-on people in New York and here, but in between is a wasteland."

"There're two Sioux Indians going back to South Dakota with the idea. I talked to them," a happy voice reported, while another one said, "I turned on a cop. He was a nark too."

Another person disagreed. "It's not a wasteland. There're a lot of turned-on people in those little towns. They've heard about the Haight-Ashbury and they want to come."

"They shouldn't come here," the editor persisted, and then, like the professor at the church meeting, he asked tall Peter how the Hip Job Coop was doing.

"It's over. Not enough good energies to keep it going," he said. He was too intense, too dramatic a person to be down long. Regardless of the Coop's money trouble, Peter was walking the street again, crying out, "Hail, brother! The Haight loves you! I love you." He was memorable in his green, full-length djellaba. "You like it?" he'd ask when complimented; "somebody, a good friend, laid it on me, and I'm grateful, brother."

In that period he walked the neighborhood almost all the time, as though, if he didn't, something bad would happen. "The street is a rough motherfucker," he said. "It's a survival-of-the-fittest trip, but it's my feeling that you can't lose in the Haight, because Haight Street is God-fingered; it's a pulse, it's like a cosmos, it's a respiration trip. Here's where you get the best stone of all, because the best stone, the best groove of all, is just to look into the eyes of your brothers and sisters on the street and smile. That's the best dope of all, but I'm not going to put down anybody else's trip— smack, acid, speed, whatever it is, love."

"I've got no love left in me," a fat old woman with a German accent said, stopping him on the sidewalk. There was no beauty in her. Warts and wild hair, flesh like bread rising in the pan. "I have no love left in me."

"I see love in you, sister. Don't you believe in God, sister?" Peter asked, looking hard into her eyes.

"Ja, ja, I appreciate him, but I have the feeling he didn't do right with me. My fifteen-year-old son was killed by a drunk driver and they put me in the insane asylum."

"You must love anyway, sister. I see love in you. Love, love, flow, flow, love, flow." Peter's voice gentled off and it tranquilized the old woman. Quietly she said, "I'll try. Thank you," and went off down the street.

Jerry appeared. Still terrified, but it hadn't worked in Topanga Canyon, so he was back to sell some dope and flee again. "Owsley's left the city," he whispered. "Oh, he's a very heavy cat."

"A heavy cat," Peter repeated.

"When you're in the room with him, he doesn't talk much, but he gives off heavy, groovy vibes . . . an' Peter here is just about the heaviest cat you can meet, like, man, people come to him and he soaks up their problems," Jerry hushed in air-rushing syllables.

"At night, as darkness comes, the fear is moving in earlier," tall Peter said, moving on down the street. "There's no grass and there's more drinking, more breaking of bottles. It would only take one cat who thought he saw a black panther carrying a gun. The fear is coming earlier. There's only one group in the Haight that has defied this negative trip and that's the Hell's Angels. I've been in jail with some of them. They're acting as the policemen right now, not to control the flow but to protect people. Oh, there are some strange vibrations, fearful ones. The Diggers tell me the bloods are collecting huge energies; they have a very negative trip they must take, and, when they do, we'll get the thousand-petal, white lotus flash."

### KIDNAPERS SPREAD
### FEAR IN SARDINIA

**Rome, Aug. 27 (AP)—Bandit-ridden central Sardinia is gripped by fear in its blackest week of ransom kidnapings and vengeance slayings this year.**

### SARDINIAN BADMAN'S
### WORD FOR TOURISTS

**Cagliari, Sardinia, Oct. 4 (Reuters)—Sardinia's top bandit, Graziano Mesina, yesterday assured foreign tourists they will not be molested if they accept his invitation to visit this Mediterranean island.**

## LIZ TAYLOR'S
## NEAR MISS
## IN SARDINIA

**Porto Conte, Sardinia, Oct. 8 (UPI)—Elizabeth Taylor's dressing room trailer plunged over a 150-foot embankment into the sea yesterday, only seconds after she stepped out of it.**

Night at the Free Medical Clinic. The clinic is up a flight of stairs in a converted apartment. Down on the street there is talk of trouble from the Negroes in the adjoining Fillmore district. For some reason, the Negroes who live in the Haight itself are regarded as less threatening.

It's not because the hippies know the Negroes in the neighborhood. Contact is almost nonexistent. They don't realize that most of the black people they see live next door and not in the Fillmore, which is defined as dangerous territory; but the smoke from the fires of Newark and Detroit has irritated the eyes of the suburban youths in the dope colony.

### SPADES ARE PROGRAMMED FOR HATE

—Acid aphorism, Summer 1967

"Teddy, Teddybear!" a bearded young man calls, running down the apartment hallway to the room that serves as the clinic office. "Four spades in a car with a machine gun parked just down from Tracy's. What're we going to do?"

Teddybear hangs out at the clinic, doing the voluntary work of answering telephones. It also makes a good place from which to deal dope. The straight doctors who ostensibly run the place and give of their labor free have strict rules against holding and dealing, but their grasp of what goes on is vague. They have a lot of medical work to do when they're at the clinic, and there are so

112

many press conferences, interviews, and speeches to be made to concerned adults about what's happening that they don't have time to find out.

"You better call the fuzz," somebody in the room says.

"No, don't call the fuzz. Call the Angels," the messenger from the confusion on the sidewalks below puts in.

In critical moments Teddybear develops an officious way about him. Only he, his manner implies, has direct contact with the important people, as though all the telephone numbers in his little book are unlisted. "I think I'll call the Gypsy Jokers in Daly City, and I'll get a-hold of Chocolate George," he says, and begins dialing the numbers where the leaders of the motorcycle packs hang out. Teddybear, like so many of the people in the Haight, has great trust in the protective power of these psychedelic storm troopers.

"Hello, Chocolate? It's Teddy. No, no, you know, Teddybear, yeah, yeah, over at the clinic. Listen, Chocolate, it looks bad here. Carloads of spades with guns cruising the neighborhood. I think there's going to be trouble. We need the Angels fast," Teddy informs the biker on the other end of the line.

Hanging up, he laments the state of things in the Haight. "I've been here since March. [Assertion of status to distinguish him from the summer visitors.] It was beautiful then. We had human love. Did you know I performed a hippy wedding? A hippy wedding is based on love, not on a piece of paper. We had music and it was in the open air before the people and God as it should be. When I came here in March you could actually feel the love here, because we're not like people think. We're not beatniks, dirty, who don't give a damn, but now it's getting bad—the spades raping our women. I personally know of two hippy mamas raped by spades. We went to the police station and they didn't even write it down because we're hippies."

Like so much of the rest of white America, the dope community believes most black men have the rape of white women in their minds. The flower children have been nurtured in the same social soil as everybody else, and their drugs don't expunge the fears and

113

misunderstandings that hang invisible over the cities. But both the drugs and the types of people drawn to the center of the drug world combine to produce some different responses to the racial crisis.

In the Haight the word "Negro" is almost never used. "Black" is employed by people tinged with New Left political understanding, but the most common word is "spade." Even the Negroes who have amalgamated into the scene invariably refer to themselves as spades—a term used without prejudicial meaning in a restricted part of the jazz world for many years—but in the Haight its use is ambiguous. It can connote nothing more than an in-group vocabulary; most of the white kids aren't in that in-group, however, and for them the word carries a mildly derogatory, mildly hostile meaning.

For them spades are very much dark, dangerous people whom they both understand and dismiss with the oft-cited aphorism, "Spades are programmed for hate." This kind of passive fatalism extends beyond race to take in all of life, where everybody is programmed and nobody programs himself. It conforms to much of the experience of the white youth, of being surrounded from infancy by human objects that obey their magnetic tapes. Mother and her automatic washing machine both appear to run on ineluctable and unknowable pre-set cycles.

This unknowability permeates the personalities of the Haight. The mechanics of the machines, of the government, of everything are unknown and therefore awesome. You can accept them or destroy them, but changing them is impossible, for you are caught in a closed system outside of which there are no ideals to measure yourself against. All there is, all that is imaginable is within the programmed system; outside of it there is nothing—and that is where so many of the drug trips take their passengers. This is the God-cosmic trip, back to the unprogrammed beginnings when there was no individual personality nor any distinction in matter and spirit; then it was all one, which is to say, all was nothing.

A state of unprogrammed being is the Haight's highest ideal. For then, it is believed, you have broken the tape inside you and are free to feel, to react and discover if you do have a self of your own. For older people who have spent a lifetime wrestling with their internal conflicts, it is difficult to comprehend people who have been reared in such fine adjustment that they are not sure they are alive, who say things like, "I was high on grass and I realized that this body I've had for twenty-eight years is for carrying my brain around." These types are always taking dope (the psychedelics, chiefly) and discovering their brains, their tissues, even their cells and being amazed. They live in a condition of dismembered hysteria questing after the parts of their own bodies.

Afflicted with such convictions, this kind of youth, who is almost always from a middle-class home, has difficulty finding the anger inside him. He is the passive, nonviolent, loving hippy so much has been written about, but he has the spades, and if the white youth can't destroy the tapes inside of him, the spades, man, are programmed for hate.

### NEWARK, A WAR ZONE!

### UNEASY PEACE IN PLAINFIELD, N.J.

#### TANKS LEAD ATTACK
#### ON SNIPER SQUADS
#### —Death Toll Mounting

Detroit, July 26 (AP & UPI)—National Guardsmen and police battled early today with Negro snipers holed up in a 200-square-block area they seized last night.

#### A CIVILIZATION
#### GOING BACKWARD

Detroit, July 27 (Times-Post Service)—This haggard city is a mirror of civilization going backward.

In the days after Newark and Detroit, the hope that the spades would burn down America hardened into a certainty until, on the afternoon of the night the killing was supposed to begin, a lithographed flyer appeared on the street. It tells much:

### SURVIVE, BABY
#### BROTHER: AN IMPORTANT NOTICE FOR YOUR SAFETY AND SURVIVAL

*Sorry to bring you down, but this is about the riots our black brothers have planned for the city. There isn't much hope that they won't occur.*
*What do they mean to you, as white hippies, et al.?*
*Riots mean that the black people are going to be busy and would appreciate your getting out of the way . . .*
*Looting will empty all the food stores in one day.*
*No trucks will come to bring more food to the stores . . .*
*Store up some right now . . . Within the black people's mind they will be fighting a revolution. If you hamper them in any way you will be their enemy. During the riot the only help they want from you is your gun.*
*If not that, get the fuck out of their way.*

The word was passed down to the silliest street hippies to be off the sidewalks by eight. At the clinic, plywood was tacked up against the downstairs glass door, and within, heavy, light-proof curtains were put over the windows. "This'll be the first place the spades are going after. They had a hearse with BAR's in it parked down in front for three straight nights," somebody explained to a visitor amazed at the siege preparations.

A block or so down Haight Street, another apartment was ready to be used as a medical aid station. Citizen-band shortwave radio communication joined the two. To make sure that everybody had a place to go, temporary crash pads were opened all over. The Print Mint—the largest poster store on the street—opened a rear room to crashers, and Peggy spent the hours before sunset supervising the removal of most of her men's store inventory. Other stores closed early.

People fled off the streets to the communes, like that of Gary

116

Goldhill, the small Englishman who did sketches for the *Haight-Ashbury Tribune* and schemed to find a way to put out a marvelously expensive psychedelic magazine.

His commune was a large wooden house with ornately cut bargeboards, right on the edge of the Fillmore. Gary arrived from the Haight like a man infiltrating enemy lines. Grant, Helmut, and a girl were already there in the living room, a space that had been transferred to Persia by hanging a white silk parachute from the ceiling. The arched ribs of the material gave the room a domed lightness that even converted the black marble Victorian fireplace into something oriental. They were, the three of them, sitting on poufs, but the Fillmore was right outside. The girl had been chased and just made it to the door.

"What gets me is that if you're white there's nothing you can do," the girl said.

"I think we should close this place for a week and go to the country. When it's over we can come back—if it's still here," Grant remarked, sipping a glass of wine. He wore ducks and a loose blouse. He could have played a blond Sindbad the Sailor in the musical.

But the anxiety from outside dominated the room. "I was beaten up," Gary recalled. "It was seven or eight kids who wanted my leather jacket. I tried to show them I wasn't afraid, but it didn't help. I said, 'Peace,' but they hit me anyway. While they were doing it a car stopped and a man put his head out the window and said, 'Kill the motherfucker.' Then he drove off."

"It's not going to be safe here. We should go to the country," Grant repeated. "I wouldn't mind a week in the country anyway."

"It happened to me too," Helmut said. "I was in the park with a girl and this black man started slapping me. I said, 'I don't want to fight,' but he kept hitting me. The girl told him to let me go because I was much younger, so he started hitting her. They could break in here easy."

Grant had more wine. "They're going to burn down all the cities now. If I had a gun I'd be a sniper. I'd help them."

117

They had some more wine. Grant opened his silver pillbox, took one himself, and offered the others the small yellow tablets before they sneaked out to the car and drove off to dinner with friends in Sausalito, the verdant and richly quiet town on the other side of the Golden Gate Bridge which reminds world travelers of Portofino.

A lot of people had no intention of getting off the streets. They scurried around looking to score acid if they hadn't been provident enough to keep a stash. There is a distinct type of acid taker who has no interest in beauty, self-discovery, or religious learning; he likes to get stoned in a variety of situations for the experience: "Man, can you think what those fires are going to look like under acid? I've never seen even a fight under acid, but wow! a riot, what a groove!" they told each other as they went about copping dope.

Even to experts at dropping it in freaky situations, acid can do funny things. The night before, some Negro teen-agers had marched up to the corner of Haight and Masonic where they'd busted a few store windows before the cops cooled down the scene. Some stoned hippies had run toward the melee to pick up the vibrations. One of them, a boy named Pete, had frozen into a cataleptic trance by the time they dragged him into the clinic.

"Pete was on a groovy trip too," said his equally stoned pal. "But he couldn't manipulate himself. He tried to flow with it but he couldn't, and now, wow! he can't talk. Man, I dug it, though. Right now I'm behind STP, and on STP you can see what's what and it's communism that's doing this."

There was one Negro in the clinic at that moment, a young woman who stared at the hippy and then remarked, "I'll bet some of your best friends are spades too."

The Negro reaction is often patronizing disgust with an admixture of amazement at what appears to be hippy stupidity. On the night the kids thought the riot had been programmed, a couple of Negro men stood on the steps of 1526, a narrow place much favored for dope taking. Speed is even shot publicly on those steps.

As the hippies floated by, one of the Negroes called out, "Take dope and shout love! That don't solve anything," but the hippies only smiled and asked for spare change. "It don't figure," the man said to his companion. "I live here in the hottest building in the neighborhood and this silly boy sits down and shoots up. I say to him, 'Why don't you just put an ad in the newspapers? There's a policeman across the street taking your picture.' An' you know what that silly boy says? He says, 'That's your hang-up.' My hang- up! I almost liked to hit him alongside his head."

Not everybody in the Haight took dope or waited for the spades to do the violence they couldn't bring themselves to do against the machines and their fathers who make and run them. Teddybear reacted like Lester Maddox. He armed himself with an ax handle and stayed in tense, self-important radio communication with the other apartment, where a collection of hippies, street commandos, and junior heistmen hid in the darkness, peeping out from behind the window shades, checking their guns, knives, and clubs.

White Rabbit wigwagged from the roof of the clinic, and a little man with a limp ordered people around and supervised the laying out of bandages and a rudimentary set of surgical instruments.

"I'm Doc, the hippy biker doctor who isn't licensed because he won't take people in an' cheat 'em . . . I've been known to stay up seven weeks at a time and do as competent a job as any straight doctor. I'm from the University of Minnesota . . . I'm a no-money bastard; I'm vulgar an' I've got the eyes of ten eagles with the words of black magic; I can kill a man fifteen ways, and if anybody touches my wife he'll die the death of salt in a thousand wounds."

The effort to clear the street failed absolutely. It never had so many people on it and they were never more stoned, walking up and down, waiting for the spades to do their thing. In the crowd that night were two different-looking men, well dressed, but not like the rest of the tourists, although they carried cameras. They were visiting Hungarian doctors, one of whom was an official of the Communist party, and how they had gotten misdirected into loveland that night was never explained.

"Where are the police?" the party official demanded to know.

"They're around."

"Well, why don't they arrest these people?" he insisted on finding out.

"They wouldn't know exactly what to do with them if they did arrest them."

"Put them in work camps. This is terrible," he said in a voice that showed quite genuine indignation. Then his tone changed, became peremptory, as though he had a claim on the middle-class American he was talking to, as if both were members of an undefined world master class that had best stick together lest it be dismembered by Chinese, dope fiends, and the unruly young. "How can you allow this? What is happening to this country? They are burning down your cities, and your President doesn't do a thing. He waits. I can understand for a few hours, but there is a time when you must use machine guns. And these people, you let them run loose. These are the same people who are doing this peace protesting, who are betraying your own soldiers in Vietnam. They should be shot."

As he said it, somebody handed him a flower. The flowers came from tall Peter of the Hip Job Coop, who was taking his own measures to meet the crisis. He and his friends were passing out flowers everywhere. "I won't tell you who laid them on me, but we're giving out ten thousand of them," Peter said, expressing his view of the night:

"We threw the *I Ching* and it said, 'Youthful Folly,' then it changed to 'Opposition.' It said gather quietly and flow. Listen to the *I Ching*. It is the prophetic book of China and it contains three thousand years of social commentary and it never lies. It tells us the constructive response is flowers and candles. Candles! When a man picks up a candle, he picks up the sun and all its energies. So flow, go down on the street and pick up your brothers and sisters and get them comforted. The good energies will come again."

## YOUNG REDS TOLD:
## EMULATE SINATRA

Moscow, Aug. 28 (UPI)—Multi-millionaire Frank Sinatra was held up as a model for Soviet young Communists.

"He hates only racism, Fascist ideology and coercion. He loves little children," said a Young Communist League newspaper, Komsomolskaya Pravda of Lithuania.

## SINATRA GETS
## NEW TEETH

Beverly Hills, Calif., Sept. 13 (UPI)—Frank Sinatra's dentist flew here Monday from Connecticut to replace two of the singer's front teeth, knocked out in an altercation at the Sands Hotel in Las Vegas.

## MIA AND THE MYSTIC

Los Angeles, Oct. 5 (AP)—Actress Mia Farrow will leave husband Frank Sinatra behind for a month of meditation with Indian mystic Maharishi Mahesh Yogi, her studio said yesterday.

There was a poem glued to the window of the Black Man's Free Store in the Fillmore ghetto. The Black Man's Free Store is a Negro version of the free store the hippies have in the Haight, only it looks like another wretched charity. It smells of castaway seconds and handouts; it has none of the suggestion of change and rebellion of the hip free store not many blocks away. It does have its poem:

> *Choose your weapons*
> *flowers or guns stand by*
> *them; learn their essential*
> *energies. Apply them as*
> *use permits. You can have*

121

*both; only you can't shoot*
*flowers and guns make lousy*
*flower pots.*

Despite the words "flowers" and "essential energies," this is not a hip poem; it is about tools and their appropriate use. They are to be used against an external enemy in the furtherance of an ideal that is greater than an individual but which single persons can help realize through conflict. The hip view of man obtaining happiness by activating his self-destruct mechanism is absent.

White druggies attribute their world-view to the knowledge they gain from taking dope, particularly acid. Negroes, people from another subculture, apparently don't react the same way to the psychedelics. Roy Ballard, who runs the Black Man's Free Store, observes, "Marijuana is groovy. I myself take it, and LSD is useful. I know a number of white kids who've had their heads straightened out by taking it. These are kids who were all messed up by guilt and the black man, but now they can do their own thing. But if a man has to depend on any kind of drug to find reality, that's bad. That's a world of fantasy. They just wish the world would be like what they feel when they're on their drug."

For Ballard, what's wrong with the world isn't what's going on in his head; it's what people are doing, and there's no drug that will straighten that out. His whole life reinforces this belief. Even while he's talking in his dusty, dilapidated Free Store, the conversations of people around him buttress what he says:

"Ain't that a bitch! Jive ass po-lice comin' in here las' night an' wrecking the place."

"Yeah, a sister got so upset she passed out and I'm trying to help her with a washbowl and this mother comes up here with a machine gun—*with a ma-chine gun!*"

Ballard is twenty-seven years old and nearly a third of that time he's spent in the civil rights movement, both in the South and the North. He met some of the whites in the Haight in jails and on picket lines during their activist days and is more favorably disposed toward "the movement"—drugs, that is—than most Negroes.

"I put down organizations a long time ago," he says, sympathizing with the anarchist pronunciamentos issuing from Haight-Ashbury. "They're a hang-up. They don't get anything done. I was a member of Snick for a year and a half . . . I went in Haight-Ashbury, spent four months there to find out what it was all about. The only worthwhile thing I could see was their free store, which we started here. The rest of Haight-Ashbury is white kids getting away—revolting against what their parents neglected to do . . . They're trying to say the only way to do it is to start over again because everything is a game . . . Black people never had it before, so they can't start all over. You might say the white kids are more advanced but also less realistic."

Ballard is talking about the section of the Haight-Ashbury world that isn't anti-Negro and considers the drug experience politically and socially relevant. It is a minority segment but a large one, and a black person could comfortably fit into it, make friends, and become a hippy. Very few have decided to do so, probably less than fifty in the whole Haight.

One reason for the paucity of black hippies may be acid itself. The drug, according to expert opinion and users' testimony, tends to hypo all physical sensations. It is not a pain-killer, but just the reverse. The senses—sight, sound, taste, smell, and touch—all become much more intense with most users. The nervous system is overloaded with sensations which arrive with such speed and variety the brain often doesn't know what to do with them—or even how to sort them out.

This may be exhilarating for people who are half-dead emotionally, for whom life is hardly more than enduring the blandness of "the plastic society"; but for Negroes such is not the case. "Man, I feel enough as it is. I don't wanta know any more than I do," said one black who tried acid.

Negroes are the last people in America to need drugs to express themselves or realize their feelings. They take smack because

123

sometimes their feelings are too strong to tolerate; and they have the catharsis of art. It is they who have given the drug world most of its language, its music, while the effete English homosexuals of the mauve decade provide the ideas of color and form from which psychedelic art derives.

Thus the hippies use black people as whites always have in America, as the people who are truly affective, emotional, sensual, and uninhibited. If you want to break out of white middle-class restraints, the way to do it has always been to go among the Negroes or imitate them. The colloquial language of the Haight is the speech of the ghetto interspersed with a few expressions from two other fugitive minorities: the homosexuals and the underworld. The word "chick," the verb "to split," the expletive "man" (as in "look, man . . ."), the deuces-wild use of the word "like" (as in "like, man, you ain't gonna make it with that chick so like you'd best split") is all ghetto idiom.

But a black man doesn't have to dress up like an Indian and go running to hippy town—there is now one in almost every city —to live an affective, feeling life or hear language like that. He can stay home. In fact, if he goes to hippy town he will find he is still in the white culture of self-restraint.

The drugs don't necessarily facilitate free self-expression. This is best illustrated by what's happened to Negro music after it's been given an acid bath by the Beatles and similar musical groups. The volume is turned up, but the notes are fuzzed over so that you have to be stoned on acid to pick up its tectonics.

(Much has been written pointing out that this music is about drugs, but it is also often played by people who are stoned and is meant to be listened to by stoned people, although a minority of acidheads are driven up the walls by their outraged nervous systems when they hear it.)

A hundred notes are used where one would do, but only at the cost of losing the tension and hard clarities of the urban blues. The emotion is either too strong or directed toward joys and pains white dopesters have never felt; but men like Muddy Waters, the master of ghetto musical idiom, enjoy only a fringe popularity.

The same holds true for dancing. "My God, my God, what are those people doing?" cries the Negro girl on seeing three hundred dopeheads on the dance floor of the Straight Theater, the Haight's Palladium. "They can't dance. They can't keep time, what *are* they doing, and they're so ugly!"

On the night in question the heads were coached before the music started "to find the moving, rhythmic spot inside yourself, and then find another, and another, and let them come together until they bring you up off the floor expressing yourselves with your bodies." The poor hips tried, rising to their feet from the floor where they had been seated during their dance lessons, but they knew no dance steps and could only stamp and flutter their arms. Some were so stoned it was enough for them to approach the stage where The Grateful Dead were playing. They stood looking up at the Dead, their mouths creased in the characteristic expression of people on acid, picking up the vibrations like a motionless cloud of drugged bats.

At a time when Negroes are fighting off dope and forcing their way out of the ghetto to get the good things that hips dismiss as so much plastic, it's hard for them to empathize with white kids who have all the Negroes want. It's incomprehensible that these whites should build a new ghetto and lock themselves up in it to take dope. They are an affronting put-down to the blacks, making a virtue of every sin the black man has been accused of—dirt, shiftlessness, sexual promiscuity, improvidence, and irresponsibility. For these things the black man has been excluded from America, and for these same things the people called hippies, the white sons and daughters of the white collar, are revered as culture heroes, as holy povertarians. So rich, so precious, so secure, so much to the manner born, they can despise the money, the cleanliness, the comfort, the balanced diet, the vitamins, and the living room carpets black people have been willing to die for.

AN AFTERNOON IN FRONT OF BENCHES,
A HAIGHT STREET HAMBURGER JOINT

Cast: Teddybear, a dope dealer; Jerry, another dope dealer;

Gypsie, a sixteen-year-old girl speed freak; Chester, a sidewalk hippy; David Simpson, a political activist hippy; Randolph, an older Negro; Malcolm Y, an unidentified black militant.

TEDDYBEAR *(grabbing hold of* GYPSIE, *who giggles):* These are the people who live in the Haight-Ashbury. The government won't take into consideration we're a people, a fucking people. We're tired of the establishment and we're tired of wars.

GYPSIE: He's my Teddybear. *(he starts to let her go)* Don't split, Teddybear. I'll give you a grape.

TEDDYBEAR *(taking one):* We're a persecuted people. The police are always hounding us. That's why everybody around here knows some law.

DAVID SIMPSON: The spades have been up against it for years. We just didn't know what the law is like until they came after *us.*

JERRY *(arriving on the scene):* Oh, wow! Wow, wow, oh wow! I was just hitchhiking on Van Ness and, like, this Rolls Royce, man, with a chauffeur, man, comes up and stops, and wow! the guy in the back—he had to be a banker or something—wow, asks if I want a ride and when I get in he opens up this gold cigarette case and offers me a joint, and was it good, man! I just leaned over and kissed the dude, gave him a big kiss.

TEDDYBEAR: We can't lose.

JERRY: The sun is shining today. It was out of sight—I just came from my shrink. I told him I wanted a letter keeping me out of the Army. He said he was glad I was honest and he'd give me one.

TEDDYBEAR: See, where's the Bill of Rights? It applies to everyone but hippies.

DAVID: That's not true. It doesn't apply to colored people either.

TEDDYBEAR: Well, they're hippies too.

GYPSIE: It don't apply to speed freaks.

TEDDYBEAR: She started geezing [shooting] when she was twelve and she's sixteen now. She'll die like the rest of us, but sooner unless we can help her.

GYPSIE: You can put down I'm very happy because Teddybear loves me.

RANDOLPH (*he has been listening all the time*): I believe I take acid so I can pretend. You don't have to pretend, but I caint talk good English. If I had good clothes and a fair face I wouldn't grow no beard and stay here.

CHESTER: Sure you would, because you're a hippy and a true Christian.

RANDOLPH: You people have taken the Bible and broken it down so you can understand and go higher with God, but our people have been deprived of it, man. (*enter* MALCOLM Y *who listens*)

DAVID: Not our people, just *the* people.

RANDOLPH: Our people, yeah, our people, gotta have help, man, ya understand. We want nice coats and pastel striped ties, and they've got to stop killin' the brothers, ya understand.

DAVID: Well, who's doing the killing?

TEDDYBEAR: The establishment.

RANDOLPH: You're the highest power, white folks. You been talking English sixteen hundred years. The black man hasn't been exposed. He gotta catch up.

MALCOLM Y: I think you're insulting black people. I see you here dressed in costumes wearing African prints! (*to* RANDOLPH) I really don't dig black brothers and sisters getting hung-up tripping with these junkies.

TEDDYBEAR: We're your brothers too. We're hippies.

MALCOLM Y: The best thing you white brothers can do is get out of our neighborhood and go down on Van Ness to do your begging.

TEDDYBEAR: We love everybody. We love you.

MALCOLM Y: I don't want you to love me. Love! I know what *I'm* going to do. I'm going to train my people to kill you and you and you. (*points a finger at each of the whites*)

A WHITE VOICE: I can't talk well. My teeth have been knocked out by the cops, but I still believe in peace, don't you?

MALCOLM Y: Peace! Peace! Crap! You're street bums. You better go get your hair cut, get a job, and train your people to defend themselves.

127

THE WHITE VOICE: I'm just a stoned, happy hippy. Let's talk hip.

MALCOLM Y: I don't know anything about being hip. You're sick . . . disgusting!

TEDDYBEAR: Do I look like a hippy?

MALCOLM Y: Yes. A hippy bum that doesn't do anything.

TEDDYBEAR: I spread love and understanding.

MALCOLM Y: I understand you, and if I see you again I'm going to kill you. *(he exits)*

CHESTER: I profess Christianity myself, and I know that spade. I saw him in Watts two years ago. He was one of them that was trying to start the riot.

CHUCK *(the hash slinger in Benches, who's been listening; he makes a face):* Welcome, welcome. This is hippyland, land of love, land of tolerance and integration.

Santa Barbara, Calif. (AP)—Municipal Judge Frank Kearney dismissed a charge that 18-year-old John Tower threw a "substance" at a police car.

The arresting officer, Donald Sweet, said the substance was "a flower: to wit, a daisy."

\* \* \*

"We know the intellectual nihilists—they have been our teachers. We know the dream of demolition—it is the American dream, and we are still moving in it. But how can we awaken from it? The vertiginous nightmare of early morning seems to hold us forever. Yet even while we are falling through space, clutching our absurd bluebooks and draft cards, we dimly sense what it might be like to throw off the blankets and walk on the cold honest floor, and we know, even while we are falling through space, that the price of awakening will be a painful act of the will."

—From "White Student, Black Theatre," by David Robbins, *The Bowditch Review,* Summer–Fall 1967

The females, the children, the noncombatants, the poet Richard Brautigan, who has blond moustachios, moved off to one side of the dusty church playground. They didn't want to get hurt while the young men fought.

There were six or seven of them overpowering each other with their masculinity. Roberto was drunk out of his mind on mountain red. It had been he who'd built the sturdy wooden dragon in the churchyard for the neighborhood Mexican kids to play on. He'd built silently and pleasantly, for he is that kind of a person; now, with the celebration of the dragon's completion, he was bombed, staggering, so full of alcohol and fight that he almost tumbled into the pit where the roast suckling pig was cooking. Brautigan wore a high-crowned felt hat which he left uncreased. He wore a vest and he stood to one side like a nineteenth-century statue without a pedestal, an *objet d'art* neglected, put in the back of the barn like a rusty threshing machine. He is a fine, ironic writer who was ubiquitous during the summer in San Francisco. He may make the ultimate sense of what happened in that city.

Brautigan predates this generation and finds his beginnings in the Beat Era of a decade ago, but the rest of the men are Diggers, members of the unorganized group of politically aware people in the Haight. There are people styling themselves Diggers wherever there is a scene—Long Beach, the East Village, Detroit. The San Francisco Diggers are the first, save only the original seventeenth-century sectarians who coined the name. When they get organized —which they sometimes manage to do—they give out free food, clothes, and crash pads. It is a form of acting out the demonetized, communal society of their dreams.

The young men didn't hit each other but wrestled in the dust, harshly and painfully trying to pin random opponents. They were being worked over by an abstract anger that abates itself by causing pain to particular people. That is why they hurt each other with flying tackles, but because it wasn't anger at individuals, they put a limit on their violence and got their satisfaction from twisting headlocks and the feel of the other man's body as he wiggled to get his face out of the powdery dirt. They stopped short of serious

129

injury, but Roberto did almost get accidentally roasted with the pig.

After they finished their fighting, they went back to turning the pig and basting it with mountain red. The children and the women came back toward the fire. Night had fallen and it was chilly. Richard Brautigan moved closer, and Emmett Grogan sat on the church house steps wearing a magnificent necklace made of the complete spine of a snake.

He wasn't talking to reporters. They had mistaken him this spring for the leader of the Diggers, when he was more of an imprecise, inspirational force. They had written about him suggesting it was he who had declared the "summer of love," and this had caused much jealousy. After Grogan had left the city to hide, Tobacco was still going around the Haight accusing him of sopping up the publicity all for himself.

They can't forget the mass media. The media encase them and form them. Many of them can't express themselves in any other form. While they were roasting their pig they were also working on a free newspaper in which the thoughts came out in headline exhortations:

SAN FRANCISCO TO BE FIRST FREE CITY ON THE PLANET
BY THE END OF '68 OR MIDDLE OF '69 THE LATEST
HERMAPHRODITIC DEITIES FUCK FOREVER

One of the best efforts to come out of the scene is a tour de force novel called *INFORMED SOURCES*. The entire work, distributed free, is done in the wire-service formula jargon that suggests why they were fighting in the dust, why they feel so imprisoned by an infinitely tautological culture that they can't stand and can't break out of:

ALL POINTS

INFORMED SOURCES NEWSFEATURE WRITER SOLOMON HERSHEY IS PREPARING A TWO-PART NEWSFEATURE ON A TYPICAL DAY IN THE LIFE OF A TYPICAL INFORMED SOURCES STAFFER. PLEASE HAVE ONE TYPICAL STAFFER IN EACH BUREAU MESSAGE A RECORD OF HIS ACTIVITIES FOR A TYPICAL DAY, INCLUDING ANY INTEREST-

ING CONVERSATIONS, SPECULATIONS, OR MOODS THAT MIGHT OCCUR
DURING THE 24-HOUR PERIOD COVERED. LIMIT MESSAGES TO 50
WORDS.

NY (GENERAL DESK)
PR610PES

FUCK INFORMED SOURCES!

ALL POINTS

CLEAR FOR LAW AND ORDER DAY GREETING. PUT MACHINES ON
SINGLE SPACE.

NY (TRAFFIC)
PR606PES

CLR 604PES . . .

IS58

FOLLOWING IS GREETING FOR LAW AND ORDER DAY.

```
. $$$$. . $$. $$. .$$$$$$. .$$$$$$. .$$$$$. .$$$$$
.$$$$$$. .$$. $$. .$$$$$$. .$$$$$$. .$$$$$. .$$$$$$
.$$. . . .$$. $$. .$$. . . .$$. . . .$$. . . $$. $$
. $$$. . .$$. $$. .$$$$$$. .$$$$$$. .$$$$$ . $$$$$$
. . $$ . .$$. $$. .$$$$$$. .$$$$$$. .$$. . . $$$$$
.$$$$$$. .$$$$$$. .$$. . . .$$. . . .$$$$$ . $$ $$
. $$$$ . . $$$$ . .$$. . . .$$. . . .$$$$$ . $$  $$
```

It is a novel about the destruction of the social system expressed
only in the system's terms. It is scary and nihilistic, for nothing
new is added. There is no vision; there is only the ripping out of
the wires of the teletype trunk and the use of them to garrot the
operator. But the drunken fight in the dust is an effort to break
out and find another form of expression.

"Okay, now those relationships are clarified," said Peter Cohon,
one of the fighters. "We feel better. We do it that way because
some things have to be done totally. It was good and there was no
fear because there was no malice. If you grow up through twenty
years of marshmallow, plastic, and hopscotch, you want to have
an end to it. I want to lay life. I want to taste it, beat it, feel it,
kill it, fuck it, and I want to have all these things done to me."

131

Peter makes no distinction between his brawling in the dust, fighting his way out of his plastic flesh, and his broadest social and political perspectives: "Personal confusion is directly relevant to social confusion, so when I feel a contradiction I do something about it. That's why I must take this system apart. Otherwise I'll end up with the same guilty feelings that college students have. I'd like to live a life that is free, so I begin living that way. I don't do it to teach or propagandize, but because I want to. To live an alternative that is totally outside the alternatives of this culture is a profoundly political act."

What he is saying could also have some profoundly disturbing political consequences if he is articulating the feelings of more than a forlorn band of hippies living out their brief moment of public attention. In truth, Peter and the Diggers are on the fringes of the dope world of the Haight-Ashbury, although it was they who coined and popularized the love slogans that the mass media picked up and offered the world as epigrams of hippy philosophy. What happened was that the ideas the original Diggers proclaimed when they invited American youth to the Haight were entwined in a flash-fire kind of social movement that got completely out of their control and made them, the founding older brothers, irrelevant to the dope peddling, the avarice, and the human exploitation that substituted itself for their fraternal communitarian dream.

It was for this reason that in the middle of the summer, after the papers started reporting "hippy" murders, you began to get stories out of the Haight saying the "real" hippies were taking flight to rural communes and that ersatz, plastic hippies and teeni-boppers had taken over. In some sense the stories were true. People like Peter had been pushed to the side; but their eclipse is temporary, for they represent a current in American culture which is only squashed or detoured in one place to re-emerge in another.

It is a current of emotive, affective politics; it is politics of the gut, of feeling, of unqualified conviction, of the compulsion to act out the disposition of the soul in public and political ways. It is a politics that finds dichotomies damnable and hypocritical, that demands a perfect consistency between private and public life, a

132

politics without distinctions or subtleties—without craft. It is one of the prodigal consequences of the age of affluence when many people are not trained by the necessitous tactics of scarcity to put a check on their moral perceptions.

This in itself is not new. It is the affective stream of history that provides us with our passions and our moral point of view. Without it, all government would be administrative mechanics operated according to morally neutral, natural laws of human behavior. There are no such laws, but for a long time in America the non-affective political myth has been the conventional wisdom. Out of it has come the notion of consensus, bipartisan foreign policy, non-partisan public administration, the belief that expertise can replace ideology.

The other view of politics as a Zoroastrian struggle has never died entirely. The Far Right never surrendered. The John Birch Society and the Minutemen with their cries of treason and their secret stockpiling of arms have always believed, like Carrie Nation and the temperance crowd, that moral truth justified breaking the law or pulling down whatever part of the government stood in their way. The Left capitulated, however. In place of trumpet calls for action regardless, it accepted rationalism and began to say, "You should pay your workers more because if you do, the system will operate more smoothly and we'll all profit by it."

Now comes Peter to join in making a new sort of affective politics of the Left. The first aspect of it to strike most observers is its aristocratic tinge. Whether of the Diggers or the plain, stoned, apolitical hippies sitting on the curbstones in their dopey fog, everybody exclaims of them, "Oh, but they're middle class!" Peter exemplifies this. He isn't a proletarian communard who wants to abolish money because he hasn't any. A graduate of Grinnell College who grew up in a New Jersey suburb, the son of a stockbroker, he says, "I come from an overprivileged home."

Such studies as have been done on young, white, radical militants indicate Peter doesn't have an unusual family profile. A heavy percentage come from upper-income homes, often from professional parents. What this suggests is that leisure and money are

133

producing some unlooked-for types of human beings. For the last decade, ever since our social seers began to worry about the plushy results of automation and money, the cry has been to teach people how to use their leisure "constructively," which always seems to translate into adult education or salmon fishing. We have filled our newspapers and magazines with warnings to businessmen that early retirement can lead to cardiac arrest from boredom.

In the past, of course, the idle rich seldom died of boredom but rather frequently from vice. From this point of view, what happened in the Haight can be seen as the children of the new moneyed middle class copying the older corruption of the upper classes. Certainly that seems to be the way that sex, drugs, and alcohol are being used, and it is demonstrably true that modest suburban homes can now produce ne'er-do-welling playboys along with the very rich. The sportive style in the Haight resembles jet set and movie stars at play. Except that they cost less, hippy-costumed be-ins atop Mount Tamalpais aren't so different from costumed balls on the Côte d'Azur.

But upper-class opulence doesn't invariably bring forth *la dolce vita*. It may also produce people with the time and resources to germinate exquisitely filigreed sensibilities which are moral and political as well as personal. Wealth is also conducive to the development of the artist, the aesthete, and the saint. Thus the anguish of the nineteenth-century Russian in Tolstoy or the American tycoon's daughter in Henry James is now available to middle-class youth.

None of this is prelude to dismissing today's anguish by saying it's not new and that, by faulty logic, it's therefore not important. It is new, if only because so many people now have the opportunity to cultivate their souls in unhurried leisure. It is also new because its content is new.

In the recent American past, radical revolutionaries have had vast but still limited objectives. They've wanted perhaps to overthrow the government and divide the wealth, but they haven't wanted to destroy everything and start over with nothing more than a tepee and a flint knife. Many of today's radicals do. Their mood, and their critique, is one of dead pessimism for everything. They are convinced they are trapped in a huge mechanism for synthesizing bombs and artificially flavored orange juice. They are disillusioned with all, and because their despair is panoramic, they aren't able to answer the questions put to them again and again, "What's your program? What would you do if you were President?" They can only reply that they'd abolish the presidency and then shrug their shoulders and wander off in search of people who don't ask silly questions.

This bleak mood, this faithlessness in the exhausted possibilities of the society, appears to have dominated the souls of American youth for nearly twenty years. David Riesman, writing of "The Uncommitted Generation" of the 1950's, observed, ". . . these young people have come to feel that . . . nothing, except the family, deserves their wholehearted allegiance . . . it is taken for granted that a sensible fellow, indeed an honest one, will prefer suburban domesticity and a quiet niche to ulcerous competition for large stakes, despite the view from the top and the interesting climb."

The "Silent Generation" bet on the close, personal relations of domesticity; home and hearth would provide the grace to quicken the soul. But that generation's younger brothers and sisters, its own children, found the very preconditions of American family life so deadly they murdered the relationships of the people in it. They abandoned the family as a hope of salvation and went out to build a new society with new kinds of families or none. In the process of joining the Peace Corps, building a Haight-Ashbury and a civil rights movement, they have shaken the Silent Generation's faith in the rightness of its own youthful decision for cool withdrawal into warm and private family life. One of the reasons for the adult world's slowness to condemn what its youth is doing must come from this sneaking reappraisal of what it did, a reproaching thought that it may have settled for too little, that a rich domesticity will finally be poisoned if it's secured through

135

mutual atomic terror and world famine, that it is not enough to send people Christmas cards saying a donation to CARE has been made in their name.

Yet adult America has found it very hard to follow this politics, even when trying to be sympathetic. Few people who aren't part of it can get past saying, "Well, it's not ideological," which usually translates to mean, it's not communist, so we don't have to worry about *that*. At the same time it strikes outsiders as irrational, internally inconsistent, and so devoid of programmatic content as to be useless for any kind of application. From the point of view of mid-twentieth-century rational man, affective, confessional politics would have to be so. Confessional politics begins with the disposition of a man's soul, not with his relationship with the economic or political order; for a very long time it has been disreputable in America, something for Negroes, Nazis, and nuts. Now it has returned in some shapes that are hard to dismiss—as when 35,000 youths storm the Pentagon to "stop the war machine and burn down the house of death."

This form of politics abrogates the distinction between public and private, substituting a psycho-moral consistency for the logical consistencies of the rationalist. It destroys other compartmented separations, seeing culture, economics, politics, family life not as an "interrelated whole," to use the academician's phrase, but as inseparable. The New Left confessionalist outrages liberals who want to do one thing at a time; the confessionalist rejects this because any single reform or change is to his mind bound to be corrupted by its surroundings. In the past, confessionalists have often found the only way to satisfy their all-or-nothing morality was to turn quietist and establish some kind of communal life that would save them even if the rest of the world was going to hell. The Haight has hatched its form of secular quietism in its veneration and imitation of American Indians. Peter Cohon has a streak of it in him, but a better exemplar is Ron Thelin, the young man, twenty-nine, who with his brother started the Psychedelic Shop, the first head shop on the street.

136

Ron believes in and can talk about his solution to the human dilemma: "My vision for Haight Street is a world-famous dope center. In every little store . . . the kinds of stores we would have on Haight Street would be like fine teashops where there are big jars of fine marijuana, where there are chemist shops with fine psychedelic chemicals . . .

"Some people in talking about the Indians, they say that you can never go back to their way of life, that it no longer exists, it can't happen. Well, I don't look at it that way at all. Right here on our own continent we have the Hopi Indians who have been living peacefully and are living in the same place they have for many thousands of years.

"When they have meetings—I have been to meetings of heads of the clans of the Hopi Indians—they all sit around quietly, very peaceful. A man will speak for five minutes, fifteen minutes, or three hours, and everyone sits around quietly and listens. When he is through there is usually a little quiet, and then someone else will speak. Right here on our own continent we have a spiritual people who, I think, are the spiritual heads of this continent, who know a way of life that is peaceful. And as a model of life we can learn from the Indians. We can learn a model of the way of life that is based on the tribal sense of family organization, of social organization that is not a large mass of individual family units, what are called little boxes, that children go to school, mother goes to coffee, and father goes to work. It's completely insane. These aren't meaningful relationships.

"The direction I see it taking is getting back to the land and finding out how to take care of ourselves, how to survive, how to live off the land, how to make our own clothes, grow our own food . . . how to live as a tribal unit.

"This may mean a man and wife relationship. This seems to be workable. There are instances where a man and a woman can love each other truly for a lifetime, but I think that is rare. Something equally valid is a tribal unit where there is a contract between maybe three families, and where sex relations are shared equally

137

under that contract. This is in a larger context, the village. I see thousands of small villages all over the world, with cities as trading centers.

"Perhaps at this point we see the relevance of the Diggers and a free frame of reference. That is, money people, the people who think through the eyes of money, cannot see any activity or human involvement unless they surround it with some kind of relationship with money. This is the most difficult thing to transcend . . . doing things for free instead of for money. It is a difficult thing to work out, but as soon as you can start to do it and figure it out, the more you do things because they turn you on, because it is the right thing to do . . . that is the criterion . . . that is the right thing to do. Peter Berg [one of the more prominent Diggers] was right: 'Establish the social facts first, and the economics will follow.' "

As Ron Thelin states it, the hippy Indian trip ceases to be bizarre, though it remains farfetched even for the largest majority of the New Left. Yet elements of this political vision reappear time and time again in the new white radicalism. One of the most common is the aching demand for human relationships that support and satisfy the soul, a primary group that isn't a "unit" but one that yields loyalty, love, and personal completion. This marks people like Ron off from economic communards, the syndicalists who have wanted to destroy the money system because it isn't divided evenly. Ron would destroy it because it divides people; before everything else, he and the youth who think like him crave human solidarity.

Confessional politics, be it under the hand of Muhammad, Wesley, or Ron and the radical romantics, tends to divide creation between the sacred and the profane, kosher and *tref*, good manna and bad, the helps and the hindrances of the soul. They do not talk about the greatest good for the greatest number, or progress, or the relative advantages or disadvantages of anything. They start with individual salvation and build their network of value judgments from this concern. Thus Ron speaks ideas that are always popping out of certain segments of the New Left to the surprise and puzzlement of many nonbelievers:

138

"Turn on, turn on to new relationships, turn on to new styles, turn on to different metaphors, turn on to Hare Krishna chants, turn on to Zen Buddhism, turn on to dancing, let go, relax. Psychedelic experiences at first are a kind of a jar, a kind of wakening needed to understand all the programming that has gone on.

"There has been a lot of programming. The child is programmed as soon as he is old enough to walk around. It puts him in a tunnel. When he is fresh and free he is programmed to get an education, get a job, get a home, get a car, buy a grave plot, die. That tunnel blocks out everything.

"Let's understand this. Learning is a chemical process. Psychedelic chemicals are tools of learning. It is a matter of learning how to use the tools. Everything you put in your body affects your brain.

"Food is another terrible thing we have been programmed to believe in. The markets are filled with food that has preservatives and junk in it that affect your consciousness. Organic food that grows up from Mother Nature, the way Mother Nature intended for it to grow, *really* affects your consciousness.

"I had a friend who committed suicide. He wasn't high at the time, but it had very much to do with a psychedelic experience. What happens is that everything you were programmed to believe in, everything you were programmed to learn turns out to be a shuck. But now lots of us in the Haight-Ashbury have made big steps in the direction of groping for new forms. We are dealing with new forms of social organization, of economic organization, architectural organization . . . the entire spectrum of life and its relationship to the tribe."

Ron's speech is elliptical, a jumble of nonsense to infidel ears, an entanglement of prophecy, dietary laws, and rebuke; its value lies in revealing the recurrent themes of this brand of politics, not as a complete exposition of it or as a statement most people in the Haight would accept or even understand. A very large proportion of the people who showed up there were apolitical types who memorized a few slogans and spent their waking hours in the serious pursuit of pleasure or solutions to their own personal

139

problems. But Ron Thelin and Peter Cohon represent a minority who are as much connected to campus radicalism as to hippy dope.

This new form of politics demands to be acted out. It must be affective. It must align the soul and one's place in society in a consistency of action. Sometimes this can be done by acts of cultural warfare. So the Digger Abbie Hoffman drops shredded money from the balcony of the New York Stock Exchange onto the arm-waving money changers below. Ron Thelin suggests, "The thing to do is like turn on the city. Like stop signs. Stop signs should be God's eyes. Surely people would stop for God's eyes. A bunch of psychedelic rangers could do it easily with some spray paint cans." The San Francisco Diggers pass out mimeographed sheets on the streets asking:

ARE THE MOTHERS OF AMERICA AVATARS OF DELILAH? . . . THOSE PREFERRING CLIPPERS TO TRESSES HAVE REACTED WITH THE SORT OF RIGHTEOUS INDIGNATION ONE COULD EXPECT IF THEIR OWN BALLS HAD BEEN THREATENED . . . THE SHORN MEN ARE JEALOUS BECAUSE THEY THINK YOU'RE GETTING LAID MORE. THEY'RE RIGHT, BUT THEY MUST ALSO REALIZE IT'S YOUR WHOLE WAY OF BEING AND NOT JUST THE HAIR OR ELSE THEY'D BE HOME NIGHTS PULLING AT THEIR HAIR INSTEAD OF THEIR DICKS. YEAH, IT'S JEALOUSY BABY. DON'T GET BUGGED—JUST BE BEAUTIFUL AND LONG MAY IT WAVE!

This is all a species of war against cultural form, and for many who do it, it is a reasonable second step after the psychedelic drug experience, an act consistent with what you may learn under the influence of these chemicals. The psychedelics often attack the sense of form of white, middle-class American youth. They eliminate time as a form—that phenomenon is almost universally reported. But they also seem to do the same thing with shape, either by producing hallucinatory distortions—legs growing out of shoulders and arms out of hips—or by blurring the lines that indicate form. They can also attack the form of the personality, the you in you, putting in suspension the elements of consciousness that make you a recognizable and comfortable friend to yourself.

140

They can stop the lifelong dialogue you have with yourself and make it quiet in there, an experience some people find magnificently revealing but which can panic others across the doorway and down the stairwell of madness.

You do not even have to take this kind of dope to arrive at the conviction that all possibilities—except the most satanic one—have been wrung from the present arrangement of society. Disillusioned youth is often pictured as being unable to move beyond the destruction of form. Some have, as with the Indian cult, which can produce its own synesthesia, mixing the ritual of personal salvation, the destruction of the present order, and social reconstitution in some interesting ways. Study this poem of Gary Snyder's as an example.

A CURSE ON THE MEN IN WASHINGTON, PENTAGON
OM A KA CA TA TA PA YA SA SVAHA

*As you shoot down the Vietnamese girls and men*
*in their fields*
*Burning and chopping*
*Poisoning and blighting,*

*So surely I hunt the white man down*
*in my heart.*
*The crew-cutted Seattle boy*
*The Portland boy who worked for U.P.*
*that was me.*

*I won't let him live. The "American"*
*I'll destroy. The "Christian"*
*has long been dead.*

*They won't pass on to my children.*
*I'll give them Chief Joseph, the bison herds,*
*Ishi, sparrowhawk, the fir trees,*
*The Buddha, their own naked bodies,*
*Swimming and dancing and singing*
*instead.*

*As I kill the white man*
*the "American"*
*in me*
*And dance out the Ghost Dance:*
*To bring back America, the grass and the streams,*

*To trample your throat in your dreams.*

*This magic I work, this loving I give*
*That my children may flourish*

*And yours won't live.*

HI NISWA VITA' NI

The square world, if it bothers to pay any attention at all, dismisses such sentiments as anachronistic gibberish—which they assuredly are from a formal, political standpoint. From other standpoints, however, they reveal recurrent thematic material from both the dope world and the new confessional politics of white youth.

The poet sings, "So surely I hunt the white man down in my heart," and who is this white man? He is a plastic, suburban boy from Seattle, a boy who must be exorcised in much the same way that baptism removes original sin. The "white man" the poet is talking about was born with a stain on him. It wasn't something he did, something that is his fault, but baptism won't work to remove this fault because, as Gary Snyder announces, "The 'Christian' has long been dead." The Christian, then, can't destroy the white American.

The poet proposes to perform this rite by the Ghost Dance "to bring back America, the grass and the streams." In other words, the dance is the means for conveying people back through historical time to the time when there was no time, the time of innocence, the time of first creation. This must be one of the oldest and most universal of human myths for, as Mircea Eliade explains, "The radical 'cure' for the suffering of existence is attained by retracing one's footsteps in the sands of memory right back to the initial *illud tempus*—which implies the abolition of profane time."*

The *illud tempus,* the paradisaic time for these young people, is the pre-polystyrene age. Their Elysium has no dancing girls, no sparkling wines coming out of every water tap. It is a time of "the fir trees . . . naked bodies, the grass and the streams." It is a time of collective dancing and singing, the bison herds and Chief Joseph, the noble savage, again resurrected by morally depleted, faithless Christians. But this isn't the passive nostalgia for the "natural" that we've seen in times past. There is an active principle here. The faded French nobleman looked at *his* savage as though the Indian were in a tableau, an unhappy reminder that in exchange for his lace and buckles he had lost pre-Adamite bliss; but Gary Snyder, if not for himself at least for his children, is going to get it back. In his poem, he'll give them Ishi, the Buddha, and "their own naked bodies," now handsomely encased in the finest transparent plastic. This he will do by "killing the white man, the 'American' in me." (The "American" is always between quotation marks because the real American of the *illud tempus* is the Indian.)

This combination of carnality and violence is not only a way of getting back your natural self, which has been adulterated with artificial sweeteners, but is the natural state of man in Eden. "I want to lay life. I want to taste it, beat it, feel it, kill it, fuck it, and I want to have all these things done to me," says Peter Cohon, for only then can he or the poet feel the electricity of life in his dead nerve endings. So much of the testimony on behalf of what acid does declares the same thing. "You haven't eaten, you haven't tasted, you haven't fucked, you haven't seen colors, your fingers haven't touched rock and soil until you've had acid, and then you know you're alive and you know what life is," is the rhapsody of one young acid dropper.

In the poet's conception you return to *illud tempus* by killing the white man, by "trampling your throat in your dreams," and

*Mircea Eliade, *Myths, Dreams and Mysteries,* New York, 1960, p. 51. A full understanding of what these people are up to religiously can't be gotten without reading Eliade.

also by the Ghost Dance, that is, by inducing a shamanistic trance. The chant and the dance are immemorially old ways to free the spirit from its present entanglements and sense of mortal sin, to allow it to return to primordial time. They are to be found all over the hip fringes of the New Left, where you may discover Allen Ginsberg or less famous people with their little thumb cymbals leading these devotees back to the affective state of man at the moment of creation. If these rites also call to mind Hitler leading the echoing chant in the Nuremberg amphitheater, there is no denying the similarity. Another method of going back to the time of no time is dope. A frequently reported theme by acid takers is the experience of going back in their lives to their childhood, their infancy, and finally to the "cone of conception," as one boy graphically described it. But however you get back there, once you have picnicked in those gardens you have the ground of experience for the affective type of politics which distinguishes this group and perhaps even our mid-twentieth-century era.

The crux of the problem in confessional politics is how to live your faith. The faith is ahistorical; it cannot, like the Christians or communists, temporize today in the belief that it will be justified later. It must be lived purely in the now, the present moment, without thought of building a political apparatus that will prepare the way for the day of resurrection or justification.

David Simpson tries to live his heterodox political faith. A young man in his late twenties, he became something of a Haight Street celebrity, not because his longish hair was held back out of his eyes by an Indian headband, but because he got busted and successfully defended himself in court. He was busted for handing out leaflets to the tourists which read: "Middle-Class Brothers! Loosen up, let God flow through you. Remember, we are with you as you drive through the valley of the shadow of death." At the trial he explained, "I was trying to reach out across the void that separated us in what was then the only possible way. Most of the people I wished to communicate with were locked in their cars staring at me as if I were some strange tropical fish flashing at them from my tank."

144

For a few days there was a fair amount of interest in the cheeky young man who'd risk a jail sentence to take on judge, jury, and prosecution in his hippy costume. There were some articles in the papers, amused, tolerant stuff, and David seemed content. He went about Haight Street inviting people to the trial and devoted himself to preparing for it and arguing it. He carried his point too. He made the authorities look pompous and got off with a ten-day suspended sentence.

After the trial David was seen now and then on the streets, not taking bows but hustling from one place to another on some Diggerish project. And then he was gone. When he turned up again at the I/Thou Coffee House, he said he'd been to Chicago for the National Conference on New Politics. Few things fail as completely as did this gathering of white liberals concerned about the war, old-line radicals, angry blacks, and white radical, political confessionalists. Nothing was retrievable. The whites turned over control of the convention to a minority of demanding blacks who had insisted on controlling the conference because they didn't think the whites would be so guilty and confused as to give it to them. Once they had the power, they didn't know what to do with it, so black and white, in argumentative discord, spent the better part of a week confusing the national news media, which had come believing this was the central committee of the protesting eruptions manifesting themselves everywhere.

To the meeting at the Palmer House, David the Digger came. "I had a wooden flute in one hand and a tire iron in the other," he said, "but they told me I couldn't sit there. 'Why not?' I wanted to know. 'Nobody else is sitting here.' Then they asked me who did I represent. 'What do you mean, who do I represent? I represent myself. Me.' They said I couldn't sit there and accused me of having a weapon. I told them, 'This isn't a weapon, it's a stage prop.' We argued some more, until I drew an invisible circle around my chair and said, 'I declare this a liberated area. If necessary I'll defend it with my life.' They went away then.

"During the convention I wore a sign that said FREE on it. People would come up to me and say indignantly, 'What do you mean FREE? Who do you represent anyway?' Nobody there could see what was happening. You know, in the hotel lobby I saw a black kid who was selling papers walk up to a white radical, spit on his jacket, and tell him, 'Buy this if you want to help my people.' And the white reached into his pocket and said, 'Sure, sure,' and bought it.

"I tried to find a black man who'd walk down the aisle with me, both of us stark naked, and stand in front of them all and beat the shit out of each other. One guy said he would, but he backed out at the last minute. That meeting . . . stupid, petty, radical bureaucrats, bastards, cowards, playing the game of politics, defending irrelevant, abstract ideologies at a time like this when it's come down to man to man, to life and death."

When David got back from Chicago he seemed to have dispirited moments when either his faith failed him or he failed his faith. He still talked his language of plunging personal commitment: "I told them in Chicago they should scratch their balls in public, dance together, fuck a brother, act . . . but I don't know, I'm getting to the point that I almost won't be able to talk anymore. I'm of another race, not black, not white, maybe I'm of a race that's not here yet, a race without a name. In America you can be a hippy, a doctor, a fireman, but you can't be a man, can't be free. I was lucky. I came here to San Francisco and I met a lot of brothers and we haven't bloomed yet, so we haven't been cut off like the beatniks and the Wobblies were cut off. My immediate family is now fifty people, and there're a couple of hundred other people whose lives I have a stake in. So I'm not cut off yet."

This last David said one night in his apartment on the steep hill above Haight Street, where he lived with a girl named Jane in a domesticity that was more bohemian than hippy. He was in the kitchen cooking, enjoying the feel of the food under his fingers, the sounds it made on the stove, the smell. Little Negro children who lived on the block would wander into the apartment to watch TV or play. They were welcome, part of the community he would build, but none of it gave him pleasure that evening. He spoke of moving, said in the doomed spirit that tinctures the radical con-

146

fessionalist that he had guns locked up in the next room, stored there for the bloody days and smoking nights that many now wait for, the time of national expiation and revenge. He was depressed. There were baskets of tomatoes in the garage, he said, gotten free from farmers in the country for the picking, but nobody would lend him a pickup truck so he could carry them around the city to give them away. It had been different not so long ago, before the summer and the thousands of people. But now, David remarked, you lent people tools, lent people things and they didn't bring them back, didn't care. The communal solicitude had waned.

"You know," David continued, "I look around and I see all sorts of persons with visions, apocalyptic visions, like an Indian sorceress I know in New Mexico who sees the apocalypse coming in the fall. Astrologers are having visions which in the end are explosions. I talked to one a couple of weeks ago who said the human race is on the verge of perfection. Krishna told him so. I myself feel the old formulations don't mean anything anymore. I feel a kinship with Blake, a feeling that I am my own God, the ultimate creator. There is nothing else, there is nothing else. I create myself daily, so maybe the ultimate basis of my life is an aesthetic one, maybe I should see beauty where it is. I don't know, I don't know what that means in political terms. Maybe it doesn't mean anything, but I have to be involved in politics because I have to eat . . . I took my flute to Chicago and many times my only recourse was to play it . . . As I said before, I may not be able to talk much longer."

David Simpson suggests a rare individual resiliency. It's in his body, a compact blond form, an impression that he gives of working a life pattern out for himself, a young man who will be able to winter the long nights of the soul. He has his community, his tribe, but an important part of his life appears to remain private by choice. There are others who seem to need people much closer to them to sustain their political life. Such a one is Lennie Heller.

Twenty-four years old, the son of a Brooklyn butcher, he is the head of, or at least the principal person in, the Berkeley Resistance, a loose national organization of young men who defy the draft by burning their draft cards and other acts of absolute public defiance of the war and the military system. The lines tying the Berkeley members of the Resistance, across San Francisco Bay, to the Haight-Ashbury are weak. They know some people in the Haight; they may go there occasionally for a meeting in a church; they have a mild interest in some of the things that happen there; and some of the people in the Resistance grow their hair long and have beards, but that doesn't prove much; some of the people in Resistance chapters have fooled around with dope but it hasn't held them. But in style, mood, and their underlying confessionalism, they are related to the Haight.

Lennie's given name is Stewart. He changed it somewhere along the zigzagging line of his life in an act of identification with Lennie Bruce, the comedian who died of drugs, exhaustion, persecution, prosecution, and introspective mania. There are many people in the Bay Area who say they knew Lennie Bruce, claim to have watched him in bed with girls in the Hotel Marlton in New York or insanely studying law books to confound the closing circle of district attorneys, judges, and cops that were an obsessive preoccupation with him in the final part of his life.

Lennie Heller was an admirer from afar, but his friends say he can imitate Bruce perfectly. The comedian himself wasn't funny; his humor dissolved into a projection of the amplified horror of his own cognitions. Lennie Heller is something of the same. He can start off being funny in a gentle way, less by wit than intonation and gesture, but very soon he paints himself, not horrified like his namesake, but frightened. He comes across as a melancholy swashbuckler trying to alleviate a persistent, static fear. He says of his anti-war activity that he does it "not to construct a paradise but to destroy an inferno." He tells the candidates for membership in his political brotherhood, "After you've done it, burned your draft cards, you won't be afraid anymore."

Lennie says he isn't afraid. He declares he has committed his act and he doesn't have to think about it anymore. When they come, they come and, "I'll laugh when they put the handcuffs on

148

me on the train to go to jail, and I'll laugh all the way in. I'll get out and come back and expect to get welcomed and get all the gratitude, but they'll call me an Uncle Tom. They'll say, 'Why didn't you shoot somebody, why didn't you blow up a draft board?' But you stand up on a roof with a rifle and kill a cop—that's a desperate act—he's got a family too. I'm not going to do that, drink vodka and toast the revolution."

As with David Simpson, it's hard to understand what Lennie will do. He will—he did—commit the formal, illegal act of burning the card, and by so doing he will free himself and take his place in a special community of loyal brothers. It's Lennie's memories, his feelings that are vivid things about him. His father the butcher in debt, living high off the hog, hiding his failing business from neighbors, the last heart attack; that's vivid as Lennie tells it. His days at the University of Connecticut, president of the interfraternity council, laying girls in the back seat of cars, his disgust at himself are vivid. His academic wandering through pharmacy school, film school in Los Angeles—he tells those adventures so they sound plausible. What he feels is real. "Sometimes I go down to the induction center in Oakland and watch them go in like they're going into a concentration camp. They're beaten. A tiny, little guy, a sergeant, tells them not to take the leaflets and they're afraid of him, and they could knock him out with one punch. Those guys going to the induction center. I remember one guy with acne on his face all covered up with makeup, and the cops. All the cops have bellies and guns and long sticks. They're not fighting me, they're not fighting a real enemy. They're playing a role. They're living it all over again, forty years old, back in World War II with boot camps and whores in Germany. That's what they were doing the day they beat up everybody, but it was bad—the chicks coming back to the campus [Berkeley] with blood on their cheeks, girls you still have a sexual feeling for, describing all those atrocities, what the cops did to them."

Lennie can be found in the Berkeley Resistance office, a minute suite of rooms in an obsolete office building on Shattuck Street. There is a sign by the door saying "All Resistance members who have turned in their draft cards are absolutely, fundamentally obligated to do at least the minimal tasks required to keep our brotherhood alive and moving. Therefore: When you enter this office go directly to the work bulletin board and do what needs to be done. No one needs anyone to tell him."

Whether anybody obeys the sign is questionable. Whether there's any work is questionable, but there is a brotherhood, Lennie and Dickie at least. Dickie is a street-wise Negro from the slums who knows the lingo of "blowing black" but can't seem to summon the animosity for anti-white invective. They are the kernel of a community of sorts, and revolving around them is a group of others, a few years their junior. One is the son of a wealthy lawyer who reared him on trips to Europe, prep school at Groton, everything the upper class gives its children. Several others are the sons of doctors, children of moneyed families.

In gross outline their short life histories seem to resemble each other. They're all good students—one is a National Merit Scholarship semi-finalist—all got into good colleges and made good grades. None of them give the impression of being in especially violent rebellion against their families. The rich boy's father disagrees with what his son is doing but concedes the right, perhaps even the obligation, to obey the voice of conscience. Another boy's father actually is contributing money to the Resistance. The third boy's mother is a pacifist.

As case histories their curricula vitae aren't unusual for student radicals, except perhaps in one respect: all of these boys have quit school. It more often happens that student radicals don't leave school until they're thrown out by the administration. By and large they are such good students that even at a place like Berkeley, a campus synonymous with the word rebellion, demonstrations are unheard of during examination periods. Almost every serious study of campus militancy has shown the radicals to have better-than-average grades. One of the reasons the universities with the highest and most demanding standards are the centers of protest is that radical students can meet the high entrance requirements and are drawn there by their academic reputations.

The Resistance stands somewhere between the affective life of the hip scene and the self-denying discipline of the university campus. As such it exposes the drawing power of the absolute confessionalism on certain students, but it also underscores the impermanence of young people in their commitments to the number of modes of living open to them. The watching bystanders seem to think that dropping in or out, burning a draft card, or deciding to shelter yourself under the protection of draft exemption carries a finality with it. But many of the people who do these things, if only because they are so prone to live in the present tense, don't appear to think so. They move in and out of college, in and out of the dope world, of protest and radical politics, testing themselves, looking for what seems right to them, keeping their options open in the sense of not pledging themselves past the moment of time they are living in. Unfortunately, they are often operating in situations where others take them at their word. They break the school rules and they are expelled from the university; they burn their draft cards and they are indicted. No allowance is made for future change. Strangely, the largest organization, the federal government, has been more lenient than other institutions. Charges will sometimes be dropped—even if the boy is standing before the judge for sentencing—if he agrees to go quietly to war.

These young people are regarded as misguided, pathological, but most of all rebellious. Youth rebellion is the starting point for explaining their behavior, both for professionals and the public at large. That explanation doesn't fit the known facts without considerable forcing.

Peter Cohon remarked one day, "My father is a liberal, but he never did much about what he believed in. I do." The systematic studies of student radicals' family backgrounds show a high proportion of parents sharing their children's political beliefs at least in part. The parents are less likely to be "radical," but they are far more liberal than the parents of students unconnected with protest and disruption. For perhaps as many as half of the radicals, the data indicate that, rather than rebelling, the young people are carrying out precepts they were taught at home. Even this may not be the full picture because it doesn't account for boys like the lawyer's son who comes from a politically conservative family but one which also puts high store on living in fearless obedience to conscience.

As a universal explanation the rebellion thesis doesn't hold up, although it's a convenient one for those who would like to avoid discussing the issues that the radicals raise. By defining them as "youth in rebellion" they can be considered a species of psychological problem and dismissed. The other great danger in using words that carry psychological meanings in any political discussion is that these neutral-sounding, clinical terms may disguise epithets. We say radical youth is in rebellion, the John Birch Society is pathological, and the middle of the road is balanced between extremes.

The complicating factor is that affective politics drives people to act out their convictions in ways that make speculation about their personalities irresistible. The Minutemen assemble arms depots and drill by night; there have been two attempts to destroy the Berkeley draft board with fire bombs. Since such shenanigans have no tactical importance, it's reasonable to account for them psychiatrically, but even then the resulting picture can be badly skewed. Were the three clergymen who rushed into a Baltimore draft board in the fall of 1967 and poured human blood over the papers in the filing cabinet insane?

While many who fall within the hip penumbra of radical politics can't be classed as rebels against their families as far as their values are concerned, they often break very sharply with them in how they live and carry them out. Amorphous communitarian endeavors like the Resistance were not the means the parents chose in their youth, but this break in life styles extends to the nonpolitical majority of kids making hippy scenes. Take the case of Linda Fitzpatrick, the eighteen-year-old girl who, with friend Groovy, was murdered in the boiler room of an East Village tenement in New York City. The victim of this most celebrated of hippy murders was the daughter of a rich Greenwich, Con-

152

necticut, family. For some time before the lives of Linda and her friend Groovy ended—naked on the cellar floor, their heads bashed in—the girl had been living a life that sounded like a lurid caricature of the hippy way, shacking up with a couple of boys in a smudgy, six-dollar-a-night hotel room, taking speed and acid, making the pilgrimage to the Haight-Ashbury—a complete break with her Greenwich background, where they may have sex and they may use drugs but not that way. What's interesting about Linda's case is how little a part politics or social criticism seems to have played in her decision to leave the easy living of home for meandering, hippy penury. The reporters who flew off hither and yon to reconstruct the final months of Linda's life found nothing more political than a pencil scratching in the hotel room she once lived in that said, "War Is Hell," and there's no particular reason to believe she wrote it.

Linda Fitzpatrick also failed to display the huge craving for human solidarity that marks off the errant radicals of today's youth. In Peter Cohon it exhibits itself in the rolling, wrestling pile-up in the dust; David Simpson's disappointment at the lack of spontaneous cooperation is a species of it, and Lennie Heller shows the same need. You wonder, with somebody like Lennie, if one of the reasons he burnt his card was to commit an act far enough outside the pale so that he and the small number of others would, by cutting themselves off, be forced into an unbreakable fraternal solidarity, a solidarity which would be a touchstone to the unconstricted self-realization that runs thematically through the hip-radical world.

"I want to say to you people who've turned in your cards or who're going to tomorrow that we're going to have a high school of our own, we're going to have emergency services," he said one night in the Lutheran Student Center at Berkeley before a big draft-card burning service the next day. "So if you know what you want to do with your life, teach or whatever, tomorrow you're going to be able to start doing it. The Resistance is not only burning draft cards, it's making an alternative life. That's why we talk about making a community—a soul train I guess you'd call it. So

153

after tomorrow you don't have to be afraid anymore. We're going to have a community house so we'll be able to provide food and a place to live and a share of whatever we collect—you know, some money to buy a shirt or go to a movie every so often. Of course, if you want, you can go to France—we'll try and help you, and they'll teach you French if you go over there. They've had a test case there and it's cool for draft resisters. England's pretty good, so's Denmark, but Germany is bad and so is Belgium."

When Lennie talks you feel nothing will come of it, that he knows it and so do the people he's talking to, but that they need at least the promise of community before they can formally pit themselves against the legal engines of the United States government. However, at the other end of the San Francisco Bay Area in Palo Alto, there is a Resistance chapter which has become a commune. "The Peace and Liberation Commune is actually nine or ten guys," explains Dennis Sweeney, who, like Lennie, is twenty-four; but he's spent his young adulthood in a very different way—three and a half years at Stanford and considerable time with Snick in Mississippi. He was there in the summer of 1964 when Snick cracked open the state. In the process, Dennis nearly got his head blown off by a bomb in the McComb civil rights headquarters. Then he was a pretty blond boy, charming but vague, the way youths can be before they have fastened on to themselves. Eventually he left the South; he doesn't say why, but you guess that charming blond boys from Stanford must have found less and less room in the darkening black man's movement. Going back to school, even with a wife married out of the civil rights movement, was, he says, very difficult; finally it was too difficult. For returning veterans colleges make concessions; they understand that the transition from manhood back to *in loco parentis* can't be done immediately. There are no such programs for returning radicals. So Dennis aged, tried to do school, tried some acid, tried some more school, and found his vocation again in the politics of social change. Once more, as in Mississippi, he could be one of an endangered few as he took up the task of winning someone else's struggle. Dennis, as the only son of a serviceman killed in the Korean War,

154

is exempt from the draft by law; he does what he does out of interests that aren't immediate in the objective sense.

"The guys in the commune are very diverse," he says. "Stuart and I met in a traditionally political way, but one guy's a poet who is becoming a buddha. Another, who's originally from Santa Clara, played in a rock band in Sweden, and David Harris was the president of the student body at Stanford. We're diverse but we get along. We don't have any personal property. We pooled all our dough. One guy was in a train accident and he got a $9,000 settlement, so we bought twenty acres of land in the Santa Cruz Mountains. We have a couple of printing presses and we run a print shop. We never have meetings to talk about the commune. We see it as a basis for working in the outside world. Although we're diverse, we're all sort of straight out of the Stanford scene, and that makes us feel secure. It's important that the people who are doing this thing with you come from a similar background and understand you . . . very different from Mississippi. The commune's very important to me."

All of these young men—David, Lennie, Dennis—are what the FBI like to call "hard-core cases," people whose confessional political beliefs have become a way of life. There aren't many such people. They are, if you count them as hippies, even a decided minority of this group; but they have the power to influence much larger numbers of people, to pick up and play on the harmonics of emotion in an extended youth population. They can, for a day, or even for a week, enlist sizable numbers to do as they do. At the October 1967 March on the Pentagon, a member of the Fugs, that East Village rock music ensemble of poor poets and political spielers, stood on a flatbed truck announcing to a large group of the marchers, "For the first time in the history of the Pentagon there will be a grope-in, a seminal culmination of history." The crowd was appreciative; to a substantial proportion of them the language and thought were appropriate. There was no grope-in (group sex), but several couples were seen having relations on the Pentagon lawn, while other people urinated on the walls of that building which Lewis Mumford once described as "an effete and

155

worthless baroque conceit, resurrected by . . . United States military engineers and magnified into an architectural catastrophe." Horrid as it is, this product of "Bronze Age fantasies of absolute power," to quote Mumford again, you don't go urinating on it at a political demonstration unless a wild power is unloosed in you, and muezzins and priests of confessional politics have that power over an important segment of this generation.

Our recent social history suggests we would have drifted into a time when affective morality would play an important part in public life. But the nature of the two most painful issues, war in Vietnam and racism in America, certainly would have called it forth anyway.

No way exists to compromise a war, so that short of calling it off entirely there is no way to deal with it. You can't split the difference between the war and peace party. For the last generation the American government has tried by fighting "limited wars"; but they are limited only in the minds of strategists and tacticians who know they might be fought over larger areas with even more destructive weapons. For actual participants or young men facing conscription, limited war is a nonsense term. The draft is involuntary servitude regardless of the type of war you are drafted into, and the loss of a life, a hand, a pair of eyes is a limitless tragedy for the person who sustains it.

In these circumstances, the due process of decision-making breaks down utterly. A majority vote, public opinion poll, or plebiscite in favor of the war can't bring its opponents to accept the verdict and go. get their heads blown off. Instead, a suicidal, anything-goes political situation is created in which people begin to say, "I'll serve my time in jail rather than in the Army. I'd rather have my brains bashed in by a cop in front of an induction center than by a grenade in a jungle." The punishments for resisting the war verge on being equal to the risks you run in fighting it. It is a situation made to order for the most infuriated, unbridled kind of affective response, the sort of response that says, "If I've got to go, I'll take a couple of them with me."

The public and the press have gotten a whiff of this response and have called it nihilism, particularly when it has come from the mouths of the younger generation of ghetto Negroes. For they also believe that the only decision left to them is the time and manner of their own deaths. They have not only the war and conscription to reinforce this feeling, but also the riots, where most of the black snipers turned out to be imaginary while the bullets of the police did not.

This is not the first American war to be opposed, or even opposed by the sort of inexpedient, soul-satisfying affective response this one elicits. Present opposition is unusual because it finds its nurture in the youth culture with its affective values, especially as they are symbolized and summed up for the world at large by the Haight-Ashbury.

Assuming the war does end and its domestic effects aren't absolutely disabling, the question remains as to whether affective politics will end with it. For the better part of this decade, political observers have felt a change coming over American politics. They've not been able to put their finger on it, other than to suggest it has something to do with youth and a new style. During John F. Kennedy's presidency they were reassured that he was the change they sensed; but he is gone and the premonition of change remains. The Haight-Ashbury suggests that the change isn't a need for youthful political figures but the coming into existence of ardent idealists, the Peters, the Dennises, the Lennies, though perhaps in less exaggerated form.

The existence of vast numbers of idealists could strenuously tax our system of government and provoke some appalling crises. Our system works on a day-to-day basis in large measure because so few people care to mess with it. Between a third and two-thirds of eligible voters don't bother to go to the polls, and casting a ballot is the absolute political minimum. The percentage of the population who are moved to do anything more than the minimum is so miniscule that the job of running the country is left to 2 or 3 per cent of its citizenry.* If that percentage of political participants

*For a truly able discussion of these political facts see E. E. Schattschneider, *The Semisovereign People: A Realist's View of Democracy in America*, New York, 1960.

ever takes a significant leap upward, no one could guess what would happen, but it would be revolutionary.

Heretofore, when this has happened, it has strained our institutions—slavery, unionism, prohibition, votes for women. We've recovered and gone on because the insurgent demands have been such that they could be met with programmatic solutions, with formal changes in our laws and institutions. This time we may be faced with demands that it is not in the power of government to meet.

The unprecedented possibility lies not only in rearing a generation of political activists but in the basis on which they might make their entrance on the public stage. There is a sign painted on a wall in Harlem which reads, WE HAD FULL EMPLOYMENT ON THE PLANTATION TOO, BABY. That sign summarizes the dilemma that mass participation in affective political movements can create. That sign says in effect, "Regardless of full bellies, good schools, and nice homes, we're sick in the soul with racism. We're unhappy." But how does our political system deal with misery of the soul? At its best it is geared to make "equality of opportunity," that is, to give as many people as possible as much elbow room as possible to find their happiness, and when it has tried to go further it has run into the slogan, "You can't legislate morality." You can, of course, but the results for the last three centuries in the English-speaking nations have been abysmal.

Yet compared to the psycho-political demands of white confessionalists, the most extravagantly poetic black nationalist makes reasonably precise demands that legislatures may find the means to satisfy. So much of white radicalism is the projection of a tortured spiritual state onto the general society. Some of the things they talk about are remediable through the ordinary ways of government: air pollution, food adulteration, wildlife conservation, cutting students in for a share of the power in running universities; but the other, the deeper things that agitate them baffle institutional action. David Simpson calls out, "Free! I must be free!" yet when you hear him you wonder if it isn't freedom that brings him to the desperation of Doukhoborism, the Russian spiritualist sect whose members burn down their own houses and run in circles around them, naked as jaybirds, whenever they get mad at the government. When he calls out for freedom he is speaking of a social freedom, but what his life stance suggests is a superabundance of freedom of the mind, a freedom that has developed into an isolated consciousness which is driving him crazy, driving him to cast back into the ground, into the tribal, traditional time when men may have been more of a collective mind and personality. This theme is often picked up by the people who accuse hip intellectuals of being anti-rational, but perhaps it's less that than that they're going insane locked up alone with their detached, free-floating brains.

But whatever it may be when it translates itself from private pain to politics, it's unanswerable. It may also come at a bad time for America. Not only does the Far Right practice its own brand of confessional politics, but the largest subculture in the nation, a subculture which has always been hyperaffective, has now snapped alive politically. The black people are overthrowing their restrained, white-educated and -indoctrinated leaders for the most gorgeously emotive spokesmen. So a judge in Newark, New Jersey, puts the prototype of the new black man, writer LeRoi Jones, in jail for the maximum sentence, not because he was found with a gun but because of the words he's printed. It was bad law, as the emotionally stable newspapers pointed out, but the judge understood that the playwright's rhetoric was a threat to him and his system.

The system is built in part on the exclusion of confessional politics. That is one of the things the First Amendment is about. The wars of religion led to the decision that what we now call "subject" passions had to be removed from public life and made purely private. If a new, secular confessionalism is going to sweep over us, it may be much more difficult to contain. The old passions had a dogmatic ideology which made them easy to recognize and outlaw. Given the commonsense history of the American people, the majority will probably resist the most frenzied strains of this virus, but social conditions facilitate its transmittal, and even now it has caused considerable disruption and consternation.

There's a tendency in those who aren't bitten by this bug—

parents, deans of students, skeptical classmates, sympathetic narks, white liberals—to try reason to quiet the emotional holocaust. It rarely works. It may make matters worse with people who have been driven wild by a surfeit of rationalism. It also fails to work because, as hip intellectuals will tell you, the carefully manufactured chains of reason are without affect, and therefore without the power to convince. The dullest speakers in America are the leaders of the status quo. Even at their political conventions, when they feel compelled to make a stab at affective communication, they turn into bombastic hambones whose insincerity gives goose pimples to their own followers.

The effective oratory in the country comes from the affective political groupings—the Far Right, the Negroes, the Far Left. White America, as well as black, sits in front of its TV sets and enjoys listening to the black torrent of threats to burn down the courthouses and overthrow the government. They are threats delivered with high forensic artistry. Undoubtedly it is admiration for the strong poetry of the black man's language (as well as sympathy for his cause) that has caused hips and white radicals to copy and adopt it. The whites, however, have developed a nonrational, affective communication of their own.

Some of the communication is visual, as with the poster art which frequently contains savage political and social criticism—always in unanswerable form. It is nondebatable assertion. How do you argue with the famous poster of poet Allen Ginsberg's hirsute face topped with Uncle Sam's red, white, blue, and starred top hat? You don't; any more than you can argue with the equally popular, larger-than-life-size poster photograph of Che Guevara. It's as unanswerable as the slogan "Che Lives." The hip intelligentsia borrows from Marshall McLuhan to describe such communication as "nonlinear." Be that as it may, it is communication in which the ideas aren't broken down into separate, analytical parts; subject and predicate, indistinguishably welded together, come at you in one affective wave. There are no pieces to take out and examine, no ascertainable linkages between thoughts and objects, no form, no procession of ideas to a demonstrated conclusion.

It is a form of communication designed to get you to react. Its epitome is advertising, the most nondebatable, unanswerable form of communication ever invented; but it works, and we're looking at a generation that has been formed by it.*

"I go on peace marches because they're groovy. I flash on the experience, watching the straights blow their minds. Oh, it won't stop the war. Nothing will stop the war. The war'll go on till it shakes America to pieces, and that'll be groovy too. One day the lightning will ignite the smog over Los Angeles—it will, it will, you don't know how much energy is stored in the smog—and there will go Los Angeles. The city will be destroyed in a fire storm, and those of us left alive will do flat-footed dances with the plains Indians," says a boy one afternoon on Ashbury Street. The ideas are coherent but they're not rational. They're the matching and mixing of self and biosphere in chains of association that lead to acts that negate all previous definitions of sanity and insanity. Like Harry.

Harry first made himself evident the night at the Straight Theater when Chief Rolling Thunder and his braves danced. David Simpson and his friends were behind the festival. They'd spent most of the summer complaining that the Straight Theater should stop charging money for rock bands and do something free for the community. Money would take care of itself, so let the Straight Theater people, balancing between bankruptcy and ostracism, put on an Indian night. A lot of people came and a lot of people were stoned. When the Indians finished dancing, the audience started. They took branches of water oak used to decorate the hall and did airy, floating things with them in the flashing lights. To end the evening, the manager played a Fred Waring type of rendition of "America the Beautiful." It broke the mood, this gesture of pop art patriotism, but most of the young people held their oak branches straight up in a posture of respect and sang the words. Some of them had tears in their eyes, but that could have been the acid.

They had just turned on the overhead lights when White Rabbit

*Probably the best discussion of this kind of thought can be found in *One Dimensional Man* by Herbert Marcuse, Boston, 1964. This is a book, incidentally, that has had large influence on the nonconfessional wing of the New Left.

and Harry made eye contact. The manager was trying to get volunteers. "If you help us clean up you will be rewarded with karma and extra brain cells. If you collect enough extra brain cells, you can trade them in for a new head," he was saying, but White Rabbit and Harry kept looking at each other. Marvin couldn't cut between them. Marvin was the fat insurance salesman from Miami who'd dropped everything to come to the Haight and run around barefooted wearing a beanie cap decorated with a ridge of white feathers. He was planning to drop back in and get a California insurance broker's license. He wanted to tell White Rabbit, who'd been going off lately and getting jobs, about it, but White Rabbit kept looking at Harry and Harry kept looking back at him.

They went up Haight Street, the two of them, to the Turkish coffeehouse where you could go upstairs to the little balcony looking down on the espresso counter, sit on pillows, drink coffee, eat baklava, and smoke pot. "Right now," White Rabbit said slowly, still staring at Harry, "I'm on a survival probability level. I have a strong feeling something is going to happen when the peace march arrives in Washington [October 1967]. I had a dream that the White House was going up in flames. Owsley was rapping the other night that when you take acid you're switched into the future. He's working to invent something that will switch everyone on all the time, and then we'll have peace and turn the world into a Garden of Eden."

"You're stoned," Harry said, but he didn't stop looking into White Rabbit's brown eyes.

"I'm stoned," White Rabbit agreed, "and if you're really stoned too, we can pass molecules through each other's eyes and play games."

They passed molecules into each other's eyes until White Rabbit, his optical clamps still fastened on Harry, said, "You heard the Indian chief, didn't you? You heard him say they'd predicted San Francisco would be under water in 1966 but a group of them got together and turned on and stopped it."

"We're all children," Harry replied.

"You too have the mark of Cain," White Rabbit told his eye

mate, and heavy tears formed into lazy globules in the noseward corners of his eyes, trembled and fell over themselves running to the end of his pointy, Errol Flynn nose, whence they fell on uneaten stuffed vine leaves.

Harry continued to look back at White Rabbit and made a sniffling laugh. "I don't eat much," he said.

"Are you stoned on your own," White Rabbit wanted to know, "or did you use a chemical? I'm stoned on you."

"I'm stoned on him," Harry answered, referring to a boy who'd followed them from the theater and was utterly incapable of bringing out sound when he opened his mouth. "You know, I tell teeni-boppers, 'You don't need anything, just look around, it's everywhere, everything that'll get you stoned.'"

"Oh, to dream the impossible dream," White Rabbit sang. He had a fine voice, romantic tenor, and he was always singing Rudolph Friml-ish kinds of lyrics.

To the impossible dream, Harry broke off the stare and responded by saying, "You know, it's a funny thing. Man is the only animal to put himself in prison."

"But someday," White Rabbit felt he should add, "we're going to be immortal too. The reason is because some day we will be able to put our molecules back together. We'll collect our dust from the sky and reassemble ourselves."

Harry didn't want to talk about his molecules. "I want to talk about myself. I'm a poor boy. My father is a baker and my mother is a candlestick maker, and the only job I've ever had was as a grocery boy at Gristede's in the West Village. I had to borrow the clothes I have on so I could go to the St. Francis Hotel for dinner. That's right, that's where I went to dinner. This afternoon at the Straight Theater I was listening to the Indians rap against the establishment, and there was this very straight cat from New Jersey, so I turned him on to macrobiotic food, rice and vegetables. Afterward he said, 'Now let me take you to my place where I eat.' We went to the St. Francis and I had to borrow these clothes to get in there because I don't own a tie. I have to have my hair short so the cops don't pick me up as a runaway. I'm a minor."

163

White Rabbit announced he had to have $20 to pay his gas bill. That seemed comprehensible to Harry, who found five in his pocket and gave them to White Rabbit, saying, "That's all I can afford."

"Oh, gee, wow," White Rabbit replied, "you're giving me a contact high," and then the two went off to the Big Sur where Harry went dancing naked on a bridge over a stream. While he was running around enjoying his free body, a man with a gun came out of the woods and ordered him to put his clothes back on. Harry refused so the man pistol-whipped him.

To call the cops and complain would, to Harry's mind, have been cooperating with the hollow norms that make you wear clothes, go to Evander Childs High School in the Bronx, and sit through Hebrew school memorizing the sounds of words whose meanings you don't know for your bar mitzvah. "They taught us the sounds and the letters and never told us what they meant. Nobody knows what the words mean. At my bar mitzvah I was up at the head of the congregation saying words I didn't know and they didn't know. I could have been saying 'Go fuck yourself' in Hebrew and we wouldn't have known. You're supposed to have five cantors sing at $20 apiece, so for $100 you're a man, but that's not what it takes to be a human being."

Harry came back and made his cultural counterattack. He became the best-publicized hippy of the week when he went over to the campus of San Francisco State College and held a one-man "nude-in," as the papers called it . . . took off his clothes and sat in obstinate, naked dignity until the cops busted him. Then a girl took off hers in sympathy. They busted her. It was the big local story on TV that night.

White Rabbit hopped around trying to make bail for Harry. White Rabbit had been busted once, for "being a person out of control of his body," by the Berkeley police.

They put Harry in the mental ward. "But I got out because I gave the psychiatrist five joints so he said I was sane. Did I ever put him on, did I ever! He asked me how much pot I smoked, so I told him two packs a day and he wrote it down in his notebook.

They took me from the hospital to the jail where they have all those leather-jacket queers. One of them looked at me and said, 'You're my old lady.' I laughed.

"Still, I like San Francisco. New York's a hard scene and very hard this summer because it was such a dry season for acid. Even pot cost $20 a lid [better than twice the West Coast price] and it was very mediocre stuff. All the acid was cut with smack or coke, which makes it a very physical trip—nothing for the head. But that's New York, a smack scene, a paranoid scene and with reason. A lot of my friends went to jail. I can't understand it; here's New York supposed to be one of the most liberal states and they bust everybody. It's a police state."

But Harry emerged from jail and hospital neither brutalized nor docile. The affective political personality is indomitable: "If I'm in jail for one cause and you're in jail for another, we're both doing the same thing. We're both fighting the establishment, because the important thing is that we're both in jail. Today I went back to San Francisco State and did the same thing they busted me for, jumping around on the lawn. I was just as naked, only I was hiding it . . . I had my clothes on."

> **Heard from an Army Colonel stationed in Washington, as follows: "At last, when my children ask 'What did YOU do in the Vietnam war, daddy?' I will be able to reply, proudly, I defended the South parking lot against the hippies!"**
> —Herb Caen, *San Francisco Chronicle*
> October 26

The gong was beating through the fog. You could hardly see Jimmy hitting it, even though he was in front of the Psychedelic Shop. Lining up behind him were the blue-and-white phoenix pennants for the daily march down the street and into the park to restore the good vibes. Every day, at what would be sundown if you could see the sun, they stood there for a half-hour or longer while Jimmy hit the gong.

165

Peggy heard it and marched around her store, declaring, "I'm going to freak. I'm going to freak. I have to freak. I will freak. I must freak. *I am freaking,* and that's official. There's nobody left on this street but tourists, speed shooters, and bong gongers. Oh, I'm going to close early. I don't know what I'm going to do, or what I'm doing. I'm stoned. It's awful. My God, it's awful. I'm so stoned I can't remember if I bought the house or not. Michael was supposed to close the deal today. He called up to tell me if he did, and I can't remember."

Kimmie came in, shaking her head and saying the street was too freaky; but then she began jumping up and down, stiff-legged, and whispering to Peggy, "Guess what I have? Guess what I have? Coke, pure, beautiful, white coke, coke, coke, coke!" Peggy closed the store and the two of them, laughing, rolled behind the counter so they couldn't be seen from the street and sniffed the coke. "Ohhhhh! I love coke. It's soooo good. It makes my knees nice and rubbery," Kimmie whispered.

Down the street, Ginger was in an amazonian passion. She was a very tall, heavy girl, who still had a good figure and the loudest, hoarsest voice on the street. She could penetrate fog and traffic four blocks without straining. She used to hang out barefooted in Benches and paint psychedelic pictures on the ceiling for the management, but then Hank, Chocolate George's buddy and one of the Hell's Angels, took her for his old lady. She stopped dying of cancer of the stomach, took to wearing boots and a chain around her waist. She was always embattled, but henceforth happy.

> ". . . isolated sufferers try to solve by with-
> drawal what the joiners of deviant . . . gangs
> try to solve by conspiracy . . ."—Erik Erikson

She was standing on the corner of Haight and Clayton, bawling, "Dirty Dick's been busted for assault. Hank and Chocolate are on a run. We gotta get Dirty Dick out of jail. I was busted last night for beating and robbing an old man. Me! They took me down to

Central Station and told me, 'You're not a chick.' Me! Look at me! Look at my boobs! 'If I'm not a chick, what am I?' I said to 'em. 'I am too a chick.' An' they said to me, 'If you're a chick, prove you're a chick.' I said, 'Uhhh, uhhh, that's not where it's at. The matron checked me out.' But they still said, 'If you're a chick, prove it.' An' I said to them, 'Do ya want me to take my blouse off?' They said, 'Yeah,' an' I told 'em, 'Uhh, uhh, that's not where it's at,' but I did. I took my blouse off an' they said, 'We still don't think you're a chick. Take your pants off.' Then I told 'em, I said, 'I'm not taking my pants off, you go ahead an' book me as a female impersonator.' "

Papa Al came down the street. He had both White Preacher and Black Preacher with him. Black Preacher was the guy Papa Al most favored in the Haight. He was very quiet, barely audible most of the time, and he had slashing scars on both upper arms. He said he got them in knife fights. He didn't like White Preacher. "Can't be two preachers on this street; there's only one that should carry that name and be here to meet; took this preacher a long time to win that name; a man's going to have to cut me good to share this fame; can't be but one preacher on this street; the other's gotta change his name, or I'm gonna cut him neat," said Black Preacher, who talked that way a lot of the time.

Papa Al had started a street commando commune. He didn't pay the rent but he functioned as den mother. Black Preacher was the untitled boss. He could do it because everybody liked him and was afraid of him. Not because he told anyone he was tough; they knew it. It was a black, Harlem toughness that didn't have to announce itself; it was obvious from the way he did everything, from walking down a street to entering a room. He wasn't a black black man, not a race man; he didn't, as they say, have any of that rap. He didn't need it; he was past integrating anything; he went where he wanted. He was as popular as he cared to be. He kept his distance, and the more he did, the more the others tried to get close to him.

But Black Preacher didn't want the responsibility of the commune. He started bringing up girls and balling them in front of his old lady, Elaine. Then he locked himself alone in his room to shoot,

167

said he did it because Gypsie was strung out on it and he couldn't help her kick it if he didn't know how it felt.

"I don't get strung out on any speed; there's no chemical I need. I like the buzz, I like the rush; I don't gotta have dope an' I ain't no lush. Don't tell me what's a danger an' what to do; I got my strong body an' my stronger will—ain't like you," he said one day, but that was before he'd locked himself up in the room. Everybody was afraid to go in and get him. Not even Papa Al would mess with him, so the commune got worse and worse until there was a raid and Gypsie and a couple of the others were busted for having points and, the street said, a pound of crystal. Black Preacher had slipped away and nobody knew exactly where he was living, except that it was in the Haight. He liked it in the community; it was easy for him to live off of it.

White Preacher was something else. He wore a bandana around hair black enough to be Indian, as he claimed he was. White Preacher was always saying, "I voted on the Indian council even when I was in jail. I was brought up by the Trappist monks an' almost became a priest. I have a bachelor's degree in sociology an' I can work for the welfare. They can't say, 'Look at this bum'; I can work." His face was pitted and scarred; he was missing some crucial front teeth, which made the remaining ones look like poisonous ivory knives; his skin was pale and his features long and sharp, not like an Indian's. He had the biker's swagger, stomping around with knees bent as though he might still be on his bike. And when he turned, he didn't twist at the waist; he kept his shoulders and torso rigid and rotated his hips.

White Preacher lived down in the Fillmore with Lil' Wally. They said the Angels had beaten him up and told him he couldn't live in the Haight anymore. Now he was a Gypsy Joker. Nobody who wasn't crazy and a speed freak went at night to visit White Preacher's and Lil' Wally's crystal palace, as speed houses were called. When he wasn't high, Preacher was paranoid, and Al said he was too dangerous to go near when he was up and roaring. Like a lot of people strung out on speed, Lil' Wally and Preacher seemed to know their limitations. Most of the time, when they were doing up heavily, they stayed inside and away from people. Speed shooters can be violent when they're surprised.

In the afternoons you could go visiting. Lil' Wally would be asleep with his old lady in the bedroom. White Preacher would be stomping, stamping, and muttering in the kitchen, working on a piece of leather to sew on his originals. Originals are the clothes a man wears when he's initiated into a bike club. Nobody could be sure that White Preacher ever had been taken in, but he had originals—horrendous, dirty rags he was always patching and scraping the crud off of.

It was late afternoon before Lil' Wally and the girl moved under the blankets. They made themselves visible, bones under naked white skin, red sores covering them. Methedrine will do that, produce those sores, and the freaks get hung-up on them. They pick, pick, pick at them, the way they endlessly string their hippy beads or do those infinitely detailed and precisely disorganized pen-and-ink drawings.

His girl was nothing to see—cow flesh and sores—but Lil' Wally's body was a tattooed piece of self-expression. There were lots of animals, mostly carnivorous, but more to the point was the dotted line around the base of his neck with the words CUT HERE and an arrow pointing to it. Leaping out of his pubic hair and covering his guts was red fire and black flames, probably the best he could do because most speed freaks agree crystal makes you impotent.

When he wasn't feeling too paranoid, White Preacher took a certain pleasure in doing up in front of strangers. He made his geezing into a dramatic presentation as well as a clinical recitation. "I made this fit [outfit, paraphernalia, syringe]," he'd say. "I wouldn't do up with nothing I didn't make myself. I even sharpened the point. See, two things you gotta remember, if ya don't wanta have trouble with your veins: you gotta use a real sharp needle, an' ya gotta be clean. See, before I geeze, I always clean the area where I'm going to do it with alcohol. You won't see most geezers doing that, but look at my veins, clean, good, not sore, nothin'."

Then he'd fill his outfit with crystal diluted in water. He used an eyedropper with a needle attached to it, and instead of a plunger he'd expel the dope by pressing a baby pacifier inserted over the other end. "It gives you more control," he'd explain. "I'm a needle freak. I'm flashing on the needle right now, just holding it up and looking at it."

"Gypsie's a needle freak too," someone said to him one day, while he was geezing. "She doesn't need sex. When she puts the needle in, she has a climax."

"That happened to me once," White Preacher said, as he concentrated on getting the needle in the vein, which was jumping around. "I came so much I had blood. Oh, I missed. See, this vein's calloused. Now, now, yeah, I got it . . . I'm in . . . oh . . . oh . . . oh."

Black Preacher got a look at Ginger bellowing on the street and faded, but White Preacher stayed. Ginger came tromping and yelling, "It's all messed up, Papa Al. We're gonna get Dirty Dick outa jail. We're gonna march on the police station, all the hippies and the bike riders. That's what we're gonna do, Papa Al."

"Whatever's right, Ginger."

Ginger said the word had gone out to assemble across the street from Benches. The time for the meeting came and went, but no one appeared but Allen, the ex-postman and MP, and Rici, who, the two of them explained, was Allen's speech writer. Apache showed up. He was an ex–bike rider turned hippy and he came to everything. Papa Al was gradually turning him straight. He finally got him married to Rusti at All Saints Church, where they had a reception afterward. As a wedding present, Lucky and some of the others said they put two acid tabs in the "A" and the "R" of the frosting letters that spelled out "Good Luck Rusti and Apache."

The gong-banging, phoenix procession now began to move down the street. Ginger tried to stop them. "Hey, hey, Dirty Dick's in jail!" Jimmy hit the gong some more. "We gotta march on the police station!" Gong, bong, buzz, bong. "Aren't you with us? Aren't the hippies with the Angels?" Ommmmmmmmmmmmmmm. "The hippies are supposed to be with the Angels. Come on, you guys, stop! We're going to the station." Ommmmmmmmmmmmmm and gong, bong, buzz, bong, they passed down the street into the fog, the tourists, and the misty headlights of the idling traffic.

"Oh, Papa Al, what are we gonna do?" Ginger wept. Somebody bought her a beer and Al suggested they get paper bags to collect bail money from the people on the street. It was agreed, and even White Preacher took a bag and began hustling the tourists and hippies for money. The first person he asked was Cowboy, who was wailing, "They set me up for a grass bust at my old lady's house. I walked in there and I saw sixteen keys of grass under the bed. There isn't sixteen keys of grass in the Haight-Ashbury tonight. The narks put it there. They're setting me up for a bust."

"Grass don't show me nothin'," White Preacher said. "I can't stand coke, but I dig opium."

"They set me up. You don't think it was my old lady?"

Preacher commiserated: "Isn't a person who righteously comes to your place, geezes, and then makes a set up. Isn't a person . . . hey, you freak, put something in this fuckin' bag for Dirty Dick."

This last was to Donn of the long red hair, the kangaroo hide vest, and the magic staff encrusted with jewels and petite amulets. "I'm empty. I haven't got any money. I'm one of the real ones."

"Fuck you, what kind of a trip are you on that you won't give righteously for Dirty Dick?"

"Oh, I've been on a devil's trip. I'm real up tight. I'm going to stomp on some of those cats in the East Bay for what they did to my girl. I didn't know they were doing it because I was in an STP house on Telegraph Avenue. Then I was so bad, they carried me over to this meth freak house, which is a burn-out drug. I know the girl there. I used to love her so much I wanted to ball her, but now she can't keep her jaws together. It was not only a meth freak house but homosexual too, which is a reversal of nature."

"You're a fuckin' meth freak to talk that way," Preacher said, coming up under him, squinting and showing his ivory knives.

Donn reared back and answered like the prophet, "Meth is a death drug invented by the Nazis to kill men. A death-self-destruction trip."

"Yeah? Well, I'm on speed right now, and I was practically

171

raised by the Trappist monks, then I went to the Dominicans and then I went to the Benedictines and I got up to my final vows."

Donn fled and White Preacher continued his assault on the tourists for money. His looks alone scared some of them into contributing. There were about ten of them running up and down in front of Benches, collecting money and drinking beer.

"We're trying to raise a little bail money," cried Allen, who'd landed in the Haight about five weeks ago and was making it on his savings and a part-time job as a toupee salesman. He was wearing a blue, quilted windbreaker and some of his merchandise, as he called out, "Well, if you don't have any money at least give us a smile."

"Forget the politics and raise some money," Papa Al said, while he himself collected dope samples from passing friendly dealers. These he put into his plastic pouch, while he asked friends if they could get him a little information about so-and-so, or so-and-so.

"If elected, I promise constitutional reform and general amnesty for all people busted on narco charges," Allen declared. "That's from the speech Rici's writing me. I'm going to be the first hippy congressman."

When White Preacher got enough pennies and nickels in his paper bag, he went off down the street, trying to count it and put it in his pocket. Some of the others did the same. Ginger ran back and forth, shouting again, "They're burning me, Papa Al. They're burning me, they're burning Dirty Dick, they're burning the Angels . . . Oh, Papa Al. They're bastards, aren't they? What am I going to do?"

"Ginger, I'll buy you a beer."

### METHEDRINE SHOT
### KILLS S.F. YOUTH

San Francisco, July 27—A 17-year-old San Francisco boy has died of serum hepatitis after sharing a communal needle at a Methedrine party, it was learned yesterday.

Henry J. Kaiser, "the Bay Area tycoon," as the papers called him, and Chocolate George were buried on the same day. Chocolate's funeral was more lively. The best beloved of the Angels was killed in a traffic accident on Haight Street. It was said he'd been on the way to the Fillmore to collect some money owed him, because a girl named Flower had or hadn't done something. It was very confused, but Ginger blamed Flower for Chocolate George's death. While Chocolate was dying in a hospital coma, Ginger and her girl friends, biker mamas with names like Amazon, Frizzy, and Sexy, jumped Flower in Benches, shaved her hair off, stripped her naked, and threw her out into the street. That's how Ginger described what they'd done the first time; the second time, she said they put her in a car, took her down to the Fillmore, and "threw her out to give the spades something to feed on." Ginger was very unsettled because Chocolate had been Hank's best friend.

The *Berkeley Barb* ran a drawing of Chocolate with a halo and a heart, looking like a canonized saint. In the article they said the dead Angel in his coffin looked "like Attila the Hun. A fur cap hides his bare head, shaved when the doctors tried to repair the skull Chocolate broke when he flipped over the handlebars of his Harley." It was a big affair in a number of Haight-Ashbury circles. Papa Al, who was involved with a tall, red-faced young biker named Hutch in a new anti–juvenile delinquency, anti-runaway operation, broke off his picking up stray dope and stray people. He came and so did guys from half a dozen other bike clubs, their mamas in their pussy holders: the Gypsy Jokers, the Cossacks, the Galloping Geese and the L.A. Angels (all the way from L.A.), the Misfits, the Nomads, Satan's Slaves. Teddybear was there and Apache, but not people like Peggy or White Rabbit or Damien from the God's Eye.

Mona of Mona's was there with her roommate Bonnie. Mona had run one of the wildest, wide-open dope houses in San Francisco until she was busted. The two of them alighted from a taxi, complaining they'd forgotten how to wear straight clothes. The way they acted, nearly toppling over on their spikes, playing with garters, and Bonnie, who was pregnant, working at her girdle, they looked like a couple of girls who weren't used to anything but bathrobes.

"Oy, Jesus!" Mona exclaimed, reminiscing about the bust that put her out of business. "The cops broke in the door. You shoulda seen what we flushed down the toilet. There was enough there to keep the State of California high for a month. My sister wiped the fingerprints off and threw her gun out the window, but the cops did miss the cocaine under the kitchen sink."

Before they closed the coffin to take Chocolate to the crematorium, Mona saw Teddybear and said, "Oy, Jesus" again. "Do I remember him! Yeah, back at the Cafe Mustapha, 1502 New Utrecht Avenue, Brooklyn. He'd come in in his mohair suit and his attaché case, trying to play electronics executive, but he'd be stoned outa his gourd."

On the way back, the girls picked up Pancho, who said he had a gram and a half of DMT (a short-trip psychedelic) on him, but nobody had any grass to smoke it with. Mona said they had a little pot left at her house, so they went over there and scraped the last leaves out of the dope stash. Bonnie was yammering about Chob's old lady. "D'ya see her? She's on a bad trip. She's wearing Chob's necklace. That shoulda been buried with him."

"No," Mona disagreed. "She was a true old lady. They loved each other. It started at my place. Anyway, he was cremated. Boy, I wish I had Chob's old roach clip. I wonder who's got that."

They smoked dope until it was used up and Bonnie said, "I'm wiped out."

"Mona," Pancho wanted to know, "did you get off?"

"Not like I usually do—outa my gourd."

"I'll get ya off in the park. There's no more grass here."

They almost forgot to go to the Golden Gate Park where the Dead were playing free at Chocolate George's memorial farewell party. The girls got hung-up showing off their things. "My thing's beads, though you'd never know it," Mona said, showing her beadwork. "And my thing's clothes," said Bonnie, sitting in a chair, holding one strand of hair in front of her, trying to split it down the middle.

174

There were hundreds in the park meadow. They drank beer. mountain red, and smoked the last of the grass. The Angels threw ice from the beer tubs at the hippies, who kept their distance. Even so, they told Felicia to take down the peace symbol she carried at the end of her staff or they'd shove it up her. They beat up one Negro and took the pants off one girl.

"Oh, you missed the best part of it," said Papa Al. "They were down on the grass eating her. It was a nice thing to do for Chocolate George. Oh well, whatever's right."

## NUDE PAIR SENT
## TO HOSPITAL

**San Francisco, Sept. 30—The hippies who tried to start a nude-in at San Francisco State College were sent to San Francisco Hospital for psychiatric examinations yesterday.**

Steve Christenson was fidgeting and almost jumping. He threw his weight from one foot to another, a boy being allowed to help Mother bake Daddy's birthday cake, and the aquamarine-colored substance on his fingers looked like frosting.

Steve is twenty-five. He was bouncing around the door to the English basement apartment on Clayton Street, half a block off Haight, because he was God-almighty nervous that the wrong people might enter and the stuff on his hands was acid. Steve and his friend Hutch had copped big—two grams. It would make up into somewhere between seven and eight thousand doses.

Past Steve in the yellow-painted kitchen, Hutch and the two other young men were seated around a table capping the acid. The LSD itself, mixed in a harmless calcium compound, was in several large transparent plastic bags. As it was needed, it was spooned out of the bags onto several ordinary saucers where the three men laboriously capped it by putting the powder into half a gelatin capsule. When they'd filled it, they inserted it in the other half and chucked the finished product into a bowl. The gelatin capsules were stored in the refrigerator until they were needed. The cold kept them stiff and easier to work with.

175

The atmosphere in the room was jerking paranoia. No introductions, no names; if you didn't know who the people were, you didn't find out; but one of them was the most valuable of all Haight-Ashbury people: a chemist, an actual maker of lysergic acid diethylamide-25. Why he was there wasn't clear. Chemists make a great deal of money and they don't have to pick up free dope by capping. He may just have been a friend, or he may have been out of production for lack of raw material, or he may have had a secret financial interest in this batch, but he was there, a bitter-talking guy. His manner made you think of a defrocked priest or a disbarred lawyer or maybe an abortionist. "If you stay here, you're going to get stoned, whether you like it or not," he said. "This stuff is one of a class of compounds that are called aromatic, which means it gets in the air." He looked at his aquamarine fingers and added, "It also gets through your pores."

"I'm getting finger cramps," the chemist remarked, flexing them. "You know, it's a lot easier with a pill press. They cost about $9,000 if you want one that the government can't trace. The FDA knows the serial numbers and the owners of every press that's sold. They come around and see what you're doing with them, and if you don't let them in, they're back with a court order. They're nice, though. I have a friend who has one. He's wiped out now. A lot of the money Superspade had on him when he was murdered belonged to my friend."

"Do you think the Mafia killed Superspade?" somebody in the room asked about the murdered dope wholesaler.

"Don't be ridiculous. I know Superspade had at least $50,000 on him when he was killed. The people who killed him are the people he went to cop from. It was simple robbery. You don't have to go inventing gangsters. Listen," the chemist said in a particularly saturnine tone, "three-quarters of those kids out on that street would kill you for $2 if they got you alone and they had a weapon. Love generation! What crap!

"I was in this business when it started, before Leary came along getting himself up as some kind of second Jesus. That acidhead hasn't got twenty functioning brain cells left, but when I started

176

we didn't drop it to see God or overthrow the government. We did it because we liked it. I still take acid sometimes, but I get my hair cut and I'm still in the middle class. I have middle-class values. I told my wife the other day, if I ever came home and found a man in her bed, I'd kill her. You know what she answered? She said she was glad, because it meant somebody cared enough about her. I'm the same way. I want to belong somewhere."

On the street, things were much less tight. The news that there was a vast amount of acid around seemed to be sifting out. Hutch had said that the people he copped his two grams from had eighteen more, so that even the small dealers got whiffs.

Teddybear got his fat self in motion. He'd have to move fast before the people he knew learned they could cop directly from Steve and Hutch. Once they found out, they'd bypass him and buy direct, so he'd lose his 10 per cent commission.

"I don't make a commission," he said, as though he'd been accused of a crime. "I just get 10 per cent of the dope. I wouldn't take money from my friends."

"Dope is money, Teddybear," his companion said out of the corner of his mouth.

"Well, if you want to look at it that way, I guess you can," he answered, but he was distracted by somebody he knew whom he took off to the side and whispered at, probably trying to get the guy to come up with some front money. Acid is a no-credit, no-Diner's-Club-card business.

The availability of acid isn't constant. When the market's tight, the people on the street get tight, and when it's loose, they smell it like ozone from San Francisco harbor and loosen up themselves. The mood communicated itself to people who weren't involved. Love, the dyed redheaded Persian girl, who must have been in her forties and sold "loveburgers" from her streetside hot dog stand, had caught the spirit.

"Hello, baby, how are you, love?" she called, walking with her two little dogs up Clayton Street. "Oh, baby, I'm stoned. It feels so good. You know what I'm stoned on? Good Persian hashish. The very best there is. You try it sometime. You'll never drink again," Love promised with a giggly laugh, forgetting the times she'd gotten juiced.

Even Lefty, the chief of Alibaba and the Forty Thieves, had picked up the vibrations. Lefty said he didn't turn on, didn't even allow dope in his place. The outfit he ran was one of those amorphous Haight-Ashbury benevolent societies, which was supposed to do unspecified good, although all you ever heard was the membership talking about getting high. Lefty was having a party, a spaghetti dinner where a miscellany of street commandos, petty dealers, and uncategorizable oddballs socialized by talking about the great fights they'd been in, promising each other they would devote themselves to trying to return the mass of runaway kids in the neighborhood to parents who didn't seem to want them.

On the corner of Haight and Masonic, Papa Al took in the scene outside the Drogstore. There was much merry dope selling. "My, my," he said. "I haven't seen the children trade that openly for a couple of months. Usually they at least try to pass it under a blanket or a coat or something." As Papa Al smiled his smile of twinkling cruelty and made sarcastic remarks, Teddybear came up to him. "I need protection, Papa Al," he said, as though a sniper had him in the cross hairs of a telescopic sight.

"Tell me, son," replied Papa Al, "who's going to save the State of California the cost of putting you away?"

"No, no, Papa Al, I'm serious. I've got a thousand dollars on me. Will you walk me down to Hutch's? It's not my money. I don't want anything to happen."

"Well, it so happens I just do have a little protection on me," the older man replied, and put Teddybear's hand against the pocket of his zipper jacket. The dope pusher could feel the hardness of a revolver. The two proceeded to Hutch's, where the older man announced, "I've got a customer for you, but I don't think his money's any good. You'd better take a good look at those bills."

"I've got a thousand dollars on me . . . actually, a thousand and five," Teddybear told Steve. "How much are you selling for?"

"Two dollars apiece."

178

"That's too much. We want to sell them on the street for $2.50 a cap."

"Well, how about $1.97?"

"I'm buying in quantity."

"I don't have any trouble selling acid at two."

"I've got the cash on me," Teddybear replied, and there was more haggling until they agreed on $1.75, after which he took himself off into the living room, where blue stroboscopic light shone down on the mattress, and with pencil and paper attempted to figure out exactly how many caps it worked out to.

While Teddybear coped with arithmetic, more people knocked on the door; most were coming to buy, but one hippy couple had heard and arrived without money simply to window shop. The strangers were pushing Steve up tight, though Hutch didn't seem to mind. At length, Steve said, "I want everybody who's not buying out of here." Some people left, but Papa Al stayed to negotiate. Could Steve get him acid? How much? Two thousand a gram? Guaranteed righteous stuff, Steve assured him, adding that he was barely making any profit himself. Al said it sounded pretty good; could the cop be made tomorrow?

"I'll have to phone," Steve answered, and there began a round of telephone calls and people going in and out. "Now look, this has gotta be sure," Al cautioned him. "These people will be coming all the way out from Washington, D.C. . . . Yeah, I'll get them here tomorrow, if you can definitely hold the acid."

Time passed with more telephone calls. Then Hutch said the market had broken as a result of the appearance of the aquamarine acid, and now there were blue acid and other kinds of acid making their appearance. He went over to a white enamel slop pail near the refrigerator, took off the top, and came up with several handfuls of dope. "Samples," he said. They were passed around and special interest was shown in a new product, which had the acid impregnated on sheets of paper. Six shots to a sheet. It would be put out in book form so that the dealer could rip out however much the customer wanted. (To turn on you merely chew the paper.)

179

"Funny nobody thought of that before," somebody said.

"Yeah," Steve agreed. "That's how everybody's turning on their friends in jail."

"Right you are," Hutch put in. "Don't read your mail. Eat it."

The tightness in the room had abated. The men were holding out their acid-covered fingers and saying to each other, "Wanta lick?" Everybody took licks but the chemist, who declared, "I'm getting cramps in my fingers. Somebody else'll have to do this." He got up from the table, flexing his hands while he discoursed on how he was in the acid business for the money. "But it's not as easy as some people think. It's hard to get lysergic acid. The government has stopped the sale of it. Of course, there're a lot of people who are bringing it in from Europe. Once you've got that it's relatively easy to convert. There're cookbooks that'll tell you how. It helps, though, if you know laboratory procedure. If you're not a chemist and something goes wrong, you won't know what to do . . . There is a way to make lysergic acid. An article in a certain English journal of chemistry describes the procedure for growing fungus and turning it into batches of about one hundred grams."

The chemist put on his jacket and left, as did Papa Al. When Al returned, only Steve and Hutch were in the apartment. Teddy-bear, they reported, had gone with his acid in a bag and was off somewhere with his friends capping it.

Hutch was pretty well stoned, but not enough, apparently, because he produced hashish from a coat and beer from the icebox. As the dope and alcohol made their way around the kitchen, Al, having concluded arrangements with Steve, picked up the phone and called Washington. When he hung up, he reported that they would wire the cash tomorrow morning and a courier would arrive to pick up the merchandise in the afternoon.

There was only one more customer that night: a plush hippy from San Diego who was wearing a blue silk, lace-trimmed Russian blouse shirt. There was a mumbled exchange of recognition—words and names—as he explained they had mutual friends from whom he usually bought dope for the market down there. After he left more hashish was smoked, the beer drunk, and Steve asked Papa

180

Al if he could show up tomorrow with some of his gun-carrying friends to lean on a guy who'd burned him for $2,000. Steve kept saying in the most amiable way that he really thought he'd kill the guy.

Al equivocated about the request, while Hutch smiled and said, "Hey, man, I'm stoned, stoned, too stoned to drive."

The next morning the cops raided the place. Steve and Hutch were busted. Most of the dope was gone except for a little hash and about eight hundred caps. The police also found two twenty-two-caliber revolvers and a thirty-two-caliber automatic. Teddy-bear, Papa Al, and the chemist got away.

Not long ago an Oak Park, Illinois, housewife idly asked her baby-sitter if she'd ever taken any of that LSD stuff—there's been so much in the papers about it. The teen-age girl replied no, she hadn't, it was too expensive, $17 a dose in her high school.

If Larry Burton had heard the conversation he would have been perturbed by the price. "One of the reasons I sold acid," Larry once said, "is because I believe it's important that as many people as possible get good dope at reasonable prices."

Henry Ford felt the same way about cars, and both he and Larry did their best to bring a product that once was within the reach of only a special few to the American mass-consumer market. Until recently, Larry was, as they say in the Haight-Ashbury, a very heavy dealer.

For an extended period of time Larry was selling more than ten thousand acid tabs a week. In one three-month period his business grossed over $100,000. He offers these figures himself, but other people who know the dope industry corroborate them. (Larry estimates that fifteen other dealers in San Francisco were doing business on the same scale, which, if he is correct, means at least a half a million acid tabs were being sold every month there.)

The actual Larry Burton has no resemblance to the stereotyped dope pusher. He has no Cadillac, although at one time his income was about $800 a week; he never went around with snarling bodyguards; he doesn't talk tough; he has never met a gangster or had anything to do with the syndicate, and all his sentences parse.

They should. Larry is a graduate of Reed College, Oregon, one of the most respected liberal arts schools in the country. His senior thesis was about topological squares. From Reed Larry went on to the University of California at Berkeley, where he completed a year of graduate work in mathematics.

If he fits a stereotype it's that of a mathematician. Slightly built, a bit stoop shouldered with glasses that always magnify wondering, naive eyes, Larry is both timid and cerebral. The timidity is reflected in a slight hitch to his otherwise articulate speech, and a small, irrelevant laugh which introduces itself from time to time in his conversation.

"I've always had difficulty relating to people," Larry will say of a childhood and growing up that he regards as too studious and

182

too withdrawn, too preoccupied with the arcane, tautological symbolism of mathematics.

"I played Marcus Aurelius Stenchfield in a play in my junior year in high school. He was a character who had beautiful girls falling all over him. That play was a turning point in my life because Marcus Aurelius Stenchfield was where I was really at . . . I didn't get along with people at all. I had to prove I was better than everybody else, and unfortunately I was often successful. I always got the highest grades in my class.

"The play pointed out to me that I was closing people off. I saw myself with a choice of being a famous mathematician or a mediocre one but a well-rounded person. That was when I first started smiling at people.

"I was a junior in high school before I had my first date, and I was a senior before I kissed a girl. The summer after I graduated from high school—I was the class valedictorian—some girl practically had to rape me before I'd have sex with her. Then it took me a year and a half to recover. You know, I used to be over at one girl's house at midnight and she'd start reading dirty poems to me and I was afraid to kiss her!"

Larry has figured out when a girl wants to be kissed. At Berkeley he got mixed up with the Sexual Freedom League and has had his fling at what are usually called orgies because the term blows the straight world's mind. "I enjoy group sex activities, but not with a bunch of people who are just there to ball, you know, where you have a lot of horny guys and a few horny girls. But if it's a group of people who really dig each other it can be beautiful."

People in the Haight respond to criticism of their sexual practices by pointing to what they consider furtive and sneaky couple-swapping in the suburbs. The mass media don't write much about that but concentrate on them, they assert with some justification.

"By and large," Larry has decided, "I've devoted the last three years of my life to cleaning up my hang-ups, and I think in the last few months I've climbed above average. That is, I have fewer hang-ups than most reasonably well-adjusted people."

Larry says he's happier now than at any time before he began taking acid and got into the dope business. If he has any regrets, they're not obvious. "Acid works to resolve cognitive dissonances; it's unifying," Larry explains, as he reveals himself to be a person who spent most of his twenty-two years trying to find his own obtunded feelings but always blocked off from them by mathematics, by ciphered abstractions.

"One of the things acid does is bring you into present time," says Larry, talking of his first LSD trip as though until then, emotionally anyway, he had lived in no time—unless it was the vague future time of post-doctoral years that young professors in training live in. "The second time I dropped acid was on a Greyhound bus going to Portland to see a chick. I had some math work to do so I said to myself, if I really dig mathematics I should enjoy doing it when I'm stoned. I found I couldn't do it, so I decided to give it up. I finished the semester at Berkeley and left school."

Exactly how these drugs work on the nervous system is still in serious doubt, but it may be that not even a universal mathematical genius like Archimedes could function on acid. Judging from the testimony of many acid users, one of the first capacities to be impaired or held in suspension by dope like pot and acid is the ability to manipulate any kind of closed system of symbols. So what Larry thought was insight into himself may have been the action of the drug; but the desire to do what he felt like doing, not what he *thought* was good to do, seems to have antedated his acid taking. Those "cognitive dissonances," the internal contest between Apollo and Dionysus, the conflict between knowing deeply in a specialized, professional sense and knowing broadly— these themes have been at war with each other inside Larry for many years. "I used to want to know all there was about one thing; now I want to know at least something about everything."

There are other elements at play in Larry too. One day he said, "I think I might have been an original mathematical genius if I'd had the right person to study under in grammar school, but there wasn't anybody, and I could only go so far on my own. I was held up in an important period, and you know in mathematics you usually do most of your original work before you're twenty or so."

Larry is not the only young academic to feel the pressure to be an Einstein or else consider himself without value. There are other young people in the Haight who judge themselves by standards of accomplishment realized by only a few thousand individuals in all of Western history. These, you might say, are the Promethean dropouts, people who condemn themselves because luck failed to endow them with the rarest gifts of the mind. When Larry left school he got a job as a computer programmer, and "I started in the business by selling acid to my friends so I could get mine free. I used to buy it in $100 lots. Then I had more money and I bought a $500 lot and started selling it in $100 batches. It was easy to do because basically with acid you never have to push. There is always more of a demand than a supply."

Many people get into the business the same way. They buy a kilo of grass, sell enough to their friends to cover the cost, and smoke up the profit themselves. At this stage they are still amateurs; they're not really part of the distributive chain in which the ultimate consumer is somebody they don't know. From this point they graduate to professionalism. The part-timer will sometimes deal purely for a monetary profit, not merely to keep himself in dope. He's in and out of the professional market either because he has a straight job or because he's too busy with other things, like going to school or just grooving on life on Haight Street, to want more than a marginal amount of money.

Another reason that many people remain part-time dealers is the difficulty they have copping, that is, buying dope from a wholesaler. Small dealers are virtually immune from arrest; it isn't worthwhile blowing a hard-to-come-by police cover to arrest some kid who's selling five or six lids (a few ounces) of grass a day at $8 a lid. Big dealers, wholesalers, are another matter. As a result, they're very careful whom they sell to.

Copping dope isn't easy, and very few small dealers have more than one reliable wholesaler they can cop from. If that wholesaler is busted, the little dealer's supply is cut off until he can make another contact. Meanwhile, he's out of the dope business.

One of the ways you can grow into a big dealer is to build up a reputation for honesty, for keeping your word. The same premium is placed on personal integrity in the dope business as in any business where contracts aren't legally enforceable—like gambling, prostitution, or politics.

Larry suffered many of the hit-and-miss vicissitudes of the smaller dealer, but he's a reliable, well-organized, truthful person, somebody you'd prefer to do illegal business with. He grew big in grass and acid. (These are the only two commodities he's ever sold or used.)

"I had three full-time people working for me. It was very challenging. It takes remarkable ability to handle money and organize people like that. It was a big business, so big I never saw the dope, never touched what I sold. I sat at a desk and took care of the arrangements."

By this time his business had become completely wholesale. He wasn't even selling to people in San Francisco. His buyers were in Seattle and Washington, D.C. They would come to San Francisco or Larry would have couriers deliver to them, but shipping contraband is a lot harder than shipping automobile parts.

Larry's description of what it requires to get a shipment of grass across the border into the United States will give you an idea of what's involved: "You have to have a reliable American down there to cop from the Mexicans. Mexicans aren't trustworthy. They'll take your money and then turn you in for a bounty. We had somebody there full time.

"Usually the purchase is made in the desert. You don't pay until you get the merchandise. Whoever's receiving the shipment comes armed . . . it's usually two people. They're Americans, of course. The pot is transferred once and sometimes twice before it's taken across the border, so that the Mexicans can't tell the guard what kind of a car it's coming across in.

"It's often taken across in private cars. The ideal thing is a late-model car with a husband, wife, and a baby. A passenger car can hold about one hundred kilos of grass . . . you'd be surprised how much empty space there is in an automobile. The door panels are taken out and it's stuffed in there. The same thing is done with the seats. It's even put behind the hub caps. There's a lot of work

186

involved in that. In that heat the grass will smell like a Mexican compost heap and the smell will give you away. Before the grass is packed in the car it's sprayed with a pine scent, then wrapped in plastic and aluminum foil. It's also brought across the border by bribing the guards. The usual price is $5 a key.

"They can make a lot of money that way. I knew one person who was buying five hundred keys a week. I'd estimate that San Francisco consumes a ton of grass a week."

Larry is a good businessman. He is also, like a number of other people who deal dope and are called hippies, a student and practitioner of and a believer in certain metaphysical ideas that have found their fullest expression in China and India. On the floor of his bedroom, next to the mattress he sleeps on, Larry has a copy of the *I Ching*. On top of it are the three coins used in the intricate system of divination. The *I Ching* is more than two thousand years old. It can be used for ethical insight; it is also used as a guide to the future.

> *If a man carries a burden on his back*
> *And nonetheless rides a carriage,*
> *He thereby encourages robbers to draw near,*
> *Perseverance leads to humiliation.*
> —From *I Ching* or *The Book of Changes*

Of the verses above, Confucius wrote, "When a common man uses the appurtenance of rank, robbers plot to take it away from him."

Translated into the occidental terms of the Haight-Ashbury, the words might be construed to mean, "When university intellectuals exchange their calling for dope pushing, they are laid open for robbery."

Robbers and others have drawn near Larry, but if the *I Ching*, the oracle of bronze antiquity, cautioned him, he couldn't understand, for not too long ago the police came knocking on his door, busted him for dealing, confiscated his dope, and impounded his money.

Many people in the acid world have taken up the occult sciences, *I Ching*, tarot cards, astrology, and numerology. Their interest flows from their acid experiences which, they believe, have given them new sensitivities and glimpses at ways of knowing and feeling that the categorical rationalism of the West fails to pick up or even denies. Acid people, for instance, often believe that they can catch "vibrations" emanating from others.

Larry now views his academic studies as denatured—inhuman beside the important points of life. Acid set him to reading Eastern religion and put him in pursuit of cabalistic learning.

The straight world has put down these spectral investigations by hippies as so much nuttiness, forgetting that the newspapers print horoscopes daily.

Nevertheless, Larry didn't pick up the bad vibrations when he should have. "I was set up," he says of his arrest. "It was funny because I wasn't dealing at the time. I was out of the dope business, but the wife of one of my customers from out of town got in touch with me and said she just had to cop. I didn't know that her husband, who was a good friend, had been busted and that she'd made a deal with the police.

"It was a funny thing. I had to go to a lot of trouble to get it for her because I didn't have any dope. I had to make a lot of phone calls to get it. When she came to cop it, she brought a man with her, and later I found out he was a narcotics agent."

As Larry tells the story he was not arrested at the time, nor for months afterward. "They waited until I was back in the business, dealing big. When they raided my place, they only had an arrest warrant, no search warrant. But they got all the dope I had and $3,000. They confiscated the dope and I never got the money back. I was wiped out," Larry concludes.

### LOOKING AT DANGER

**Vienna, Sept. 5 (UPI)—Franz Petrus, 20, acknowledged leader of Vienna's hippies, pleaded in court he kept marijuana at his home just to look at. "We wouldn't use LSD or marijuana," he said. "It's too dangerous."**

Ordinarily, intelligent people in the dope business never keep money or merchandise where they live. For a considerable period of time Larry operated that way. This was when he was in a ring headed by a mysterious girl named Marge whom he doesn't say much about. Marge was in a position to cop acid wholesale— probably one or two transactions away from the manufacturing chemist—while Larry's sources were smaller and less reliable. They formed a partnership with Marge the dominant member.

For a while everything went well and they made a lot of money. Then there was trouble, if Larry is to be believed. You can never be entirely sure. The stories are never told quite the same way twice; all the parties to the transactions aren't available for interviewing, and events are omitted or changed to hide identities. A general pattern holds true, however, in the careers of most dealers. Endemic in the dope industry is the double-crossing, the informing, the suspicion, the emotional instability, arising perhaps from taking the drugs and certainly from everybody's precarious legal position.

"There was a time," says Larry, indulging in the arcadian reminiscences that stamp him as a Haight-Ashbury old-timer, "there was a time about a year ago when all acid dealers were my neighbors, people I trusted, but that's not true now. The change was due to a complex set of factors. When a scene starts it can be pure because it's small, but when a scene grows there are fakers, charlatans, and mountebanks. If you sell H [heroin] you do it for the money, but if you sell acid you sort of believe in it, you're sort of a preacher. At least that's the way it was."

There are some dealers who fit Larry's description of people who only want to make a modest amount of money, but there aren't nearly the number of such philanthropists as the dope world would like to believe. Most dealers charge what the traffic will bear; even so, only a small number of people dealing big and close to the source of supply make money. Most dealers, like Larry, may make it big for a while, but then they're burned or busted and wiped out.

Often financial disaster overtakes them because they've been stupid, which means doing business on credit or drawing the police's attention by doing something mildly nutty when they're stoned. Even those who stay straight and smart can't always avoid the traps that go along with any illegal industry. One of the most hazardous is the hippy costume. There are many reasons for wearing costumes which have nothing to do with dope, but dealers will say that it helps them in their business. It is the dope equivalent of the cigar store Indian or the bright yellow Shell sign at the gas station; but it attracts narks as well as customers.

Marge was a speed freak, or so Larry says. Acidheads look down on speed freaks as little better than old-time junkies—dangerous, erratic people who aren't to be trusted. Consequently, Marge, strung out on speed, apparently reached a point where she was too disorganized to cop acid for the dope ring. She may simply have grown suspicious of Larry. Acid and pot can induce paranoia, but prevailing opinion is that speed is almost guaranteed to do it.

In any event, the operation broke up. But not before Marge accused Larry of having burned her for several thousand dollars in acid, which she had supplied but he hadn't paid for. Larry claims it was her fault because the word got out among their customers that he had no more acid to sell—and they had no reason to pay their outstanding bills once they knew they couldn't cop from him anymore.

Some time later, Larry says, Marge revenged herself. Though no longer partners, both were back in business and Larry, with several thousand dollars, went to cop some acid from Marge. With the help of two men with guns, she took his money and wouldn't give him the acid. Even now Larry sometimes fantasizes about getting even with Marge.

But most of the time he's more detached: "In the long run nobody makes money in dealing. With all the money I made and lost, I haven't come out much ahead. I think dope paid for my hi-fi set, and that's about all."

Of possessions he has few: some records, some books, his hi-fi, and an old, lovingly and psychedelically painted Volvo, which he has upholstered in paisleys. In his wallet he carries a picture of the pre-arrest Larry—head encircled in blond hair, dripping with

190

beads. Now he is clipped short and most of the time he wears a business suit, de rigueur for his job as a computer programmer where they know nothing of their employee's short, glorious past.

He lives in a little apartment across the Bay in Berkeley where the bedroom is hung with madras prints. The tentlike effect, with the rugging, the candles, and the smell of incense, is more Bedouin than Hindu.

With him is Kathy, the dark-haired daughter of an Army officer. "My father's the kind of colonel who wears his blues on Sunday. He only lives to get his star," says Kathy, who lived on the sidewalks in the Haight for three weeks until Larry found her and took up with her.

With another dealer who's awaiting sentence, they are trying to start a "love center," a place where disturbed kids in the Haight can go to talk out their problems. It's a surprising endeavor for Larry, once such an ingrown person that he seemed to his friends to shrink back from even walking the streets. But acid, everybody agrees, can change your personality, and Larry has taken a lot of it in the last couple of years.

"I usually take it about once every seventeen or eighteen days. You feel when to take it from your body's rhythms, unless you're really dingy," he explains. People might say that Larry is dingy. He does convey the impression of one who has changed, perhaps lost a certain acuity and power in his thinking, as though he has gone limp in his personality.

"After I got busted, I felt relieved. Maybe you don't realize the tension you're under because it's illegal," said Larry, who pleaded guilty at his trial.

Larry's relief seems deeper than that. It's more like a release from a lifelong internal strangulation that had held back his metempsychosis into a new life.

"I'm not going by the name Larry anymore," he said. "I'm using my karmic name, Lomand. It means to use understanding. It's not a name that is given to us. It's one that we find out. My karmic name used to be Lom, which means to gain understanding.

"There is at least one plane of existence parallel to this one, that is to say another space we're not normally aware of, but it's possible by expanding your consciousness to come into contact with it. There are people there who know of our existence, so by getting in touch with them you can learn your name. The higher your karmic existence, the more rapidly you change and your name may change. A woman on the other plane named Eob told me my name."

Kathy has a new name too: "My name's Saqui. I don't know, but I have the vague feeling it may mean bewildered."

### WE'RE CLOBBERING THEM
#### By Bob Considine

Saigon (Hearst Headline Service), Sept. 10—
Stop griping. We're winning this lousy war.
It is not, repeat not, a stalemate.

### MICE ARMY ADVANCES

Sarajevo, Yugoslavia, Aug. 21 (UPI) — A
rampaging army of millions of field mice destroyed an estimated $400,000 worth of crops
in Bosnia, it was reported yesterday.

### MOUSE ARMY DAMAGE SOARS

Priboj, Yugoslavia, Aug. 27 (AP)—Armies of
hungry mice were on the move in parts of
Yugoslavia and Sicily yesterday. In the
Sicilian capital of Palermo rodents have
sacked food stores, destroyed vineyards and
killed chickens, pigeons and rabbits in their
pens.

### AIR WAR AGAINST MICE

London, Sept. 6 (Chicago Tribune Service)—
Airplanes spraying poison are joining the
battle against an invading army of yellow
mice on the march in central Yugoslavia.

The plankton were the simple hippies, the stray teeni-boppers, the runaways, the summer dropouts—the microorganisms without power of locomotion that hung in the heavy water pond of the Haight-Ashbury waiting for the more complex creatures to inhale them into their mouths and ingest them into their bellies where they could be food. Often there would be attempts to teach the plankton how to avoid being consumed.

The *Los Angeles Free Press* ran a long piece called "How to Survive in the Streets." It was reprinted in the Haight:

> *In the street you are subject to all manner of problems which do not exist if you have an "indoors" to go "outdoors" from . . . In an emergency—if all else has failed—it is possible to sleep in the daytime on the roof of a tenement or apartment building . . . Better than a roof is a garage. These may be rented from between $7 to $15 a month— ostensibly for storage. Don't make your garage a hangout as this draws heat. Communal apartments are nice—if they work. Most don't. If you have the bread to get one, an old panel truck or step van can be lived in. Park your truck out of the "action," lock it, and don't hang out by it. Don't sleep in a passenger car: it is a bust.*

> *Change your socks every day, and dust your shoes with Essenex powder. Take care of your feet. Sandals are fine during the day, but will give you colds if you wear them at night. Make it a rule to take a bath every time you get a chance and to wash your clothes at least once a week. Laundromats are good places to meet people.*

> *Don't shoplift. The people watching for this are better at watching than you can ever be stealing. There are two apparently easy ways to make money living on the streets: whoring and selling dope. Both are to be avoided at all cost. Dealing will always get you busted and whoring will spoil your sex life.*

The plankton that caught on fast wouldn't play and got out of town. Some of them were disappointed and just went home; some continued the quest for the hippy El Dorado. The really beautiful people, they were told, had split for Mendocino, the Santa Cruz Mountains, communes in Utah and New Mexico. They followed. Others shrugged their shoulders—another shuck, but all advertising is deceptive and the trip west was worth it.

Many stayed.

Sunshine stayed. She said she came from Montana or Wyoming. She was as pretty as her name, but she wasn't smart. She couldn't whore so she caught pneumonia. She was all right as long as she stuck with Pan, the boy who had spread his blanket on the lawn just past the pillars where you leave Haight Street and enter Golden Gate Park. "Get your hippy dope pipes here! Genuine hippy dope pipes," he'd call out, and people would gather around and look at the merchandise displayed on the blanket. Sunshine seemed to sparkle while she was with Pan. She always wore high-topped moccasins and she looked like he took care of her, but they broke up. Pan was on a very heavy Indian trip and Sunshine was one of those born, joyful wasters. His new old lady, Little Bit, was squawish and submissive. Sunshine thought you could do anything and the bills would never come due. They never had for her. She was so pretty, and you could see somebody had spent a lot of money on her once. Her teeth were perfect, and her hair and complexion were holding up.

When Pan got rid of her, she went with this tall boy with a cough. He was stoned a lot and he couldn't look after Sunshine. She wore out her moccasins and started coughing too. He probably loved her; they held hands a lot, but they were getting sicker. One night they were up at Brian's and Mike's, lying on the bed stoned, with fevers, trying to make love and not being able to do more than shiver. Pretty soon after that the boy left. Sunshine got so sick she had to go to the clinic. By then she had pneumonia and she knew there was something wrong with her. It surprised her that she could get so sick, but they had to put her in the hospital anyway.

Bill Graham was the man people in the Haight said swallowed the biggest mouthfuls of plankton, when the subject came up—as it did all the time—about who was onto the most money. Graham foresaw that light shows and acid rock could be bigger than esoteric guruism and put them in the Fillmore Auditorium, which promptly became the Dome of the Rock, the most famous place in America for music and dance in this decade. As a tourist attraction, it is probably better known to youth than the Golden Gate Bridge. It turned out that Graham was an excellent businessman. The Haight accused him of making millions and of displacing its own chosen people in the Fillmore Auditorium in favor of richer, squarer tourists.

"The tourist doesn't know Jim Kweskin and Roland Kirk [musicians]. And this is where we differ from the psychedelic lights and love birds of America. I don't want a total hippy crowd, I never wanted it," says Bill Graham. "The earlier crowds with colors and the plumes and the costumes and the stuff on their hair and their faces, I still would like them to come. But I also want the guy from Madison Avenue, from Montgomery Street, because that's the balance. The hippy who comes in here, he's already extroverted. The guy who comes in here with shirt and tie and who's really stiff, if he can come in here and turn on to the environment and the talent, and when he leaves here, his tie is down to *here* and he's sweaty and he had a good time, that's *it*."

The man who's probably made the most money—legal money, anyway—out of the hip phenomenon and who has perfected the art of exploiting it gives the whole thing a harsh lick with the back of his tongue:

"The Haight-Ashbury scene now is tragic. Take a look at Haight Street! The only beginners—God bless 'em!—who have gone back to their original concept are Ron and Jay Thelin of the Psychedelic Shop. You know, when we first started they were very nice—they sold my tickets and they set up some of the posters. They had them all over the wall, and then they became a freak shop. They voluntarily retracted and went back to what they had been . . . the Far East, the cultures, the religious books, Indian records, better jewelry, and so on. All the other shops, what's happened there? It's a lot like the old cigar factories on the Lower East Side (rebaptized the East Village) in New York. 'Make the cigars, shut up, make the cigars.' You know . . . 'Make the sandals, come on, it's going to be a hot summer. When the bus stops we've got to have every size.' And the loveburger and the sunshine burger and selling stuff on the sidewalks.

"The ones I blame are the lovebirds who open a shop and say, 'I want to do a good thing, I want to communicate with you, neighbor—what size do you wear?' Or, 'Listen, I got something hot for you, step in the back' . . . And the guy who sits on the sidewalk banging away on bongos and 'Hey man,' and three weeks later he's still there. 'Out of sight, man, lovely, everybody should love, man.' 'What do you think of the anti-poverty program?' 'Ah, gee, it's going to be a hot summer, everybody should groove.'

"You cannot say, as the hippy does, 'I'm not going to go by your rules, I'm going to sit here and thump my bongos.' If that cat can't go to a store and buy a pound of tomatoes, what's he going to do? 'Well,' he says, 'I'll buy that.' But you can't buy *that* either. You ain't growing anything. you ain't doing anything, so if everybody's like that, you know what happens? You're gonna drown in your own shit! I want my posters printed, I call my printer. What do you think the printer's going to say? 'Love, baby'?

"There's so much posturing . . . Every time I raise my voice at the Fillmore, you know I say, 'Get in line!' Then it's, 'Hey, Mr. Graham, come on now, where's your love?' Fuck your love. One time a kid wanted to get in. 'Can I get in?' he says. 'I'm sorry, there're people waiting in line to see the Jefferson Airplane.' 'Yeah, man, but you see, I haven't got any bread. I groove, I dig, love, love, love, love, out of sight, sunshine, and so forth.' This guy went on for five minutes. Finally I said, 'Look, you can't come in. These people are waiting in line, you're no different than they are, some of them dress like you, some of them don't have any shoes.' I tried to explain to him that I pay the rent, I pay for the lights, I pay for the posters, and I'm sorry. 'If I knew you, if you had been here seven or eight times before and there was a relationship and you were short, I might let you in.' For the next five minutes I got an assault like you never heard. All of a sudden this guy who has been all love and sunshine started yelling, 'Motherfucker, capitalist bitch, don't go into that place, there's no love in that man.' Finally I looked at him and said, 'Okay, come on in,' and as he came toward me and started up the stairs he turned to the line and smiled and said, 'Isn't he beautiful? Love, man, hey, outta sight! Too much!' Well, I grabbed the son of a bitch and threw him on the sidewalk."*

*From a taped interview by Rick Nanas and Frank Robinson in the *Haight-Ashbury Tribune*, Vol. 1, No. 2.

There was a theory current among some of the schools of psychiatrists who came to feed off the human data floating in the
green waters of the Haight that the place was a harbor for rejects,
for the young culls who couldn't hack it in the general society. As
proof they referred to the female patients in the Free Medical
Clinic or the girls lounging on the sidewalks and remarked how few
of them were attractive. The truth was that the good-looking ones
were picked off fast, sometimes within minutes after they arrived.
You could see them, often quite literally, getting off the bus at the
Panhandle—the oblong piece of greensward and eucalyptus running off Golden Gate Park and through the neighborhood. The
free feeding took place here. They would line up for beans being
cooked in large, corrugated iron garbage pails, with pieces of card-
board for plates. They'd get their beans and have to eat them with
their hands. A boy would approach and ask, "You want to be my
old lady?" There'd be a flick of the eyes—or none if the girl was
hungry or disgusted enough—and she'd say yes.

The boys would find that some of the free crash pads were operated by homosexuals who expected them to put out in return
for shelter, and there was one female transvestite—quite masculine-
looking in her costume—who took home girls who were willing
to have sex with a man in return for half of his bed, but not to
have their partner reveal herself as a lesbian.

The new community couldn't shake off the sexual patterns of the

*Sexual Freedom League.

199

old; it magnified the sexual exploitations without any of the limits the larger society puts on the uses of people. The police must have spent most of their time looking for juveniles to return them to their parents, and they were hated more for it than for the dope raids, but it may have been the biggest service. There seemed to be so many kids broken up and confused by their sexual experiences. For some, those who were built for it, whose genitalia seemed unconnected with the rest of their nervous systems, it was exhilarating. "I like Mazola orgies," Frodo declaimed one day. "See, what you do is get stoned, but before you get stoned you get sheets of plastic or something like that and put them on the floor, then you pour a gallon of Mazola oil on it and everybody takes off their clothes and has a group grope. It really feels good. You don't get as much fucking done as you would otherwise. It's hard to get purchase."

Frodo could enjoy it in good health and so could the Berkeley coed who said, "Oh, those big cluster fucks! I can't stand them. I think it's revolting, you know, more or less getting punked by anybody who happens to be standing near you, man, woman, child, or dog. But four people, friends, good friends, spending a lovely, quiet weekend together having nice sex every imaginable way, slowly in the same bed, well, that's a long-drawn-out pleasantness."

Many found out that they had limits and weaknesses and fears and needs and dependencies they hadn't known about, and the elements within them kicked up and stunned and disoriented them when they had sex that didn't suit them. With some, their reaction could be attributed to guilt, violation of the official morals of society, but it also seemed to be a case of people using themselves inhumanely. "I didn't think I'd feel that way when I balled a guy," said a boy in the doorway talking to a stranger, hoping to put his disjointed head back together. "My friend said, 'Do it because this old guy wants a young boy and we should share each other.' But I didn't like it, I didn't like it and I can't forget it. Maybe I was stoned. I guess I must have been. I must have been stoned to come to San Francisco."

Funky Sam was older, in his thirties, and like a lot of the older ones he knew himself, so he knew he just wanted girls. Funky lived in a commune on Central Avenue with Jan, his old lady. He was one of the few people in the Haight who could claim to be a drop-out inasmuch as he'd dropped there from the beginnings of a career as a lawyer and administrative assistant to one of the best-known members of the California State Legislature. Funky made few claims, however. "I'm one of the youngest and most energetic dirty old men there are in the world, and I'm going to make a lot of money so I have a lot of chicks to ball," Funky would say, and Jan would smile a tolerant, wan smile.

They had a great living room in the commune. It was stuffed with art nouveau and it had a hi-fi tape player, a lot of what looked like Tiffany, and two wheelchairs so you could sit comfortably and, if you were the restless type, roll back and forth across the room instead of pacing. There would be occasional collisions. "I enjoy balling. I like it with single chicks, and I like orgies . . . You have it wrong. It's not exhausting. When you go to an orgy you're not fucking all the time. You fuck when you feel like fucking, and nothing's imposed on anybody. If you hit on a chick who doesn't want to, you don't."

"The first time I went to an orgy, I was scared. I felt ambiguous," said Jan, who had a deep voice and unambiguous manners, like a woman who might be able to have five children and always get dinner on the table on time. "I felt like, well, just like I wanted and I didn't want to. Now sometimes I enjoy myself and sometimes I don't. When I'm at one and I see someone who's embarrassed because they're there for the first time, I try to make them feel relaxed."

"I'll predict," Funky broke in to say, "that in another ten years we'll be having sex orgies in Candlestick Park. If you have a sexual experience by yourself it can be very moving, but if you share it with someone else that makes it more intense. Not that I find watching all that terribly exciting, but the more of the senses you use, the more's happening to you, seeing, touching, smelling, tasting . . . But, as I say, I'm the youngest, most energetic dirty old man in San Francisco. I'll ball with any chick, sure, a fifteen-year-old if I can achieve rapport with her—hedonism, but I wasn't born that way. When I was a kid I was told that if I played with myself I'd turn into a cripple. I remember the first group grope I went to was with some guy and his girl friend. We'd heard about wife-swapping in the suburbs, so we got to talking and we all ended up in the rack. Next time was when somebody from the Sexual Freedom League said they were putting on an orgy for *Playboy* magazine and why didn't we drop by? There were about thirty to fifty people there, some dancing, some balling. We came into this long hall where there was this one chick in the middle of the floor, naked. Then somebody said to go downstairs. I met a chick I knew there. She said, 'Come on,' so we balled. Most of the couples were fucking in a big pile. There was a lot of grass and I guess I was high. I got very paranoid, which I'll do on grass sometimes, so I didn't really like it that much."

Funky must have balled a lot of chicks and Jan put up with it, though more and more she gave the impression of being in the classic woman's bind, making his meals, looking out after him, and getting balled herself when Sam didn't have another chick around. The relationship had one virtue: it wasn't sneaky. Sam would bring the chicks home, some of them astonishingly beautiful young girls with the tenderized facial expressions acid sometimes induces. The real loving smile. They'd be up in Sam's bedroom, postered, painted, and wired from floor to ceiling for marvelous acid hallucinations. He'd be on the bed, tripping out doing something like painting a picture, and the chick would be sitting there too, her back propped up against the wall, smiling, ready to have a desultory, wandering conversation with you. You always thought that if you'd ask Funky, he'd lend you the chick. He never seemed proprietary about his chicks.

In the end Funky betrayed himself and lost his life of ease. He was probably too chick-hungry. Funky wanted a million dollars, because, he said, if he had a million dollars he'd be able to keep himself in chicks forever. That led him to start Funky Features, a poster company. His first poster was based on a Beatles' song. It was an ugly thing, though Funky, who had good judgment in many areas, didn't know how awful it was. There are only four or five good poster artists in San Francisco, and Funky's artist wasn't one of them. It was a vulgar parody and it sold like hell. Funky couldn't get them out fast enough. He was on his way to making money, running around getting distributors, talking to wholesalers, working out joint promotions with record companies, getting deals from the printer. He still talked a good game, and he still had his beard and his tight pants, but he was another businessman scooping it up as fast as he could and getting laid on the side. "Yeah, I know," Funky would say in self-defense, "but when I get my million—that won't be long—I'm going to spend the rest of my life fucking, and I plan to live a long time."

Jan moved out. Funky had a new old lady, a remarkable olive-skinned girl who looked like an Israeli heroine soldier. She was from L.A., and there was no easy way of telling how Jan really felt about it. She just moved around the corner to a big dope house and started dealing grass.

Hip or straight, the essential feminine role is intractably the same: the old ladies of the Haight doing the cooking, the sewing, and the house cleaning like the young matrons in the suburbs. They walk one step behind their men, submissive, yet often retaining a ferocious protection of their idea of womanliness. The younger girls, the teen-agers, don't seem to have the trait. They'll allow almost anything to be done to them—what happens sexually still keeps them in the passive, non-initiatory role; they are laid, they are taken to a group grope, they are made to sleep with their old man's boy friends—but the older girls are not so sure. They strike you as more like Jan, interested in new erotic combinations, but not to the point of shattering the inner mirror where they see their faces. They go to the orgies a little reluctantly, and often in the same spirit that they cook for their man and clean his pad.

There are exceptions, like the lady who wrote to HIPpocrates (Eugene Schoenfeld, M.D.), the far-out doctor who does a question-and-answer column for the underground press. She wrote, "I am currently trying to get pregnant after taking birth-control pills for three years. The problem is that I live in a rather fluid household. Besides my lawful, legal-type husband, there is almost always one additional man around and frequently there are several. I would like my first child to be my husband's, but monogamy at our house is difficult and not particularly desirable to any of us. What is the best method of temporary contraception that won't interfere with my husband's sperm, but will reduce the chances of anybody else's? We'll use condoms if necessary, but that's a big drag generally."*

### HOUSE OKs PANEL TO
### STUDY PORNOGRAPHY

**Washington, Aug. 8 (UPI) — The House voted yesterday to set up a commission to study pornography, define it and recommend legislation to curb the billion-dollar-a-year trade in obscenity.**

Carol was from Ottawa, Illinois. It was impossible to tell if she was a victim or a victimizer. She looked like what the word "comely" suggests: rounded, full-bodied, not a large young woman but highly suitable as a nude study if she would relax, which she didn't. She had a stiffness about her; when she stood still she was like a young actress who doesn't know where to put her hands. She held them off her thighs, almost rigidly, almost shaking, her arms and shoulders in a slightly unnatural position. She attended the psychodrama group at All Saints Church on Waller, a block up the hill from Haight Street. The psychodrama was a therapeutic mold that fed itself off the scene.

They met once a week, anywhere from ten to thirty of them, with the shrink in charge. He was a young guy who seemed half athletic coach and half director as he led the dramatization of their lives. A different person would have his life dramatized each week.

Carol went regularly and then, one week, asked to be the subject. She was flatly unemotional, perhaps scared or embarrassed, as she discussed herself and her problem, which was, as she defined it to the group, that she didn't care for her little daughter. It had been a shotgun marriage that had forced her to forgo college; she'd only

*Eugene Schoenfeld, M.D., M.P.H., from the *Berkeley Barb*, July 14–20, 1967.

slept with him because he had sex appeal or he was nice or other girls wanted him, she wasn't sure, and when she got pregnant she wanted an abortion, but he insisted on marriage. She seemed to hate him for that. Her father was a drunk, she said, and her mother was one of those bleached-out women who work all their lives and don't know why. She'd gotten her college education and divorced her husband, but she wanted nothing to do with her daughter, who lived with her father. "I have to make myself go visit her. It's not that I don't like my little girl. I just don't feel she's mine. It makes me nervous when she hugs me and says 'Mommy,'" Carol said. Her manner was tough as she said it, insouciant, flip, ashamed of herself.

The coach-director-therapist said the first scene would be Carol visiting her little girl. Who wanted to play the little girl, who wanted to play the father, and Carol's alter ego, the whispering voice of unconsciousness who would speak Carol's real feelings? People volunteered.

CAROL: Hello, dear.

DAUGHTER: Mommy, Mommy, I love you.

CAROL: That's not the way she is. She wouldn't say that.

SHRINK: What would she say?

CAROL: She wouldn't say anything. She'd hug me and I'd bend down and kiss her.

SHRINK: All right, daughter, don't say anything. Come up to your mother and hug her. (the older woman playing the little girl does as the coach says)

ALTER EGO: God, why does she have to hug me? I can't stand it.

CAROL: That's not the way I feel.

SHRINK: Tell us how you would feel.

CAROL: I'd say to myself, "Why am I this way? Why can't I feel anything? Why don't I bend down and kiss her back? Why do I just pat her on the head?"

SHRINK (sounding like an athletic coach): Switch. Carol, you play your daughter. Everybody else remain the same.

They played on, moving from scene to scene in Carol's life, Carol correcting them for accuracy and the coach commanding

205

from time to time, "Switch!" Carol grew less tough and smirky and more masked, as though she felt nothing at all. At length Jane broke down. Jane was a large blonde woman in her late twenties, finishing her Ph.D. at Berkeley, who liked to go on about how perfect her husband was, an academic success, a business success, very wealthy, the ideal husband. Jane had no children. She was playing the daughter when she started screaming, "You hate me, Mommy! You're no mommy at all! You don't feel anything, Mommy! You have no milk or love in you, Mommy. You're not a woman, you're not fit to be a mother, you hear that, Mommy? . . ."

"Switch!" said the coach.

They went back to the time in Carol's life when she wanted the abortion. Five or six of them constituted themselves a tribunal of shrinks, social workers, priests, and concerned public to decide if she should have one. They argued the case back and forth until a scraggly hip-type, a very belligerent one, began shouting at Carol, telling her she was no woman, that he'd make a woman out of her, he'd slap her face and make her go down on him, he'd work on her for as long as it took for life to come screaming out of her mute face. She listened to him, the tiny smirk in one corner of her mouth, her skin just slightly flushed. People were yelling for him to shut up, but Carol said, "No, that's all right. I'm learning something."

"Then sit, face to face, you two, and have it out," the coach-shrink said.

They sat facing each other on straight-back chairs, a few feet apart. Carol seemed attracted to him, as though she enjoyed his abuse and hoped he'd grab her and throw her on the floor. He stomped out of the circle into the center, looking as if that was what he was going to do, but when he sat down facing her, he changed. "Don't you realize that you can't feel anything because guilt is paralyzing you?" he asked, reverting to a polite, white-collar, medical role. Her flush faded.

Carol would go anywhere to be done to. She was like a somnambulant searching for the person or the situation that would wake

206

her up. A few weeks later she went down to the Esalen Institute in Big Sur for a weekend of "sensory awakening." The institute describes itself as a "center to explore the behavioral sciences, religion, and philosophy." It lists a lot of Ph.D.'s in its catalog, and it sponsors lectures by big names like R. Buckminster Fuller, B. F. Skinner, and Sister Mary Corita; but orthodox science, philosophy, and psychiatry give the place a wide berth. Carol came back with a chap named Terry, who said he was from Bridge Mountain Foundation, a rural group for experience and self-realization. The San Francisco Bay Area is heavy with foundations, centers, institutes, and associations ready to heal the sick back to health and the dead back to quickness by every means from every civilization and every epoch. Groups even migrate across the country to locate in San Francisco. One Manhattan therapy group whose members have stuck at it eight years voted to come west, whereupon its members quit their jobs, sold their homes, packed up their wives or divorced them, and actually drove all the way in caravan. The little therapeutic community now has its very large, well-furnished apartment on Divisadero Street where the members come for their meetings and get-togethers.

"I learned something," Carol said of the Esalen weekend, and Terry agreed it had been helpful. The weekend of sensory awareness hadn't done anything, for her voice retained its deadened, remote quality. There wasn't a hint of laughter in it when she described the "Tom Jones Dinner" they'd had the first night. "That was after we'd non-verbally selected ourselves into groups. We did it just by touch. It's very different getting to know someone only by touch and feel . . . very strange but nice. We'd gone down to the bathhouse where we'd massaged each other, and then we had the Tom Jones Dinner. I didn't know what they meant, but I realized after it got started it was a new form of communication through the senses. Bernie [the novice master] wouldn't allow talking. There were no eating utensils. You had to eat with your hands. They served chicken and salad, and wine, but not enough for getting drunk. Nobody was drunk. People played with a chicken bone, two people would have an end each in their mouths. Terry started to disrobe me. I didn't mind. There was only one other male disrobed and the three of us embraced. Then people started throwing food at each other."

"I had my pubic hair full of rice," Terry recalled. "There was one gal there who got up tight by everything, so I just slapped her. The Tom Jones Dinner stopped just short of a bacchanal."

"After that the dinner started to come down and subside," Carol said. "Someone started to hum and we joined in. That broke the evening into two parts."

"There were parties in the cabins the rest of the evening," explained Terry.

"Yes, all kinds of groups formed and re-formed. I remember the way one girl was screaming and screaming, but she had a beautiful, complete release."

"You see the purpose is just to allow, to bust down, be aware, and, if you do, it feels good."

Carol nodded, although her manner still didn't seem busted down or allowing. "It's amazing," she said without amazement, "when strangers meet and touch and a bond forms. Bernie said we were to explore the area betwen indulgence and inhibition, and I think that's what we did. I found it very interesting."

"But," Terry put in, "I was really surprised the next morning at the number of people who were revolted over what had happened."

Carol said: "I think what I liked best was after the last session Sunday afternoon. Bernie asked Terry and me and some others to stay. We sat silently under the silk of a parachute on the grass. Bernie passed around a loaf of bread after holding it up for us to look at it. He asked us to hold it in our mouths until it was liquid. The sensation was totally different from the Tom Jones Dinner."

Whatever it was that pushed her still wasn't slaked. Carol said she thought she'd go with Terry to his institute, or perhaps try one of the attack groups where they practice hate therapy over in Berkeley.

Grass came back, not like the rain but like the granulated moisture of the mist, so gentle was its reappearance. But swift. In hours one night it had spread out across the community. The big shipments had come in; new, good quality grass so the people with stashes no longer had any cause to look down on the people who didn't. Everybody felt better. It was like rain coming to a farm community. Even the straight organizations were pleased. The hip doctors up at the Free Clinic commented, "It's better for them than alcohol," but beneath that was the unspoken concession that everybody—the head, the reformers, the cops, the mass media, the understanding adults, the service institutions—depended on dope. If there was no dope there would be no Haight and everybody would be out of a job. Cops need crooks, doctors need patients, newspaper reporters need weirdos, service organizations need victims to minister to. The grass shortage made the symbiotic chain of dependency obvious.

The only brown-baggers left on the street were people who enjoyed it, real juiceheads. With the return of the grass came some of the people who'd been away. Rock and The Grateful Dead came back from the Southwest and opened their house again. Donn, still with his kangaroo fur vest and his magic staff, was back walking the street, speaking his arcane rhetoric: "I've lived in a Mexican village. I've lived everywhere . . . I make people happy."

An enormous Hell's Angel walked over to him. The size of his naked arms was magnified by his leather cutaway. He listened, brown-bagging booze. "I have a friend who is going to build an ark out of concrete and I'm going to be on it. I should," Donn said. "I'm the first man to go through the California penal system with my hair intact. Long hair is a sign of freedom, and they couldn't take it off me in prison or in the Army stockades."

209

"You're all love and I'm all violence," the biker said, one hand clenched into a fist, the other hand holding up the bag, as though trying to decide whether to offer Donn a drink or kill him.

"Liquor's a downer! A bad trip! It'll kill you," Donn intoned, like the revivalist couple on the corner of Masonic.

The biker gave Donn a small jolt on the shoulder, a token of amity, and made his way toward Benches. Rock, who had been watching in case harm came to Donn, started on his way again, saying, "Donn's always talking about his girl, Jeannie, as long as I've known him. He's been all over the world looking for her. I know for certain he's been seen as far away as Tangiers and Boston." In the fall, he would be seen stoned on grass on the steps of the Pentagon.

Papa Al walked lighter too. Even though his old commune had broken up, he wasn't unhappy about it. He had a new one calling itself "The Dirty Dozen" going on Masonic. Apache and Rusti were living there, somewhat in charge. His charitable, soul-reclaiming operation had, for reasons no one discussed, suddenly transferred itself up to the room in All Saints Church, where the redheaded Trudy had run the Community Affairs Office before she visited Morningstar Ranch and split the scene. Black Preacher had dropped out of sight, off on his own somewhere, but Papa Al was in a good frame of mind, standing on the corner, cadging samples of dope from the kids and putting them in his little plastic bag. He even had an affectionate wave of the hand for Cowboy, who materialized in the perpetual traffic jam on the back seat of a little red Sunbeam sports car. Big Tiny was sitting next to him, and their combined weight looked like it would sink the poor thing. The female owner (she still had to keep up the payments) was driving as Cowboy shouted out, "She's my new old lady."

Iron Man had been busted again. There were certain busts that tickled Papa Al. This was one, perhaps because Iron Man had sent a letter of distress that he found amusing. Anyway, he was showing it around and chuckling:

*Dear Al:*

*Howdy brother! How're you?—All right I pray.*

*Al—This letter's from Iron Man and G'blessit—I'm in Wa!—jail!—yeah! They got me this time.*

*Al—What I'm in here for is a warrant on me—for failure to appear as promised—extenuating circumstances kept me from my appointed task that particular morning—and now this week—I've suffered the consequences of my negligence.*

*Brother—may you please get ahold of the "Switchboard" for me, Al—and request for me that they send a bail bondsman up to interview me—or to get me out—I've got a partial of the premium now—my bail's $500 ($50 premium).*

*Al—I need to be out of here to continue my development of a "Hobbit's" idea—It's an incorporated diggers—with efficient dependable leadership—I know you'd help a lot. Al, you've already done so much for our community—and I believe you'll continue until we have a permanent, reliable organization whose "thing" in the Haight-Ashbury will be an aid to bringing about the greatest amount of good to the largest amount of people—and much more.*

*Please help me now, Al. I believe you will—Please let Stu or Steve know I'm in here too—Thank you, "Brother Al" for anything you'll do to help me now. I remain sincerely yours, Iron Man.*

*P.S. I'm deteriorating like hell in here.*

"Too much," said Al, but he had other morsels. "Heard about Dirty Dick? Dirty Dick ran into a seminarian—or an ex-seminarian. I think it was at Tracy's. He got intrigued when the seminarian told him he was a virgin and really wanted to try some sex. Dirty Dick took him over to some girls' house and they all take off the poor character's clothes. They're laughing at him and having a good time with him when one girl is just putting her mouth on his prick and he throws up. Dirty Dick and the girls think it's very

211

funny, haha-ha! No, they weren't finished with him. They were going to get him laid too. So he climbs on top of one of the girls and the poor little bastard, who's only seen love in the movies, gets in the saddle and starts saying, ' I love you, I love you, I love you.' He thinks that's what you're supposed to say, but the girl looks up at him and tells him, 'Shut up and keep pumping, you little son of a bitch.' I guess that really broke 'em up, except for the seminarian, who didn't matter because after they'd had their little fun, they threw him out the door. I think he was a psychiatric case."

Papa Al was in a good mood. He'd borrowed some new dirty pictures off of White Preacher, which White Preacher said he'd copped off a queer. They were new, and Papa Al said he wanted to "take them downtown to have the faces checked against the files. You never know when it'll come in handy. You wanta look at 'em?"

If there was anything bothering him, it might have been he didn't have a sample of the new orange acid tabs that were just hitting the street. Neither did White Rabbit up at the clinic, but that didn't prevent him from delivering a lecture on the subject to a couple that had wandered in with a few. They wanted to know if it was righteous. "Oh, it's syndicate acid and it's very good, but they're only putting out samples now. It shouldn't be sold, so if anybody's caught selling it they will be cut off," White Rabbit said authoritatively. He didn't have his job back at the clinic, but they were letting him hang around again and he too was feeling rosy. He'd quit his job as an encyclopedia salesman and was going to deal. Everybody told him he was too naive, but he insisted he wasn't and that he knew all about it. He claimed he was a close friend of Owsley's and a number of other heavy people, but he was still hanging around Papa Al, coaxing Papa Al to cop for him. When Papa Al refused, White Rabbit was silent for a few days until he announced he would soon be copping a new drug, DMA, which "has all the advantages of STP plus; instead of staying up for thirty-six hours, you're up for two weeks." Nobody was sure if he was putting or being put on.

212

## SWINGING FOR THE LORD

**New York, Sept. 3 (New York Times Service)—The Salvation Army has opened an extremely groovy cafe on MacDougal Street in Greenwich Village, across from the Freudian Slip and half a block from the Cafe Wha? It is called The Answer.**

Papa Al got along with virtually every young person. He did not have much contact with the intellectuals and the ideologues, mostly with runaways, bikers, dealers, the people clogging the streets, Tracy's, Benches, and the House of Do-Nuts. The musicians, the creative entrepreneurs, and the orators, people who might not think his thirty-eight revolver was a *carte d'entrée* everywhere, would have been more difficult. With the older people he got along, but he didn't think much of many of them, especially Reverend Larry Beggs. He found Reverend Beggs standoffish, cold. It may have been because the two were competitors. Reverend Beggs was the co-director and public voice of Huckleberry's for Runaways, a church-supported experimental institution for minors. It was located at the top of Broderick Street in a high, thin, wooden Victorian house, an excellent specimen of the jig-cut, Hudson River Bracketed that San Francisco and Oakland abound in. Sometimes Papa Al was in the runaway business too, but not on a full-time basis like the Reverend. Papa Al worked with runaways only some of the time. He didn't have the stake in it that Reverend Beggs did. The young minister (thirty-four) really seemed to be making a big career out of it, said he'd got calls from lots of other cities where they wanted to consult with him about creating a place like Huckleberry's, an easy task because it wasn't much more than a couple of small, attractive dormitories.

What divided Papa Al and Reverend Beggs seemed to be whether to support the parents of the runaways or support the kids. The minister gave the impression of disliking parents. "I think," he announced, "it's the kids' religious inclinations versus suburbia.

What would happen if you knocked on a door and asked to stay the night in suburbia? They'd call the police. These are the kinds of homes the kids come from. These young people are sort of reaching out for a religious experience. You wouldn't want to have to apologize for reading about Jesus or Buddha, but you would in many of the families I know in suburbia. What you have working among many of the runaways is the love ethic or the peace ethic ... Of course, there have been instances when violence has transformed this ethic here in the community, but the thing that impresses me are the human resources here to continue with this ethic. The Haight-Ashbury is a community that has opted out of the other culture to experiment with a new subculture, one permeated by a new ethic."

Papa Al never talked about the love ethic. Sometimes he'd chant in a sarcastic monotone, "Do your thing, whatever's right, do your thing," and when he did, he didn't look like a man who saw them snatching Bibles out of their kids' hands in Yonkers and Mamaroneck. Of course, Papa Al was making scenes in the Haight that the Reverend probably couldn't have believed.

When the press would come, the minister would talk very much as if society was creating a vast runaway problem for which its only answer was the knout. "This is a place where you can go home without being defeated, where you can go home with a new contract [with the parents]. We feel that everyone in the family bears responsibility for the conflict. We feel that it's a waste of time just to move bodies back home without getting at root problems. Society is lazy. It delegates the policeman to handle a family problem. We feel this just perpetuates culprit mentality and resentment. All present methods are the police type of thing, where they just move bodies around. Our long-range goal is to relieve the police force of a job they're not trained to do."

The minister can be persuasive, and his view of the runaways is generally accepted in the Haight and far away from it. It is also a view that provides his new charity endeavor—and those who want to get into the business elsewhere—with a rationale for pro-

214

fessional status, for providing more than room and food for hungry, cold kids who need a comfortable flop after nights on the road or in the park. "Through our place, kids get more leverage on their parents. They call us and say, 'I'm pregnant,' or 'I'm on LSD,' but often they're faking it. They're really trying to hit back at their parents or find out if their parents love them."

Often the parents don't. The surprising thing about this extraordinary moment in this extraordinary community is not the number of anxious parents combing the place for their children, nor the number of sad little signs posted on bulletin boards asking dearly loved sons and daughters to return home, but how few there really are compared to the apparently large numbers of runaway minors. There is little caseworking an institution like Huckleberry's can do, little leverage if the parents are actually delighted. Beggs had at least one such case in his institution.

The case was Snoopy. Snoopy was a young teen-ager with an Egyptian cross dangling off his neck—the only sign of being hip about him; he didn't speak easily, and though he'd picked up some of the love ethic jargon, it was obvious that when he said certain things he knew what they meant and meant them: "The philosophy of the people who live around here—in this neighborhood—is that people should care more for other people, that there is too much hate, and that you can live without the worry and hurry that the outside world has built." The home Snoopy had run away from was a few miles away across the Bay Bridge in Berkeley, where his father, a chemist, had lacked the love, after repeated phone calls, to come and get him.

While Beggs spent much of his summer being interviewed by people writing stories about runaways, more than 99 per cent of the American juvenile population ran no farther than the neighborhood shopping center on errands for mother. Yet, in interviews the minister-administrator said things like, "A German shepherd has more rights than a kid. He can't be beaten. His sexual relations can't be restrained. Kids are restrained by the draft, compulsory education, sexual rights, reading rights, traveling rights,

215

the juvenile courts. The key here is self-determination. The generational war will get worse as teen-agers get more power and get down to the basic issues like marijuana and sex."

The cops weren't happy with this outlook; they busted Huckleberry's once and arrested the staff for contributing to the delinquency of minors. But in many places, including law schools and departments of sociology, Beggs's opinions find concurrence. Teenagers do have precious few rights; some of the evidence argues that their need to break the rules and bounds they're held in are stronger than those their parents faced. Children today grow up faster physically; they attain full growth earlier, usually before twenty, and they reach puberty younger. Puberty comes to today's children two and a half to three and a half years earlier than it did a century ago. If both science and folklore are correct in saying the sexual drives are strongest when you're young (they're certainly more difficult to handle), then the young today must be living in a very painful vise. At a time when full maturity, the time of the completion of school, is being pushed closer and closer toward age thirty, their physiological needs for adult freedom are coming to them younger and younger.

Despite the talk of a sexual revolution, the public, official side of the nation has made few shifts in values. Youth is still supposed to be celibate. Ann Landers, the country's best-known and best-read advice-giver, continues to tell the kids in hundreds of newspapers every day that they should stay out of each other's beds. Even the more sophisticated universities have been exceedingly slow in changing dorm regulations to make sex more available. A lot of money is spent on having policemen enforce virginity. Yet in a situation where you would expect opposed pressures to cause either explosive face-offs or mass desertions, neither has happened.

People like Larry Beggs use the existence of the Haight, the East Village, and smaller scenes in every city as evidence of a huge change already under way. The change is probably more advanced than this school of thought realizes, but it isn't the change they diagnose. Beginning in junior high school or the last grades of grammar school, youth finds a second, segregated life available to

216

it. This second life, which has no official standing and is only fitfully recognized as a highly institutionalized business, has the responsive fluidity to take care of pressures arising from sex as well as other psychological and social demands.

Teen-age nightclubs—places that don't serve alcohol and brag that they are chaperoned—are nationally ubiquitous. These are segregated institutions where all the forces in the culture that define youth as a class apart (music, dress, professional youth workers, youth-merchandised consumer items) can concentrate and reinforce difference and separateness. This second track grows increasingly wider and distinct through the late high school and college years. From fraternity row to motels and ski resorts and summer beaches, you will find segregated youth cantons where, out of sight of family and the larger apparatus of disapproving social control, youth lives a looser but perhaps no less institutionalized life.

The second track has grown so strong in American life that it finds an almost permanent expression in a new urban phenomenon: the youth neighborhoods. These usually grow up side by side, or even entwined, with an art colony, probably because bohemia is more tolerant and less able to defend itself against youth and, albeit fairly indirectly, the arbiter of youth's tastes. Most large American cities now have youth neighborhoods that are inundated every weekend by suburban kids taking part in the commercial street carnivals set up for them. Everywhere they are the center of attention for clergymen, cops, and educators. The Haight-Ashbury and the East Village are highly developed examples of these youth cantonments.

Before the kids came to the East Village, a certain number of artists, driven out of Greenwich proper by the high rents, had located there. But the Haight had few artists; it is almost a pure youth production, and it was used by a large number of the young people as they use the other encampments, as a place to visit, to turn on where dope was relatively safe and inexpensive, to have unsupervised, horsing fun and sex with relatively few complications. (In this last regard, many boys must have left disappointed:

217

the male population appeared to outnumber the females four or five to one.)

Segments of the medical profession, the clergy, the police, and social workers failed to view the community in this light. They saw it as Beggs did, or at least as a serious crisis. They reacted by instituting programs that may have strengthened the frequency of the very behavior that was alarming them. If the concerned and sympathetic adult population backs up such communities as the Haight-Ashbury with services like the Free Medical Clinic or Huckleberry's, it makes dropping out or running away a lot less scary and probably a lot less risky. Not only is nothing very bad likely to happen to you, but the older generation recognizes the community as part of the second track system and helps keep it going.

The demand for youth playlands is going to increase. More of the young are being asked to submit themselves to at least sixteen years in the classroom. As Paul Goodman has said repeatedly, no other society has ever made this kind of demand on its youth, and a certain number just can't take it; at the minimum they need an occasional break. Others need a different, nonacademic means of education.

But Beggs wants to demolish the restrictions in the official system, permitting youth, without stealth, to have the same freedoms as adults. It is not at all clear that youth wants this freedom, without concealment and hypocrisy. A lot of kids who can, don't live the second life that's available to them. They are virgins when they get married and it suits them. There are others who are in the second track system but not permanently. They want unbetrayed, private freedom from time to time, but then they want to go back to the discipline, order, and security of family and school. They get what they want and they leave. The Haight-Ashbury in the summer of 1967 had plenty of these: frat kids from Rutgers, high school itinerants, rich girls from Funland U. who would come, stay for a week or a month, and leave. You'd talk to them and they'd say they came without any intention of staying, that they'd heard about it and wanted to make the scene just for a while.

218

## WAR OF THE CHIMPANZEES ON
## AFRICA'S GRASSLAND

Stockholm, Sept. 28 (London Observer)—
Two Dutch scientists claim to have observed
a rudimentary form of organized warfare
among chimpanzees living on open grassland
in East Africa. This demonstrates, they claim,
how aggressive man may have diverged
from more peaceful ape-like ancestors by
leaving the forests for open plains and em-
phasizes the dramatic effects of a different
environment on behavior and cultural patterns.

In the time after the grass came back, the incessant premonition
of violence abated; so did the cold fogs. Autumn and the warm
season were nearing. A new optimism took hold. The hope of old
enterprises revived. New ones were talked of. The blue-and-white
phoenix flags were occasionally seen again, but now they were
more associated with the protests against the war. Lefty and Ron
and some of the others discussed reviving Alibaba and the Forty
Thieves. Leonard Wolf was moved by new philanthropic energy.
Happening House was at long last about to open, he said, describing plans to teach everything from muffin-making to psychotherapy,
yet always being careful to disclaim any program, any leadership.
The rules of the game required absolute respect for everyone's un-
predetermined free will.

The professor seemed to be out on the streets more often. He
looked the same: fine, wide features, the noble, graying beard of a
count of the Austro-Hungarian Empire, which, with his sweater,
gave him the look of an aristocrat summering in a pre–World War
I Dolomite mountain resort. His book was going well, he announced. Peter Cohon and the other Diggers who'd been boy-
cotting him, presumably because they didn't want people cashing
in on the scene by writing about it, had changed their minds.
"Peter appeared at my house and said he was ready. Then he
talked into the tape recorder for hours. I only had to ask him one

question to get him started. Wonderful material, marvelous, I want you to hear it," Wolf said over an ice cream cone at Quasars, the Haight's favorite ice cream parlor, endeared to all the pot smokers wealthy enough to afford its specialty at their parties.

"Then I got a call from several of the others. They'll all want to come in now and be recorded," he said, studying two girls who looked young enough to be runaways. He asked one in his mild way how old she was and where she came from. The girl, who was unaccountably dressed in a bathrobe, replied that she was twenty, came from New Jersey, and had been in the Haight for two years. Wolf, falling into one of his favorite roles as friend and understander of youth, said he didn't believe it. "You can tell me, I'm not the police," he continued, but this bit of information failed to soften her.

"Well, don't rap with me if you don't believe it," she retorted.

He backed off, licking his ice cream cone, waiting for another chance. It came in the form of a tiny Negro girl, who couldn't have been more than five years old. She wanted a dime from the big white hippy girl. "Don't give that little girl a dime," Wolf instructed the hippy, who paid no attention. "Oh, you shouldn't have done that. Buy her an ice cream cone but don't give her a dime," he repeated, assuming another role he liked, that of translator between cultures. "In her world people pay money to lead little girls astray. You don't want to teach her that."

No one seemed convinced, but he didn't stay to argue. Charitable urgings were leading him down the street toward the offices of the *San Francisco Oracle*. The *Oracle* was the oldest of the cluster of competing papers hawked through the community and across the city. Their struggle for life resulted in the biggest newspaper war the town had seen since the days of William Randolph Hearst, and the products weren't much better. The *Oracle* contained almost no news. It filled its pages with bad art, instructions for practicing yoga while stoned on acid, instructions for starting communes, instructions for going off and farming. There were long, dirty-worded diatribes and lots of Indian material and astrology. It also went heavily for inviting the youth of America not to worry but hurry out to San Francisco where all would be provided. "Already, individuals and groups who have seen deeply into the situation are making preparations. Kitchens are being made ready. Food is being gathered. Hotels and houses are being prepared to supply free lodging . . . If you have food, share it. If you have money, give it, if you have room for pilgrims to rest, open your door," the paper had printed.

Nobody much in the Haight read the *Oracle,* but its mauve, fuchsia, and orange inks made it very popular with tourists, who would buy the same issue when it would reappear on the street with its first page printed in a different set of colors. Allen Cohen, the editor, had been elevated to minor guru status by the more mystical members of the community, so, all in all, it was reasonable for the professor to get the editor's help for his newest charitable enterprise. Wolf had found an unused restaurant which could be rented for $600 and give out the free food promised in the *Oracle.* By this time the Digger free-feeding had stopped completely; there had been other attempts, but the only thing going on a regular basis was the twice-weekly bread-baking at All Saints Church.

"They're not going to starve, man. They'll split and go home before they starve," the *Oracle* editor replied in an angry way. He may have been aware of the rumors in the community accusing him of having made a small fortune with his tourist souvenir sheet. "It's a very uncreative way to do it. It's absurd to spend $600. If they're hungry, they can go to the supermarket after they close and get the food they throw out every night. Or, if you're going to feed, you could make an arrangement with Safeway to get their day-old food and feed in the park. A restaurant, that's absurd."

"You're talking about a whole different trip," the professor replied. He used hip language sometimes, but it never fell gracefully from his tongue. He sounded like a father trying to be a pal. "It would take three weeks to get Safeway to agree. Besides, the restaurant cuts any problems with the cops or the health department."

"How do I know if there's any real hunger? The people out on that street aren't hungry."

221

The professor looked surprised and said, "You talk like the straight and I'm the hippy." At which point a bona fide hippy, cuddling a little rat on his upper chest, meandered out of a door in the newspaper's circulation office where the kids come to buy the papers which they sell on the street for a dime profit each. "Are you hungry? How do you survive, how do you eat?" Wolf asked him.

"I panhandle on the street and ask people for money. Then sometimes at night I go to Tracy's for coffee and doughnuts. Charlie the rat here eats cheese and crackers. Charlie belongs to a chick, but she split so he's mine till she comes back—if she does."

"Well, we ought to find out if people are hungry," Wolf persisted. "Thing is, Allen, I can get the restaurant going now if I can get a fast $600."

"The Episcopal church can do this."

"But they're not."

"Somebody should ask them. I'm not interested in other people's material trips. I don't want to be a social worker," the editor said, dismissing the professor. Wolf left, but he wouldn't give up. He approached the long-haired boy he met on the street to ask him if he was hungry.

"Yeah, man. Got any spare change?" The professor gave him some silver and invited him up to his house to be tape-recorded for the book. The restaurant never opened, but Happening House did.

### NOBLEMAN'S SON CAUGHT WITH LSD

London, Oct. 19 (AP)—The son and heir of a British nobleman, Lord Broughshane, was held for trial on drug charges today after police testified he had been caught at London airport with LSD worth $210,000. They reported he carried a one-way ticket to New York.

So good were the vibrations that Al Rinker, George, and the others at the Switchboard decided to essay another attempt at cross-cultural communication between hip and straight. They would throw a cocktail party in the long-halled apartment on Fell Street that the enterprise occupied. Alcohol, it was of course pointed out, is a downer, but it is the favorite turn-on of the straights who would come, be served booze, and be impressed by the hip capacity to savor the finer aspects of straight culture. The same line of reasoning was always popping up in regard to the Straight Theater, which was having an impossible time getting a dance hall permit, even when Dame Judith Anderson appeared before the Board of Permit Appeals to ask them to grant it. People were always bugging the Straight Theater to put on ballet and opera in the conviction that, once it had established itself as a high educational enterprise, the permit for rock dance would be forthcoming. The approach works with parents, but not with politicians who were getting a certain amount of cynical ink in the papers by refusing the license, raveling up moral fibers and protecting real estate values.

It was to be a by-invitation-only party. Plastic hippies, speed freaks, and characters like Beast and Coyote were disinvited. Only respectables like Dr. Smith from the clinic, Papa Al, and the better class of Haight Street merchants like Ron Thelin were sent invitations. It worked pretty well, although Teddybear and a number of other, more colorful types heard about it and came. The straights invited included the Commissioner of Police, most of the city's elected officials, and their opponents in the fall elections. The idea was to detrack them from oratorical competition on the theme of extirpating the Haight into vying with each other for the hippy vote. As an exercise in *Realpolitik* it had a forlorn charm. The mass media were also invited, and a couple of *sotto voce* swingers from the two dailies appeared, as did a few sympathetic straights like William Soskin, a psychologist from the University of California at Berkeley who had done extensive work with fourteen- and fifteen-year-old acidheads. One ordinary Irish politician turned up with his wife, but for the rest the boycott was total.

There were hors d'oeuvres and cases of whiskey, enough for three or four times as many people. They had been provided by

Herb, a fat little man who said he was a reporter from the *Anchorage Daily News* doing an in-depth take-out on the scene with the aid of an unlimited expense account. It didn't matter, since in the Haight you are who you say you are: Ikhnaton, White Rabbit, Blue Flash, Buddha, Joe Bananas, or the friendly neighborhood nark; tomorrow, like the revolving lights at the dances, you can be somebody else. Whoever he was, the liquor must have cost hundreds of dollars, and though the guests worked hard disposing of it, there was always another case for the big straight turn-on.

In quiet corners, some of the people like Soskin, the psychologist, nursed their drinks and talked about the scene. "El Cerrito High School is loaded with young acidheads," he said, "and it's not the only school, but the principals almost uniformly deny that anything is going on. It makes starting a program in cooperation with the schools where it's most needed very difficult."

Soskin was one of the most unusual adults with direct knowledge of the Haight and the dope scene. It didn't seem to upset him or threaten him or sweep him or take him up on a sunbeam into the golden heart of the cosmic center of religious banality. He picked his way like a man finding room over fallen bodies— trying to discern and help.

"Taking LSD once a week is quite common for these high school kids," he continued, "but you must bear in mind, I see those who are most committed to it. The curious thing about these young adolescents is they simply don't have the sagacity to tell themselves, 'I'll take it once or twice a year.' When they start they go crazy. They know in the sessions I have with them that they can't turn on, and they don't, but in many ways I can't help them. They believe that finally acid will be found to be destructive of brain tissue; they know that acid taken in large quantities will be injurious, but they continue."

He shook his head: "You see, the problem with young adolescents is that anything strong in its effects on the nervous system isn't advisable. Not even alcohol. The cortex isn't fully developed until twenty-three or twenty-four, and it shouldn't be subjected to these substances. I don't see how acid can help causing some damage, if not biological at least in attitude formation. No, I don't think treatment is needed so much as a new kind of youth culture that is more adapted to the kids' needs. The vast majority of the kids I know are hungering for a new kind of significance in their society. They come from middle-class families that have much more social and psychological knowledge than any other generation. These kids use Freudian concepts at an early age, so they have the conceptual tools to think about themselves and their parents in ways their mothers and fathers didn't. They're aware of their own internal operation, and this makes their search as to what they are and who they are unlike the past's. Not that these young people are different from preceding generations, but they're much more sophisticated, so that the answers they seek are more complicated.

"The institutions in the high school youth culture are becoming monolithic at an awesome rate. There's fantastic pressure to conform to a lock-step system. Even the football teams are kept alive by it. With their huge investment in physical plants, stadiums, and so on, the school administrations keep it alive by hiring coaches and creating vested interests in things like gym classes. As a result, if the kids don't go for the prescribed variety of choices, student activities like athletics or the drama club, there's nothing for them to do. But a large number of the kids I encounter want no part of the old-style high school extracurriculum. What happens is that by around thirteen or fourteen these kids either buy the parental value system or don't. If they do, they buy the schools, and if they don't—and those are increasing—they think seriously about leaving. This wasn't the case when I was in high school. Then the kid who dropped out was a failure or poor or a no-good-nik. That isn't so anymore. Now I think we're in danger of allowing the dilemma of the most talented white middle-class kids to become as grave a problem as the Negroes. I want to stop it before it reaches these proportions.

"I've just seen so many of them who started on acid and then began dropping out. You can watch the retrograde development of their thinking. Again, a striking concomitant of their taking

225

acid is the price they pay of a progressive erosion of their motivation. I also feel pretty confident that one of the properties of both acid and Methedrine is the tendency to produce paranoia.

"I don't think dropping out has to be bad. Our society is adding many months to each month of what was formerly adolescence. You could develop a youth culture that would have a much greater tolerance of complexity and play. You know, there's a curious quality of play about the eighteen- and nineteen-years-olds you meet. They're open, like children, learning through play. I'm tempted to call it a regression to about the six-year-old level, but that's not the way to put it exactly. Let's just say our society is the first where the youth aren't needed. We can afford to keep them in nonproduction occupations like play, and certain kinds of play may produce cross connections in the brain in a way that wasn't possible when people had to start working and close off free experience at an early age. It's possible a new youth culture of extended play could have an effect on the mind as great as good food has had on physical stature."

Al Rinker, too, was talking about youth. "We get parents who call and say that if their runaway daughter will come home, they'll give her a factory-fresh Mustang or a college education. It's people like that we're trying to establish dialogue with." Around him the alcohol turn-on was beginning to impair dialogue, as something that resembled old-time collegiate whoopee welled up to steal the spirit of the party. Eleemosynary Herb continued to pour liquor from its inexhaustible sources, while around him there was much necking and fun wrestling. Alcohol isn't always a downer. George's girl, Joan, was profoundly taken with the stuff. "Oh God! My God! My God! EEEEEEEOOOOOOOwwwweeeeee! Why didn't somebody tell me about an alcohol high before? Jesus, I've never felt so good. Nineteen years old an' I never knew what I was missing. So this is why the straights groove on it like they do. It's much better than grass. I'll never smoke grass again," she shouted as she began dancing in high-prancing circles.

"Joan," somebody warned her, "you'd better go easy. It's best with an alcohol high when you reach where you're at to quit."

226

"I don't believe it. I want more, more, more, more, more booze, more juice. This is absolutely the best high of my life. I want everybody to know that. I'm going to tell everybody that. I want them all to know that I'm now a reformed dope fiend. Starting three hours ago I became queen of the juiceheads. EEEEEEOOOOO-wwwwwwwweeeeYYYYYaaaaaooow!"

The party was breaking up. Soskin and the straights made sober farewells, while some of the neighborhood blacks, attracted by the police who were attracted by the noise, wandered in and got sloshed by the liquor that tireless Herb was still pouring. As a reciprocal gesture they swiped some of the still undrunk bottles and then, not realizing they could have had them for the asking, ran with guilty speed out of the front door and down the steep flight of steps to the street, where one tripped, fell, smashed the bottle, cut his stomach, and got up, half limping, half running, and made his escape as he bled whiskey and blood on the sidewalk. The Queen of the Juiceheads shouted, "Awwwgh! I'm going to be sick," and was steered onto the back porch by someone more experienced with alcohol highs and told to breathe deeply for all she was worth.

Joan's post-party headache didn't last more than a day. Al Rinker's did. Not very long afterward, Herb's beneficence proved to be the charity of a bum-check artist. The $1,500 for contributions and cost of the party were written on an empty checking account, so the Switchboard, which had to make them good, went crashing into debt. Al Rinker visited super-straight himself, the district attorney, to file a complaint against the vanished Herb. The denouement was the first of many busts, disasters, panics, collapses, disappearances, freak-outs, and farewells that came to the Haight with the fall.

**BE WARNED
SOMEONE IS PASSING OUT BAD TRIPS
IN
COFFEE MUGS**

**HE IS ABOUT SIX FEET TALL, LONG
DIRTY-BLONDE HAIR, WELL**

Wendy was depressed. She'd tried selling papers, she'd tried begging, she'd tried everything she could think of but selling herself. She had a nice body and she was still talking about finding an old man, but he had to have other qualifications besides money. Wendy per se wasn't for sale, but Wendy herself was beaten down by the scrabble to get up her share of the rent so she wouldn't leave her roommates in the lurch. After four hours in front of Tracy's trying to peddle the *San Francisco Oracle* to the thinning traffic of tourists, she'd netted less than $3. "I'm tired of starving to death," she announced in her big voice that couldn't lose .its friendly, back-slapping quality even in adversity. "I'm going to San Jose to get a job building the big birds," she said, and she did.

Brian was going too. Money had been sent from home for first-class air fare back to the East Coast, but Brian had bought tourist and given every extra penny that he didn't absolutely need to Mike. Mike was genuinely downcast at Brian's going. It hadn't been an exploitive relationship. Mike was truly fond of Brian, although the young man's SDS politics seemed as ridiculously un-American as they had at the beginning of the summer. Mike had changed, perhaps because of Brian. Brian would have liked to have thought so, because on his last night in San Francisco, his useless legs stacked one on top of the other on the mattress in front of him, he was still saying he wanted to help people, even entertaining the idea of the ministry again. No matter; Mike's fatal case of cancer of the brain was cured; so was the charge against him of murdering his father. He'd taken off the priest's liturgical vestments and said he was out of the grass business. He was going to open a welding shop; Brian's money would be used, and Papa Al had promised to help.

"That's my thing, trying to help people, and it really spaces me out when I can't. Last night this super-intellectual cat asked me, 'What makes you think all these hung-up people want to be helped?' Like him. I don't know if he wanted to be helped, but I couldn't get to him—too many words, too many symbols between us. I couldn't help him, and that's sort of ego-defeating," Brian said, trying to assemble the words that would be the summation of the summer for him. "Another thing that would put me on a bummer was like when I wanted to ball, but you can't go up and say, 'I'd like to ball you,' because deep down they don't want to ball me. I never balled till this summer. This summer was the first time I balled."

You wondered what that scene was like. Brian had no old lady. Did the crippled boy simply end up buying a piece? Or did one of the girls take pity on him or get stoned one night and do it to see if it would be groovy balling him? It could have been the geezing girl who'd be in a lot to shoot up with the guys in the kitchen. Wouldn't that be just the way to get balled the first time, by a speed-freak girl who couldn't come but needed something to do to help her body catch up with her racing mind? Maybe Mike arranged it for him. He was always bringing chicks into their room and balling them. Maybe a night came when he put a bare foot in the small of some girl's back and said, "Roll off my mattress and roll onto Brian's. I want you to ball my friend. He's never been balled."

"It's not just me," Brian continued. "Even the people here are afraid of the truth. They don't want to say, 'I want to ball you.' We'll all flirt and do it like it's a dirty thing, so there's no room for love. There's this one chick at the Psyche Shop. She comes up to me and I turn her on and she turns me on, but I've told her I won't ball her unless she wants. So we don't. She wants to be half-raped. Imagine me doing that!"

He moved himself over on the mattress, his overdeveloped shoulder muscles compensating for the legs. These he had to drag by jerking and twisting his pelvis, yet there did seem to be some responsiveness in them.

"They're better," Brian confirmed. "They can hold some weight now. I might be able to stand without my crutches if they improve a little more. It happened this summer. Wow, it's been a swell summer for me. I hitchhiked down to the Big Sur, just got back. I wanted to see it before I went home. Man, it's just as beautiful as they say. On the way back, I got around all the way to San Jose. When we got to San Jose this guy asked me, did I want to eat. I said yes and we went to his house and afterward he asked me if he could ball me. So we balled each other. I spent the night there. Clean sheets, too much! He fed me breakfast and I got another ride almost straight here. It was a beautiful summer. The people are beautiful, man. It was a trip and a half."

> **... After a long hiatus, the Psychedelic Raiders have struck again: the fireplug at 25th and Rhode Island, on Pot Hill, is now painted Navy blue with white polka dots and looks quite fetching ...**
> —Herb Caen, *San Francisco Chronicle*,
> September 29

The Hip Job Coop closed. Everything was gone—desks, sleeping bags, Buddhist altar, mandalas. The storefront was locked tight with a FOR RENT sign in the window. In the upstairs apartment, everything was gone but a girl on a mattress somewhat cut off from the rest of the room by several flimsy madras-print bedspreads hung from the ceiling. She looked a little vague but with effort focused on the topic: "Peter, oh Peter, yeah. See, Garcia split with the rent money, so Peter was up four nights in a row going crazy. I don't know where he is now."

After many hassles, Raena Love, Tracy, and Ego moved out of the Hip Job Coop to the house on Laguna in the Fillmore. For a full, complete house the rent was cheap, $185, and maybe that's why they moved into the Negro section. "Spades," as Raena said, "aren't my thing. I don't put 'em down. When I was going to high school in Chicago, well, that was my segregation trip. All I ever heard around that school was that there weren't going to be any white people left. Well, that was a downer, but spades can

230

be a downer too. Those chicks in the East Village who go with them are masochists. Those white chicks have all those spade cats who beat them or hassle them all the time. I don't think integration is working anymore."

They'd had trouble finding the house on Laguna. After they found it, Tracy's car with all her clothes in it had been busted by the cops. Finally, the three of them had gotten there and rented the upstairs out to an acid band, so the place thundered with electrified vibrations but nobody minded, not even Ego.

"He's a turned-on little kid, Ego is," said Raena. "I used to give him acid, but kids don't need acid. Kids are naturally turned on. Kids are born knowing everything. I'm not even going to teach him to talk. No, he won't forget anything growing up in this environment. It isn't plastic."

It wasn't plastic; the pots in the kitchen with dried or rotting remains of cooked natural rice, the smells of rancid rags, everything putrescent and looking like it had a thousand swarming white bugs under it. They all slept in one room, including Augie Lowe, who shared Raena's mattress. This evening they were naked, lying together as Ego slept nearby. Tracy roamed the rooms reading *I Ching*.

Augie sat up and peered shortsightedly into the indistinct room before picking up Raena's remark about children: "I think people should live backwards. They should be born old and grow younger until you turn into a baby and climb back into a womb and disappear."

"Well, I'll tell you one thing," put in Tracy as she looked through the pages of the *I Ching* book, "you can't get any hepatitis or anything, including VD, if you eat a macrobiotic diet. Trouble is, heads don't take care of themselves."

"That's right," sighed Augie, "if more people believed in Buddha . . ."

Raena agreed. "That gives you absolute protection. During the riot in New York a girl went into the lotus position and into a trance and nobody bothered her. One cop even said, 'Don't touch her, she's meditating.'"

"I've been on demonstrations that could have turned into riots if the cops had known what was going on. That was when we had a fuck-in at the White House. We had it in our sleeping bags but nobody knew, because if we'd said it in advance they would have busted us or the cops would have rioted or it would have been a very heavy scene. You can't fuck with the President; you can't even fuck near him," Augie said with open-mouthed cunning, but that may have only been his nearsighted straining forward. "That was when those black farmers came up from Alabama, Selma I guess, and camped in front of the White House, but I've been on lots of demonstrations."

"If we can get a total spiritual network going they can't touch us," Raena said, but it wasn't too clear who the "they" might be. "Superspade's not really dead. The Mafia thinks by killing people they're really hurting us, but Chob's spirit and Superspade's probably inhabited two very deep, very heavy people seconds after they were killed. But a spiritual network would be good anyhow."

"I was almost going into a diabetic coma, but it says here in the *I Ching,* 'Don't use medicine on any disease you're born with,'" Tracy said. "I didn't. I needed macrobiotic food and now I'm well, which goes to show . . ."

Raena, who was on some kind of God-Indian trip, kept on talking while Augie explained future plans: "My main objective is to form a community to have people make jewelry. You have to do things like that to survive."

"Jewelry and dope, that's us," Tracy exclaimed.

"I was busted when I was fourteen years old in Bethesda, Maryland, for pushing amphetamines," continued Augie. "I'm a minister of the Neo-American Church. My title on the East Coast is Boohoo of the Bethesda Bag, but in the West I'm a Primate so I can go around making other Boohoos. I've performed two marriages . . . To be a Boohoo? You have to be a decent-trip sort of guy. You have to be a philosopher, a priest, a warlock."

"A love," interjected Raena.

"Yes, but mostly a warlock. I told three people that the spade

232

cat was going to be killed. My faith in the supernatural is greater than most people's even though I've been called a satanist."

In some ways Augie, the Boohoo of the Bethesda Bag, conforms to the not entirely inaccurate public picture of a modern psychedelic dope fiend: the formless disorganization of his life, the filth, the incoherent, metaphysical lunges into God knows where, the focus on affective experience; but in other ways he doesn't fit the pattern so well. When he cares to he's able to stick to a chain of rational thought, to understand reality as straights define it; he also fails to exhibit the dangerously erratic possibilities that a certain type of acidhead seems to harbor. In contrast, Raena, who says she's dropped acid two hundred times to Augie's four hundred times, shows all these symptoms, as well as an unnerving tendency to trip out into a bland, good-natured, vegetal state, the telltale homogenized acid personality.

Apparently, even in a physiological sense, the stuff hits different people differently, but it's always powerful. Dr. Jolyon West, chairman of the Department of Psychiatry at the University of Oklahoma, accidentally killed a seven-thousand-pound male elephant named Tusko with a small (less than elephant-sized) dose of acid in the course of some experiments on the musth disease, a strange distemper that afflicts only bull elephants but makes them go crazy. "You should have seen me there sitting on top of Tusko's head, shooting anticonvulsants into his ear while his mate, who was under restraints, was trumpeting and kicking up a helluva roar. I might have saved him if I hadn't run out of anticonvulsants. You need a lot of that stuff to pull an elephant through. I've given LSD to everything from elephants to Siamese fighting fish. When you give them some, they stop swimming back and forth and start going up and down."

Jolly West began experimenting with acid in the early fifties at the request of the United States government. At the time, some people in Washington suspected the North Koreans were using the drug to brainwash captured American soldiers. It turned out that this was one time acid was innocent, but the doctor never lost interest in the drug. When the Haight-Ashbury broke onto the national retina, he was spending a sabbatical year at Stanford University's Center for Advanced Study in the Behavioral Sciences. West immediately interested himself in the world's first psychedelic community. Besides his background in working with the drug, West had another advantage over most medical men. Years before it became fashionable, he'd been interested in civil rights, both as a citizen and as an investigating scientist. As a consequence, he'd had close and long familiarity with the generation of young people who had tipped over the American racial status quo. Social change, revolution, the far-out didn't bother him. Instead, he rented a pad in the Haight where he installed a small group of semi-hip college and graduate students to live and play participant observer. He would chug in from Palo Alto once or twice a week to direct the study and keep on top of things. As a result, Jolly West's testimony on acid and its uses is especially valuable, for he is the only doctor with an appropriate specialty who has had a chance to study dope-taking outside the clinic, in the actual youth culture where almost all of it is consumed.

"The Haight is like one great, enormous Rorschach card. You can read people by what they do with it when they come here. Some come because they want to take drugs free of economic and social necessity. They just want to cast the burden off and float and drift. Others are so antagonized, the long-haired kids who come to school and get their hair and their balls cut off, but I think most of them have some things in common. There is almost a deliberate argot which fits into a rebellion that is primarily spiritual and mystic. It's not like civil rights. It's not geared to change through action. These kids aren't even antiaction, because that implies action too.

"So much for the general background; now let me tell you about two hippies, a boy and a girl. The boy's father is a doctor; high IQ, bright, but resentful of his younger sisters, and a very fat boy. This boy's rebellion took a passive form. You could make him go to school but you couldn't make him learn. Therapy was unsuccessful. Then he began to shoot up, and as he grew taller he slimmed down, which brought him into a phase of his life when he'd hang around Sunset Strip and smoke grass. He played the defy-the-fuzz game with the other kids without getting busted, but finally he did—for walking across the street on a yellow light. They found pills on him, but they were legitimate ones for hay fever. Next he ran away from home and was taken in by a couple of waitresses who didn't know he was only fifteen. He lived *ménage à trois* with them, and meanwhile he learned about acid— took it two or three times—and then learned about pimping. Finally he got busted. The cops found marijuana on him and the court said he was incorrigible. His family sent him East to school and that lasted two or three months, when he broke the conditions of his parole and ran away to the Haight. That's where I found him and took him with me to Oklahoma City, where we sent him to summer school. I believe the thing he likes about me is that I know more about pot than he does. Altogether he's taken acid thirty to forty times in the last two and a half years. Before he took acid his IQ tested at 140. Two and a half years later he retested at 112. That's one way of looking at what happened to him; but he's much less anxious than he was, more relaxed, more concerned with the pleasures of the moment. He reminds me of teen-agers I've examined who've had frontal lobotomies, but how much of the damage is reversible if there's been biological scarring is uncertain. Today this boy likes himself better. You have to realize that lobotomies make people happy; they attenuate those inner struggles and conflicts that are characteristic of the human condition.

"Now let me tell you about my second hippy. Rosa came from a lower middle-class immigrant family in an eastern city. This summer in the Haight I think she was Princess of the Runaways. I know one night she brought thirty-six crashers into the pad. You couldn't walk down the hall of our little scientific outpost. She came out here this spring after her junior year in high school and changed her name from Rosa to Blithe. As Rosa, back East, she'd been the child of parents who practiced a very concrete Catholicism, which affected her. She was searching for Jesus but they were always saying, 'It's Saturday night. Did you go to confession?' When she got here and changed her name, she had an identity crisis of almost psychotic proportions. Jim Allen, the child psychiatrist who's been working with us on our hippy research project, first saw Blithe in the Free Clinic when she was on a bad trip. He noticed something about her, her intelligence, her energy, something . . . A couple of days later, he found her on Haight Street wandering around in a daze. He brought her to the pad, where she lived all summer. We gradually persuaded her not to take any more drugs. We even got her to the point where she wasn't smoking much grass. By the end of the summer she wanted to go back to school, here, not at home, and we managed to arrange for her to go the best high school in the city. I think the whole experience has been developmentally valuable for her. If she stayed at home, she might still be hung-up with parents, trying, probably not very successfully, to make her search for Jesus and their rules come together. Now she has her new name and her new identity and a life to go with it. She does communicate with her parents who have been very understanding. Of course, I don't think there's any question the acid did damage. When we found her she was sick and the drugs had something to do with it, but she had a convalescence living in a therapeutic community, our little scientific pad.

"As you can see in these two case histories, there aren't very good grounds for a final judgment, but overall I'm not enthusiastic. I think the people who say there is a shift of values are correct. Ask me, what are the values now? There is a much greater emphasis on the importance of primary information and a disappearance of the value of digital information. People are paying more attention to their visceral brains and less to their cerebral cortex. It may be the beginning of an anti-intellectualism like we've never seen, and what the outcome of that might be, I'd rather not guess."

West, the psychiatrist, senses the affective man and draws back. Without saying it, he allows you to imagine Id, the unchained, rabid and earthy, suddenly becoming aware that forces completely outside the Freudian trinity have crippled his old enemy and keeper, the Ego; now Id can rise, destroy his captor, enter into unheard-of alliances with Superego, and burst forth roaming the earth in search of the satisfaction he lives for. In this, Id has a great ally in the psychedelic drugs; they put Id and Superego in direct communication with each other, paralyzing the rational mediation of Ego. The psychedelics are murder on Ego control and defenses. One of the most common and easiest forms of freak-out to recognize is Ego-panic, that moment when the drugged, traduced, overwhelmed Ego realizes it's drowning; then it also realizes it has its own life principle, that it isn't parasitically dependent on the Id for energy; then it freaks and shows the whole organism the terrifying, identity-less chaos that its destruction will bring. Even the Id is scared; it can't feed itself without Ego; Superego is panicked at having delivered itself into the hands of a healthy force changed into a mindless explosion of energy. It is perhaps for these reasons that the Eastern religious masters condemn dope and guide the students back to the first oneness by instructing them in supernal Ego control.

"The use of drugs has been to permit primary process thinking," says Jolly West. "That's what a good trip is. The desideratum is bringing up primary process material, not in a case of illness for therapeutic purposes but as a fulfillment itself. That's what the hippy cult means, and if it gains wide acceptance we may go back to the bonfire.

"Now, within two years marijuana is going to be the major firing line between youth and the older generation. The establishment is going to say, 'No,' and the kids are going to say, 'Fuck you.' It's going to be very hard. We're already the most drug-taking country in the world; then add that people have always wanted to turn on. People all through history have wanted to intoxicate themselves. Even little children spin themselves on a swing to get a little dizzy high.

"Six months ago I might have been in favor of legalizing marijuana, although I still would have asked myself, 'Do we need another intoxicating drug in this society?' Apparently we need some, and for that alcohol has the advantage of exacting almost immediate penalties: nausaea, headaches, the hangover. These penalties set limits on its consumption for most people. Pot doesn't have such uncomfortable aftereffects. The other advantage of alcohol is that regardless of what it does to some of the other organs of the body, it doesn't damage the brain.

"Now I have some serious doubts about legalizing marijuana. We don't know what its long-term effects are. There haven't been any competent studies done, with the exception of one in Greece, but there they smoke cannabis indica, not cannabis sativa, which is smoked here, so there isn't exact comparability. Still, the findings are disturbing—symptoms persisting two years after the subjects have given up use. With neurological damage, whatever doesn't repair itself in a year usually doesn't come back. I may have seen signs of the same things with some long-time American pot smokers. I talked to one young man recently who told me, 'Oh, sure, I got good grades before I started smoking pot, but I had a lot of drives I couldn't control and sex hang-ups. Now I feel happier. I know what's important in my life; sex is better for me; I only need a little food. I've changed in other ways. Now I don't know what I'm going to do with my life. I know what I had lined up for myself was a lot of establishment crap.' I asked him if his thinking was any different after three years of pot smoking. 'Yes,' he said. 'I used to get all hung up with these abstractions; now I think about what's here and now. I can't remember a line in a book, but I can tell you if it did or didn't turn me on.'

"When I heard that, I thought to myself, 'There is a whisper here of lobotomy.' The fact of the matter is that tranquility isn't the natural state of man."

### 6 UNDER LSD BLINDED
### BY STARING AT SUN

Harrisburg, Pa., Jan. 12 (AP)—Six young college men suffered total and permanent blindness by staring at the sun while under the influence of the drug LSD, it was learned yesterday. Federal officials said it is the first case they have heard of in which total blindness resulted. Last May four students at the University of California at Santa Barbara reportedly suffered loss of reading vision by staring at the sun after taking LSD.

## DISCLOSURE OF LSD HOAX
## HOSPITALIZES FIRED AIDE

Harrisburg, Pa., Jan. 19 (AP)—A Pennsylvania health official's "concern over the illegal use of LSD by children" apparently motivated him to invent a story that six Pennsylvania college students were blinded by the sun after taking the drug, Gov. Raymond P. Shafer says.

Dr. Norman Yoder, 53, suspended from his job by Shafer, collapsed after revealing the hoax, a state official said, and was sent to a psychiatric hospital in Philadelphia.

Many kids were becoming anxious about hurting themselves with dope. The reports of chromosomal damage caused by acid had penetrated most heads except those belonging to the speed freaks, who didn't use much acid anyway. Dr. Smith at the clinic said the experiments weren't yet conclusive. "I could get the same results using caffein from coffee." The apostolic acidheads dismissed all the talk as establishment lies, but the kids worried. They might not like science, but they believed in it with more faith than in birth signs or tarot cards. What's more, the underground press seemed to be convinced that the dangers might be real. They began running "Watch it, Baby" articles.

"I hope I haven't messed myself up," said Candy, the girl who had bum-tripped at the I/Thou Coffee House and been taken home by Bernie and Kate. She was back from L.A. in physically damaged condition but in better psychological shape. She'd gone there because she'd fallen in love with an older guy and given him her Southern girl's slightly romantic virginity. Apparently he had the clap, but he didn't tell her, nor the three other girls he was sleeping with. As far as Candy could tell, he was waiting as long as he could before he got himself fixed up so he could infect as many girls as he could get hold of. She'd left him and come back to the Haight and was getting treated, but she was disturbingly calm about what he'd done to her. No anger, no remorse, no revenge seemed to move in her, merely resignation. You wondered if it was Jolly West's whisper of lobotomy. It was so hard to distinguish what might be the effects of the dope and what was just the common Haight-hippy passive-aggressive personality which can only kill with kindness.

"I hope I haven't messed myself up with the chromosome business. I want to have children," Candy reiterated. "I can't even talk anymore. I mean my English has deteriorated. I can't speak complete sentences. I'm always using baby words like 'Wow, gee whiz, it's a bummer.' I've lost my memory. I ran into this boy named Chuck three times in one day and I couldn't remember his name. You have, like, this overwhelming ability to trip out. Like today a lady called me over in the store and that's all I remember.

"I can think of other instances. I was on a bus a couple of weeks ago, and instead of heading toward Venice [California] I was going in the other direction toward Malibu. I had no conception of what happened in between. The same thing happened to me another time on the bus. I was on it and then I was off it, standing on a street corner. And then everybody gets acid flashes—suddenly something trips you out and you're back up high."

Acid's power to recur and persist in its effects long after it is taken—weeks and months later—is so well recognized that many kids say they live stoned all the time. Yet the ratio of good trips to bad trips, and of trips without aftereffects to ones with them, must be favorable enough to get a lot of people to play dope roulette a second, third, and fiftieth time. This observation, of course, doesn't take into account the possibility of the cumulative effect of the kind that Jolly West and others increasingly suspect. The ratios with other kinds of psychedelic dope aren't so favorable. Peyote makes most people sick to their stomachs, so there is a shying away from it, or, if they do take it, they prepare it with

240

all sorts of weird formulas or ingest it in peculiar ways, like taking it by enema. (Mescaline, a peyote extract, is supposed to give you the high without heaves.) The ultra-powerful STP hasn't won a large market for itself because of its poor bad-trip ratio; the word is out to stay away from it.

Under these circumstances, making up horror stories to tell the young is a dubious practice which may only discredit the story-tellers. This happened with pot. Adults told young people things for which there was no evidence, and now it is impossible to convince them that marijuana is any more dangerous than chewing gum.

The other side is making exaggerated claims too. It's being said that pot smokers and dope takers in general don't drink alcohol, which is just another form of dope. This isn't so. Acid, pot, speed, smack, and alcohol are different kinds of highs. They're not mutually exclusive, except for certain psychological types who greatly need one particular form. Many dope takers drink when they're high, and others, people who have been strung out on speed or smack, give it up to become booze hounds. They'd rather get juiced than stoned.

The way some people switch their poisons casts doubt on the usefulness of the idea of addiction. There were a lot of people walking around the Haight who said they'd been hooked on smack and kicked it. There was no reason to disbelieve them. There were also many fairly well-authenticated cases of speed shooters giving it up. Addiction or dependence may not be an inevitable and mechanical thing but may depend on the person and the circumstances.

There may also be truth in the assertion that pot leads people to take stronger dope. Getting stoned on pot can be very tedious if you do it often enough, and if you're in the dope culture the next step is a more interesting high. Many dope takers say they began with marijuana. But others report they got started by sniffing glue in high school. Another group—this one isn't small, either—reports they were first turned on by their family doctors. Typically, the pattern shows the doctor writing out a month or two-month prescription for a powerful drug and then saying to his young patient,

"Call me if you don't feel better." The youth takes the drug for weeks without clinical examination and does "feel" better, whether or not he is better. Then, when he runs out of pills, as often as not a new prescription is obtainable simply by phoning the doctor's office. What percentage of the dope population is created by negligent physicians is impossible to ascertain. Drug dependency caused by doctors doesn't show up in arrest or clinical records because the people have an assured supply and often are only vaguely aware of what's happened to them. Occasionally there is a scandal, as there was a few years ago with a San Francisco doctor who had worked out a kickback arrangement to turn on his patients with diet pills. Nobody knows how many women got strung out before it got so bad that the medical society had to intervene. But the more usual pattern isn't that blatant. The doctor isn't running an out-and-out racket; he's just practicing shoddy medicine, seeing fifteen patients an hour when he should be seeing five. On this kind of pill-pusher there are no restraints. He will continue, unquestioned by his colleagues, gobbling fees and opening the door to hell for a certain percentage of his patients whom he permanently turns on.

Another setting where people learn to take dope is college. Amphetamines are extensively used by students to stay awake for exams. "Universities," remarks Peter Cohon, the Digger, "are proselytizing centers for dope."

Yet there is dope and dope. Some is obviously more harmful than other kinds. You can live a long time strung out on heroin and function quite adequately. But some substances can cause brain damage and death very rapidly, even when they are used only once; and younger kids who can't find pot in this dope-hungry culture will use them. Not long ago there was a be-in in Washington, D.C., a gathering of the floral people in Georgetown's Montrose Park. The people who live in this neighborhood are among the richest and most powerful in the world—United States senators, millionaires, Supreme Court justices. Their children were in the park that day. The older youths sat in the preserve's woody copses and on the sides of a shallow ravine and smoked pot.

The younger ones, in their earliest teens, who had no pot, drifted across the park looking for a substitute. Across the lawn and down a slight grade was the Tambourine Man, the mythic name used in the youth culture for the dope provider. At first the young ones couldn't see him sitting on a bench filling balloons from his green steel bottle. There were already too many other young ones crowding around him with flat, shriveled balloons in their hands, pressing toward him, supplicating him to fill them up with the wonder-making gas.

When they grasped what he was doing they ran down to him. They pressed in and got free balloons from the Tambourine Man's girl friend and waited their turn. When it came, he turned the cock on the end of the rubber hose so that the freon-22 inflated the balloons. Even before the kids turned away they put the balloons to their mouths, letting the gas fill their lungs. Eyes watery-wide and unblinking, they held the gas in their lungs until it acted on their brains. As it did, they lost balance, began to stumble, fall down, and pass on elsewhere in a state of gassy intoxication.

The Tambourine Man was in hilarious excitation: "I've filled six hundred balloons already," he cried, "and lots have come back for refills."

"Won't it kill you? People died from it," a little girl wanted to know. She was referring to the reports that several people had died from the refrigerant, which turns to a cold liquid under pressure.

"No, no, not as long as you don't drink it," the Tambourine Man reassured her. "Don't believe the yellow press and their lies. It'll make you feel good. Remember the yellow press hates hippies."

The Tambourine Man was twenty-one, an only child, a student at the University of Maryland. The adolescents, just out of latency, demanded more gas, but the Tambourine Man was getting tired. "That's all for a while. I want to take a rest . . . you're the last one . . . Okay, I'll give you some if you want to take it directly from the tank," he said to a boy whose pursed lips were prehensile as they strained for the nozzle. "Okay, that's it," the Tambourine Man repeated. "I'm cutting out for a while. Well, a few more, but chicks only."

He gave the pleading chicks gas and then picked up his pressure bottle and walked away from the young ones. Some of them were too stoned and stunned to register his leaving; others lay on the turf which had become a tilting platter for their dizzied, revolving consciousness.

The strolling straights, adult rich from the neighborhood, sauntered through the grounds of Dumbarton Oaks and the brightly colored air of an October afternoon and into the park. They saw the scene but they didn't comprehend it. They puzzled and walked on. A few were nettled. These kids were lousing up the park. "Where did they come from?" an older man asked. "Did they come from the P Street beach? What are they doing? There's gas in those balloons. Wait, wait till the Washington power structure hears about this. They'll put a stop to it."

The Tambourine Man was off with a few others explaining why he was doing it. "It's legal. They can't bust you for getting stoned on it, so I had this idea. Why not give it away? I walked into a store and bought it off the shelf for $10. People were offering money for some, but I didn't take any."

"It's a bad high," somebody said.

"Yeah, I don't like the high from it," the Tambourine Man agreed. "You get a dead head from it afterwards."

A brunette chick was impatient with this conversation about "body highs" and "head highs," the connoisseurship of the true head. "I just want to see how high I can get. Give it to me from the nozzle and don't turn it off until I say."

The Tambourine Man did, but he stopped dosing her before she signaled. "I don't want you to take too much. I don't know what it'll do," he said, as the little chick began falling over backward off the bench she was sitting on.

## 11 POT CASES ARE REPORTED ON AIRCRAFT CARRIER

**Honolulu, Dec. 4 (AP) — Eleven crewmen have been reported involved with marijuana**

aboard the aircraft carrier Kitty Hawk,
Pacific Fleet headquarters at Pearl Harbor
said today.

When Candy got back from her amatory disaster in Los Angeles, she had dinner one evening at Annka's restaurant on Haight Street, the place that serves delicious German food, but not to hippies. Candy is a very pretty girl who looks more nubile than hip in slacks and long hair, so they let her in. She talked about her life, her family back in Baton Rouge, and her dope taking. They were, as she could easily see even at eighteen, very much interrelated:

"I was strung out on speed. At the end, before I kicked it, I was shooting three dime bags a day. Kicking it was pretty hard. I lay in the bed and had chills, while everybody was saying, 'Smoke some grass or take downers'; but, you know, pain's a funny thing. It has its own high. At first I was rolling on the bed, but then I began to flow with the pain and I could kinda sit there. For a while I was determined to become a drug addict. Maybe I was. When I kicked speed, there were a lot of people who said I couldn't take being straight; but I enjoy being straight. I'm not sure I'm going to take much dope again. I have a joint in my bra right now —that's the safest place to keep it. I've been walking around with it all day. A month ago I would have smoked it by now.

"Dope's not always easy. I've even shot Wyamine.* God, it's got a terrific rush! The kind of rush you dream about, but the rest of the time you're only sort of high, and for days I went around feeling like a butane bottle. Coming down off it is terrible . . . worse than speed. And I had a lot of trouble with my veins when I was shooting. They've about returned to normal now, but they were bad for a while, stood out from my arms and they really hurt.

"Am I going to have stories to tell my grandchildren. How I sold dope, how I sat around and shot up and caught the clap. Do

*The "Wyamine" inhaler, put out by Wyeth Laboratories, was until recently available over the counter without a prescription. The practice was to break open the plastic container, squeeze out the concoction, and shoot it. Most experienced druggies put it down as the worst sort of junk, but it serves as a good example of what can be had if you're looking.

you know, my aunt used to say I wouldn't last five seconds without anybody to pick up after me? I had my own car, charge accounts. They always thought I was too spoiled. Imagine my cleaning up, washing and scrubbing floors. At home we had a maid and I dropped things everywhere. My relatives wouldn't believe it if they could see me. They didn't think I could make it alone. You know, I want to come back with a lot of money and show it to them. They'll probably think I made it by living with an older man. I've been offered money for sex. One man offered me $100, but I wouldn't do it. I know some girls sell themselves, and they say after the first time you don't mind, that it's all the same, but there's something self-destructive about it. I'll bet you think that's funny, my saying that about not wanting to be self-destructive, but I think I wanted to be a drug addict to hurt my father. Every time I shot up, I felt as though I were putting the needle in him.

"My mother died when I was twelve. She had TB. I never saw her much, but I think she must have been very dull and proper. I think she was very religious, because that's the way my father wants me to be. He's not that way. He's a very groovy guy. If he weren't my father, I could go for him. He's got a girl friend who's twenty-two years old. She sent me a doll for a present once. I guess my father had just told her he had a very little girl for a daughter.

"My family would never believe how I made it in the Haight. Before I moved in with Richie, I lived with Reed. He's probably the biggest smack dealer in the Haight. He never hassled me about sex, though. I delivered for him, but then I realized if anything ever happened I'd be the one holding the bag. I was the one who was taking all the risks. Reed was strung out on smack. During the day he was pretty straight. He'd only shoot enough to maintain his habit. Then when he came home in the evening he'd get his high and spend the night in a corner in his cloud. Richie's straight. No dope, no sex. He just wants me to clean his house and cook for him while he spends his time over at his store doing his money thing. He's got a store in L.A. too. He works all the time and he'd get rich, but he's got this one friend who's always cheating

246

him but he doesn't know it. Sometimes I think I should tell. Richie's been nice to me, but he might not believe me. He might think I was jealous of his friend and I'd get hassled. I don't want to be. It's good where I am. As long as I take care of his house, I can do what I want, like deal. I don't do it there. I sold ten keys of grass today. I bought at 65 and sold at 70. I never even touched it, never saw it and I made $50.

"You know, when I came to the Haight I thought I'd meet interesting people, but I've only met creeps, psychos, freak-outs, and dealers. Nobody who can talk or has anything to say. I wanted to go to college this fall. I wanted to go to Tulane, a place where you'd learn something, because it'd be interesting, but my father doesn't want me to live even that far away from home, unless it's at this girl's college he has picked out, where they chaperone you all the time. I don't know. I might swallow my pride and go home for Christmas. I've shown them by staying this long. Only, I've got to get cured of the clap first. Yiiipes! Wouldn't that cause a scandal?"

Those who don't give up dope, learn how to use it. As dope usage has spread, a lore and conventional wisdom has grown up out of youth's collective experience with it. They tell each other, "Don't take dope among strangers," "Don't buy from dealers you don't know—don't put just anything in your mouth." "Learn what kind of situations you can't take when you're stoned so that you don't blunder into them and freak out."

"Freaking out" is dope's equivalent of the hangover, or getting sick to your stomach. Confirmed heads spend as much time talking about it as drunks do exchanging hangover recipes. In general, freaking out is erratic behavior resulting from a bum trip. It probably arises from many causes; a most frequent one is being high in an unfamiliar or stressful situation. Some kids will say that the biggest reason they ran away from home was that they couldn't act straight in front of their parents when they were stoned. Rather than try and perhaps freak, they split. The cry of encouragement, "Maintain!" that heads sometimes use probably derives from those tight situations with parents, teachers, or the cops.

Bad-tripping isn't confined to acid. You can bum-trip on pot, even on smack and alcohol, as anyone who has ever gotten drunk and had a miserable time will testify. The more serious bum trips involve the major psychedelics: acid, STP, and mescaline. Mescaline bum trips are rare because the dope is rare and because the people who take it are often refined types who go on mental and spiritual voyages of the sort that permits them to use even the unpleasantness for their involuted personal purposes.

So much is known about the techniques of handling people who are stoned that it has been written down. *The Catechism and Handbook of the Neo-American Church** contains some excellent advice, with some pretty entertaining psychedelic theology, for the person working with someone who's bum-tripping:

> *The best rule is to do and say as little as possible, but put the best construction on everything. If the victim [the dope taker] asks you a question, for God's sake try to answer the question instead of "treating" the questioner. Here are some do's and don'ts:*
>
> *Question: Who am I?*
>
> *Good Answer: You are my next-door neighbor, Mrs. Klotch. But I guess you are going through a period where you won't pay much attention to that and will see things from a more universal point of view. It happens all the time. Nothing to worry about. (This is a good answer only if the victim actually is Mrs. Klotch. If Vice-President Humphrey was the victim, it would not be a good answer.)*
>
> *Bad Answer: Ah, that is the question. What meaneth these cards of identity? We are all One, are we not?*
>
> *Bad Answer: You are not your body.*
>
> *Bad Answer: There is a self beyond the self.*
>
> *Bad Answer: Be still, and know that I am God.*
>
> *Bad Answer: Hey! Look at that beautiful drop of snot on baby's nose!*
>
> *Question: Are you my father?*

*The Kriya Press of the Sri Ram Ashramam, Millbrook, N.Y.,1967.

248

*Good Answer: No, actually, I'm Mr. Klotch from next door,*
  *but I guess you must be seeing things from the point of*
  *view of a little kid or something. If you want to go through*
  *some childhood scenes, I'll try to play along as best I*
  *can. Do I actually look like your father? (Wait for*
  *answer.) This LSD stuff is pretty fantastic, isn't it?*
*Bad Answer: No. (There is such a thing as being too flat*
  *about all this. It is unnatural and therefore frightening to*
  *answer a fantastic question as if it were commonplace.)*
*Bad Answer: Why do you ask that question? (This is*
  *evasive and suggestive of the sinister.)*
*Bad Answer: How do you feel about your father? (OK, if*
  *the contract is for psychotherapy.)*
*Bad Answer: Behold I am thy father, mother, brother, sister,*
  *daughter, son, indeed, I am all things and all things are*
  *ME ! ! ! ! (This may be true but there's no reason to get*
  *swellheaded about it.)*

The institutionalizing of dope consumption will contain and moderate it; it may possibly put a brake on some of the more socially destructive aspects of it, but these social constraints won't push it back onto the fringes of society, back to the days when pot was called a "dry drunk," a déclassé high for people who didn't have the bread for booze. Americans have come to like their dope and expect to have it according to their mood: coffee, liquor, cigarettes, pot, acid, tranquilizers, sleeping pills—we demand them and we shall have them.

Should dope, or at least pot, be made legally, freely available? For pot the argument is that it isn't as bad for you as liquor, but this is a non sequitur. If pot's no worse than alcohol and we know what *that* does to you, it follows that we should prohibit booze. We tried that once. The whole swirling, inconclusive debate about how harmful the various kinds of dope are is beside the point. The chances are that all of them are harmful, even pot, but what does a nation do if millions of its citizens insist on having it? If we are serious about prohibiting it, we will have to quadruple our police force. In that case, we will become a nation of cops, snoops, spies, and informers. But then, many think we are already.

We'll have to seal off the Mexican border. We'll need an army to do it, but we can't use the one in Vietnam because the reports indicate the troops, who are the same age as the kids in the Haight, are turning on like crazy too. While the Army is trying to stop dope infiltration from Mexico, we must face a second war behind the lines. Marijuana grows wild over much of the United States—particularly large amounts of it have been sighted and picked in Kansas, Iowa, Illinois, Wisconsin, and Michigan. Furthermore, there are dozens of other substances you can turn on with—sunflower seeds, parakeet food, scotch broom, airplane glue; the list is endless, and the prospect of outlawing them all is ludicrous.

The chances of convincing the new middle-class dope pushers to cut it out are nonexistent. They don't believe they can be arrested, and if they do they think their families will get them out of trouble. Or they think they're smarter than the cops and they won't get caught. But they're being busted by the thousands with awful resultant tragedies. Not long ago a judge sentenced one to a year in jail and when he did, the boy took out a gun in the courtroom and committed suicide.

Pending the day that Congress takes another look at what's happening, the turmoil, the evils that come from an illegal and therefore unregulatable industry, will multiply. When Congress does open the question for debate, the right answer will not be self-evident. Although it's popular to come out for legalization, if you're young or want to curry favor with the young, there are some serious arguments against it. Even if, as the people who want it legalized say, dope taking is a crime without a victim, to the extent that it incapacitates the taker everybody is a victim. Classically, this state, every state, maintains a fundamental right to oversee its citizens so it can defend and perpetuate itself. To the degree that these drugs are destructive by diminishing productivity, by shortening life, by lobotomizing a portion of the citizenry, the state acts wisely to prohibit them.

That is the classic argument, but there is an opposing one: the freedom of the individual to destroy himself. There is a growing feeling of having had it with the modern national state's constraint and manipulation of person and personality. The state only wishes to preserve youth in order to destroy it later in the homicidal encounters that are necessary to protect democracy. Since the end result of the modern state is the death of its citizens, or so the argument goes, it has lost the right, though not the force, to deprive its citizens of their individual liberties. In times past, when survival required the labor and the fighting ability of large percentages of the population, the state couldn't allow the right of individual self-destruction. Today this is no longer true. If these kids kill themselves, we don't need them. We don't need them to grow food; we don't need them to create new wealth in our factories; we don't even need them as cannon fodder. There is a surplus of all three. If there is no utilitarian reason to prevent them from doing something that's harmful, why shouldn't the state step back and declare this form of self-destruction an exercise in personal freedom? It's done that with alcohol; but then Jolly West's question comes back to be answered. How many of these things can we allow before, cumulatively, they hurt the society? Death by alcohol, tobacco, and automobile fumes is uncontrollable because of the vested interests that profit from them and the public that wants to die these deaths. The legalization of pot would add another item to the list, and while none of them may make the American extinct, in the aggregate they all may. The only good solution would be to raise youngsters who don't turn on chemically, but universal world disarmament will come first.

### SCIENTISTS PREDICT END
### OF INDIVIDUALISM

**Wiesbaden (West Germany), Aug. 27 (AP)— Society may well become depersonalized and desexualized within the next 50 years, two New York scientists said yesterday. Anyone who tries to be an individual "will be looked upon as odd, reactionary and anti-group."**

251

Allen, the nutty mailman, split. He used the last of his savings and bought a bike. While he was learning to ride he took a header somewhere down around San Mateo. It wasn't too bad, though. The bike was easy to fix and Allen only lost about a quarter of his face, so after a couple of days of convalescence he and his new equipment took off for Baja California. "You only live once and I'm thirty-five years old and I haven't lived at all. This's my last chance," Allen had proclaimed before he'd taken the Bay Shore Freeway south for good. But Rici, his sidekick and speech writer, languished over at Lefty's with the other remains of Alibaba and the Forty Thieves, conjured up new altruistic enterprises, and told everybody he was a war hero—the Navy Cross, two silver stars, and two bronze stars for breaking out of a North Vietnamese prison camp at the head of 175 men, whom he led southward through the jungle for six months. "Only fourteen of us survived. We walked into pungi pits, and if those poisoned sticks didn't get us, the green vipers did. I weighed 108 pounds when I got back." Everybody said the only army Rici had been in was Sergeant Pepper's, but he stuck to his story, made eyes at you that said, "I've seen death and carnage," and claimed his father, the full colonel, was killed at Operation Hastings. Rici wasn't the same after the mailman left.

Next White Preacher split. It was all bad luck for him before he left. First Hawaiian Chuck burned him. Then the Gypsy Jokers beat him up and told him he couldn't wear cutaways anymore. In revenge, or because he needed the money, or maybe because his motor was racing too fast for him to know what he was doing, he tried to set up the street for a big acid burn. He said the acid was coming from Papa Al, which increased its price until Al found out about it. Before he left he apologized to Al, who was concentrating on the Jeffery-Haight. Papa Al also seemed to be slowing down a little. He was still collecting his samples and getting his reports; he was even working his way in on a big new cop, sixteen hundred kilos, but he had the air of a man who senses his time is running out and responds by relaxing and letting up a little instead of rushing. He was still putting in those long hours, but he was talking about getting away from the Haight, and when he'd open the trunk of his big Chrysler he'd shake his head and say more often, "I can't figure it. They should have guessed by now." He'd look at the radio transmitter in his trunk, shake his head, and close it.

After Labor Day the number of tourists dropped drastically. By the end of September business on the Street had bombed out to nothing. Peggy was in an indignant panic. Her business had fallen 65 per cent. Her face was an animated, jerking, incoherent alarm. "My God, I don't know what I'm going to do. Well, I can't buy the Jaguar this year, and I don't know how I'm going to keep up the payments on the house, but my God! what scares me is where am I going to get the money to pay my taxes? No, of course I didn't save any. How was I to know business was going to drop? Well, I knew it was going to drop, but not like this! Sixty-five per cent! And the parking tickets! Kimmie just got out of jail; she gave herself up again on her parking tickets, but how am I going to pay mine? I mean, I've got to pay taxes on *all* that money I made and spent. Oh, but you have to see the house. Sam's up in the country working on it now . . . Come over here . . . shhh! . . . I don't want anybody to hear . . . shhh! . . . I copped half a gram of acid. Kimmie's up at the apartment now capping it."

"You're nuts. You oughta stick to selling pants. Summer's over and the heat's busting everybody in sight."

"Well, it's the government's own fault. They shouldn't charge so much for taxes and parking tickets. I've got to pay them somehow. They'll put me in jail."

"They'll put you in jail if they find out how you're paying them."

"God, I know. They're busting everybody. It's awful. I'm so scared. We're only going to do it this once more . . . just for the taxes and the parking tickets. It's not like I was doing it to make money or a profit."

"Do you know how the cops are operating?"

"They've got narks, nasty things. Oh, God, do you see a nark? I'll never do it again. It's the war. Wouldn't you think they could fight a cheaper war? I mean the taxes, and the spades. I'm not against spades. Superspade was a close friend of mine. I like the spades I know, but those others. Would you believe it, they've stolen $5,000 worth of merchandise out of here? It must be that much. They only steal the leather coats. I won't put them on the rack anymore, but then if they're not on the rack, customers can't see them and don't buy them."

Kimmie comes out of the crowd on Haight Street. She's muttering, "Nuts, nuts, nuts," and shivering. She's wearing slacks and a T-shirt, nothing else against the night's cold.

"What's wrong?" Peggy wants to know, her round face assuming a shrieking expression. Kimmie begins to jump up and down, prepping her stoned head to say something. "What's wrong?" Peggy insists, as her face displays a new expression of round, horrified anticipation.

"I forgot," Kimmie replies, jumping up and down some more. "Oh, oh, oh, oh, I know, I know, I know," Kimmie explains, "I'm going to cook supper. Isn't that a great idea?"

"Kimmie, who's at the apartment?"

"John and Cucuck. It's cool, it's cool. I wanted you to know about supper, that's all," Kimmie reassures Peggy. She's still jumping up and down, and as she does she sees her fingers, stops, cries, "Yummie!" licks them, and runs out and over to the apartment nearby. It is cool there, as Peggy finds when she locks up the store and comes over. There's only a spade chick, John, a slim and pleasant blond boy who was a pretty successful dealer until he ran into some bad burns and got wiped out, a couple of other close friends, and Cucuck Larue, the tiny fluff dog. They're all in a room off the living room. It's illuminated by a dull overhead red lamp. The stereo with headsets and the mattress on the floor make up the furnishings, but it's the only room in the house that is conventionally hip. The rest of the apartment is done in high camp, the period 1905–28.

The acid is being capped in the red room. People are sitting around a medium-sized gilt-framed mirror that has been taken off the wall and propped up with books to coffee table height. The acid's on the mirror, which is just high enough for the little dog to jump up and lick it. So the little dog is stoned, but also apparently bum-tripping. Anyway, Cucuck looks miserable, so that Kimmie, who's now too high to persist at capping, sits on a pouf, coos at Cucuck, "Cuku is high, Cuku needs loving."

From time to time the doorbell rings. Whenever it does, it sets Peggy off in a spasm of anticipatory terror of the police, but it's just friends dropping around to say hello. When they see what's going on they pitch in and help with the capping.

"Think how unfair it would be if we got raided," somebody remarks, "just for dropping around for a sociable evening of acid capping at a friend's house."

Almost everybody is announcing they're stoned, but their high is quiet, no melodrama, no hang-ups. They're loose and experienced heads. They enjoy the high without having to do freaky things. Kimmie can't be bothered capping the acid, but she'd be that way straight. Instead, she moves around the room lighting candles and joss sticks, chattering. The wine has worked to keep them sociably in a group.

The dope does nothing to settle Peggy. She's still on her money trip, dragging Nick the Cat, one of the guests, out of the room to confer with him about dope prices, copping, and dealing. When she isn't talking to Nick, she's phoning somebody else who copped a half-gram from the same source she did. She's hoping there was a mismeasurement or something that will allow her to get two or three hundred extra caps from the batch. When she hangs up, she runs back into the room with the mirror to see how many capsules have been filled so she can continue her calculations and computations of profit and gain. She's a kind girl. The money chase is wearing her out, making her obsessive to the point she can't keep her mind on pleasure. At the rate she's going, she's not even going to be able to get high anymore, because no matter how much dope she takes, her money trip keeps bringing her down.

"I'm righteously stoned, Peggy," John tells her. "You don't have to worry about burning anybody with this acid. It's good."

"Well, if it's that good, can we cut it and get another 250 caps?"

"Bad girl," somebody says.

"Well, I'm not a bad girl if you can get off on it. That's all they buy it for. You don't have taxes or parking tickets to pay. Do you realize, man, I've *spent* the money I should have saved for the taxes?"

They'd forgotten to cook dinner. So they went out to eat and on the way Peggy said, "My God, I forgot. There's a hippy in my hometown. She's the Worthington girl. She came back from San Francisco and Mother says all she does now is sit on the curb downtown in front of the post office, barefooted with a feather in her hair, staring out into nowhere. They don't any of them know what to do with her, so I guess they just form a circle around her and stare back."

On their way up they passed Lee, one of the Dirty Dozen, Papa Al's commune. They didn't know him so they passed him by; another street hippy or biker, an unattached protozoan necessary only as one of the many identically like him to complete the ecological life chain. Lee looked and talked like a West Virginia boy from a background of slack-jawed malnutrition, who's been section-foured out of the Army. He claimed he was the son of a rich oil family that owned wells, refineries, and five thousand gas stations bearing his name. The world's wealthiest hillbilly was living a life of ineffectual distress. "I'm bum-tripping on smack an' I want to come down," the boy said.

"There isn't anything that can take you down off smack," his friend Bob, also a member of the Dirty Dozen, told him.

"Sure there is. A cap of acid."

"You're full of shit, not smack," Bob replied.

"Don't hassle me," Lee said, and the two of them walked down the street to the Drogstore at the corner of Masonic. There was a lot of dealing going on, so soon a hassle started. Four spade kids, young boys—the oldest couldn't have been more than sixteen and the other a couple of years younger—were getting on a resplendent hippy with a waxed goatee and a red satin, high-collared Russian blouse.

"You burnt us last week, you motherfucker . . . Gave you $10 for a lid an' you never came back . . . Give us our bread back, motherfuck," the boys were saying, while the red satin hippy protested he'd never seen them before.

Before they could clobber Red Satin, Lee and Bob intervened and were leading the hippy toward the Dirty Dozen's nest while the black kids followed. Bob was promising a fair hearing to everybody and protection to the hippy. The Dirty Dozen proclaimed their thing was keeping peace and helping runaway juveniles. When they got to the apartment house, Bob and Red Satin went inside and Lee stayed with the spades. Sometimes he was coherent. Inside, Rusti was complaining that somebody besides her should show a little social responsibility about the dishes, as Bob and Apache argued over what to do with Red Satin and the spades. Apache went outside to talk to the spades, who were beginning to think that instead of justice the interveners had supplied a screen behind which Red Satin would escape. Apache went inside to talk to Red Satin and argued with Bob, who hissed that he was a dictator. Apache accused Bob of being up tight. More going and coming until Apache had gotten $3 out of Red Satin to give the kids for the burn, which Red Satin said he hadn't done. The spades took the money. They still felt cheated.

"Oh, motherfucks, we gonna come back tomorra night, an' then it's gonna be the niggers against the hippies! You just wait, motherfucks!"

Lee was still saying he wanted a cap of acid to come off the smack with. Somebody told him to go over to the Free Medical Clinic, but that seemed to be in the process of dissolving. So many of the regulars had been kicked out: White Rabbit, Teddybear, Kelly; and John, the cook, had wandered off too. Shalom gave signs of disintegrating. After all his experience watching people take bad dope, he was walking down the street when somebody handed him bad crystal and he swallowed it. Shalom should have known better. Dr. Smith gave him thorazine and after a while he stopped throwing up; but nobody felt too sorry for him because they handed him a mop and told him to clean up.

Now Kurt Feibusch had quit the clinic. It had to be a sign the clinic was dissolving or changing. The end of the summer. The

257

curtain on the scene. Not that Kurt hadn't quit before. He quit every night. Shalom would be on the phone talking: "This is Shalom, bum-trip administrator at the Haight-Ashbury Free Medical Clinic. I have a patient here. He got violent tonight at the Blue Unicorn Coffee House and his girl friend brought him here . . . No, no, he says he's never taken drugs."

"Who's in charge here? We had a two-hour staff meeting this afternoon where it was clearly decided that I would be in charge at night and these referrals were to be approved by me. I did not approve this referral," Kurt would say.

And Shalom would reply that he was the bum-trip administrator and could call for outside help. Then there would be a disagreement because somebody had given away some aspirin, and Kurt would repeat that he was the administrator at night and no pills, not even aspirin, were to be given out unless by a doctor or a nurse. Then he'd quit. There would be fights about everything—about John, the cook, feeding unauthorized personnel back in the kitchen, about keeping the door to the drug closet locked, about people sneaking into the calm room where the bum-trippers would be de-freaking and taking the ones too defenseless to combat it on astro-God-Hindu-infinity trips, there would be fights about Teddybear bringing his suspicious friends to visit, and always Kurt would quit and always he would un-quit. This time he stuck to it.

The clinic would have a different tone. It was ceasing to be a halfway house for people to rest on their way out of the Haight, or to grab hold of and use to pull themselves out, a place where spontaneous therapy would happen by virtue of people interacting with one another as they swung on the monkey bars of their imaginary, hip, medical bureaucracy. Young women, getting their M.A.'s in things like public health and sociology, were seeping in, being practical, pleasant, and untemperamental.

Kurt had been there almost every night the summer long. He was Theodor Herzl dressed as a hippy; Johannes Brahms in jeans, a black turtleneck sweater with two strands of beads, small ones, and an equally small, plain earring. At forty-one his hair was graying and he was a casualty from two wars ago. Even though he left his native Berlin when he was thirteen, he never adjusted. He still had a Berlin accent and the abrupt Berlin way. The door to the large possibilities of life shut on him nearly thirty years ago, when his refugee family arrived in England: "My parents came here, but I stayed on. After the war was over I couldn't settle down. I took some night courses or something like that and got interested in the theater, stage managing, playing small parts. Somewhere in there I got married, but that didn't last so I decided to get out of the city and spent three years working on a farm. By the end of 1953 I decided it was time to see my family again, so I came to this country. I came out here to be with my brother and worked in his custom-made hat business. After that, it was the San Francisco Actors Workshop. Then I got married again—I can't leave it alone. I had to have some remunerative work, so I worked as a coffee brewer. Let's see, what did I do then? Oh, I worked as a manufacturer's representative, selling stage and lighting equipment, and then *that* marriage went on the rocks, so I went back with my brother who had a new business, a toy store.

"Two years ago I heard about an organization called San Francisco Venture; it runs confrontation groups, contact groups. They work at increasing personal self-awareness. In this group I found out a lot about myself. I came to realize I wasn't able to continue working in commercial business, buying and selling, but that I was able to relate to people much more intimately than I had before and that, in general, I, ah, I was not alone in being beset by problems. I felt that having had people help me out, I had a certain commitment to help others."

Kurt got himself outfitted with a video-tape recorder, so that if he couldn't do therapy he might make his living assisting it: phoographing psychiatric sessions with instant replay. But the business had not gotten underway because Kurt was spending so much of his time at the clinic. Who was the doctor, who was the patient, who was helping whom?—it was never possible to know in the Haight, but Kurt had quit and was gone. Shortly after he left, Dr. Smith announced the clinic was quitting. No money.

It was peculiar. The clinic had never had any more money, but

259

it closed anyway with a cocktail party for its doctors, nurses, bene-factors, and, to be sure, the mass media. Dr. Smith was there, very angry at the Mayor for not giving the clinic money. He said he was thinking of campaigning against the administration in the upcom-ing elections, but he also reversed his field and said the clinic would reopen soon, after some benefits to raise money. There were bene-fits, but Dr. Smith didn't seem too concerned about their making money; he talked a lot about research competitors over at Berkeley freezing him out by getting some big grants from the National Institute of Mental Health, the government agency with real money.

### THE PSYCHEDELIC SHOP

**Born Jan. 3rd, 1966 ... Died Oct. 6th, 1967**
**Led one hell of a healthy life ...**
**Survived graduate course education**
**in City administration,**
**Law and Order,**
**Freedom of the press ...**
**Diggers kicked us in the ass, Thank you**
**Love to the Diggers ...**
**Hari Krishna Hari Krishna ...**
**God so loved the world**
**Once upon a time**
**There was a Psychedelic Shop**
**That tried to save the World**
**and succeeded ...**

Everyone sensed a falling apart; they seemed to react by grabbing what was grabbable or by chucking it completely. Ron Thelin chucked it. The Psychedelic Shop was closing, he announced. In its last hours its front was plastered with signs like GET OUT OF HERE AND LOVE, and NEBRASKA NEEDS YOU MORE THAN THE HAIGHT. Ron himself said he was going to India, Katmandu, some place far away with some spiritually very heavy people. The store hadn't been making it; it could have, but it had no merchandise to speak of, a few records, books, and Hindu knickknackery, and no space to put merchandise; that space was used by the meditation room, a large portion of the store given over to quiet, moving lights, car-

260

pets, and tapestries. It was a great place to turn on in, although the rules forbade it. So if you wanted to cooperate you could come in after you were stoned and lie there in the quiet. The store could have made Ron rich; it had been publicized all over the world, so much so that it was the first place the tourists wanted to see.

Ron was down on the publicity. It had, he thought, ruined the Haight. "The Indians will meet you man to man. It's the mass media that changed us from men into hippies, and then when they've done it they write these terrible editorials against us, like the one in the *Saturday Evening Post*. That editorial was the last scream of the old people, clutching, holding on, refusing to let go. The mass media made us into hippies. We wanted to be free men and build a free community. That word hippy turned everybody off, even most of the Indians. Well, the hippies are dead."

On the counter of his store was a high stack of black-bordered cards inviting everybody to the funeral:


### FUNERAL NOTICE

————•◆•————

### H I P P I E

*In the*
*Haight Ashbury District*
*of this city,*
*Hippie, devoted son*
*of*
*Mass Media*

————•◆•————

Friends are invited
to attend services
beginning at sunrise,
October 6, 1967
at
Buena Vista Park.

Several thousand of these announcements were prepared and printed by the more community-minded members of the Haight establishment. The funeral was held in the little mountainous park at one end of the neighborhood. It was followed by a procession in which the body of Hippy was carried through the community in a coffin and finally burned. It was reported that a staff member of *Playboy* magazine was one of the pallbearers and that the coffin itself contained several beards, a number of strings of beads, and two kilograms of marijuana.

"There never were any flower children. It was the biggest fraud ever perpetrated on the American public," pronounced Teddybear, dope dealer and social commentator, in approval. "And it's your fault; you, the mass media, did it. This wasn't a 'Summer of Love,' this was a summer of bullshit and you, the press, did it. The so-called flower children came here to find something because you told 'em to, and there was nothing to find.

"They got all the rules written down for them—how to dress, how to behave, what to say. They only had to turn on their television sets or open a magazine or a newspaper and read, 'Come to San Francisco, the City of Saint Francis, with a flower in your hair.' You told 'em to come here and everything would be free, free crash pads, free food, free dope. It never happened to me. The only things I got free were from my friends. Who offered free crash pads? Nobody, unless it was queers looking for boys to come over to their apartments."

"Now wait a minute, Teddybear," exclaimed the straight whom he was lecturing. "I've heard you an hour at a time on the street corner telling everybody who cared to listen what a special place this is supposed to be, how everybody loves everybody and all property are common trifles to be shared."

Teddybear stroked a moustache and pulled his goatee into a point. Then he responded, "You're supposed to be a reporter. You're supposed to get the unbiased, objective facts, not what people tell you. And truthfully, this community is based on dope, not love."

## A BIZARRE YOUNG MAN

This is the true story of a young man who grew up with all the advantages of a well-to-do family . . . As a teen-ager he seemed a normal young man, gifted and promising, with a successful career before him in the family business. . . . He was active in church work, and served a brief hitch as an officer in the Army.

Then suddenly a change came over him. Within a year he had broken with his family, and, without visible means of support, was drifting from one leaky pad to another, bearded, barefoot, dirty, and in rags. . . .

The young man claimed he was trying to "live like Jesus," all the while growing dirtier and more ragged, begging, mumbling to sticks and stones, "communicating" with anything that happened along. He dragged more and more fine young people . . . into this squalid and appalling way of life, all of them, like him, hipped on "Love, Love, Love."

Although his address was not Haight-Ashbury, but Assisi, he belongs, in a way, to San Francisco. It was named for him.

—Feature story in the *San Francisco Chronicle,* Sunday, May 28

Because of the diversity of the population that the mass media called hippies, it was possible for a reporter to find anything his editor wanted to find in the Haight. Some wanted sex, so that journalistic voyeurs found the material for many stories of prurient indignation, but just as many concentrated on what they imagined was hip social philosophy, and, above all, on love. In the smoking, fatal summer of 1967, "flower power" may have seemed hopeful in a way no message from a pulpit could be. Pro-war publications could be indulgent toward the flower children in the same manner as an anti-Negro congregation feels better for having a minister who goes for walks in Selma, Alabama, with Martin Luther King.

263

"The increasing attraction of the long-haired Haight-Ashbury hippies is in the obvious fact that what they do is generate power," wrote Ralph J. Gleason, the *San Francisco Chronicle's* social critic, who enjoys a deserved national reputation. "You may call them flower children, call them The Love Generation, call them mindless LSD idiots, call them anything you please, they are the most powerful single social movement in the country amongst Caucasians. They generate psychic force; they accomplish things and they have created a community that is effectively functioning, surviving the guerrilla attacks made upon it by the Establishment, and within the ordinary society . . . Money is losing its power to buy and thus its power to corrupt. Conformity is being lost in the Dylan ethic of 'Dig yourself' and the Digger ethic of 'Do your thing.' The revolution . . . is already happening in the street."*

Many writers lost their judgment almost entirely. In their personal despair at the condition of the world and their own country, they projected absurd hopes onto the young and then converted these hopes into facts. They wanted a change, immediate and drastic, so they vested this small band of youth with a preposterous power it never possessed. Some of the kids believed what they read and, together with the switched-on old folks from the mass media, the boys and girls fantasized they would overthrow one of the most stable societies the world has ever seen, overthrow a government nearly two hundred years old which commands a loyalty from its citizenry that is sometimes frightening and a military power that always is.

The mass media rhapsodies were harmless escapist excursions. The fact that the "establishment" organs printed so many miles of anti-establishment invective was testimony to their true nature—innocent entertainment. Dangerous thought and information has to fight to get a hearing in this country as it does everywhere. Compare, for example, the immediate indulgent reception given the hippies by the mass media with the fight the antiwar movement has had to make against slander to put its case before the public.

*Ralph J. Gleason, "The Power of Non-Politics or the Death of the Square Left," *Evergreen Review*, October 1967.

It made no difference that these flower children were armed—but not for revolution—or even that, in terms of old-fashioned police reportage, the reporters were passing up the criminal aspects of the biggest crime story since prohibition. White-collar crime, or in this case crime by white-collar people, has always been underreported by the media and the police, just as it also has always been underprosecuted by district attorneys. As an editor of a San Francisco paper remarked, "The children of some of our very best families are involved in this, and it makes handling it very difficult."

Editors' problems with the story were made worse by their staff members' divided loyalties. A lot of journalists are taking dope and turning on. They are both young writers behaving in the contemporary mode and middle-aged men who would become young again by acting like the young. Social science researchers report the same problem: staff people who are making the scene, not studying it. When *Time* magazine did its cover story on hippies, the magazine's teletyped instructions to its San Francisco bureau on how to handle the story were slipped out of the office by staff people to be Xeroxed and become public property in the Haight.

The Neo-American Church, a network of people that apparently exists to propagandize and propagate dope, writes in its catechism: "Infiltrate and take over the communications and entertainment industries." It adds parenthetically, "This objective is close to being accomplished."

The Neo-American Churchmen, who use dope as a sacrament, may be right. On September 24, 1967, CBS presented coast-to-coast in living color an hour-long marijuana spectacular. Lucky Strike and Champion spark plugs paid for the time and talent, but their products got plugged only during the commercials. The Smothers Brothers, whose show it was, had Herman's Hermits singing a song called "Green Street Green"—"Get yourself a little green." This was followed by a dialogue like, "I wish somebody would tell me what that song's about." "You know what it's about."

*This* was followed by a song called "Day Tripper," after which a spurious Haight-Ashbury hippy girl was yanked out of the audience for a little spontaneous ad lib. This creature's name turned out to be Goldie Kief, two synonyms for pot. The flower child made jokes about being high and then presented one of the brothers with a necklace made of "seeds," which, she explained, are like oregano (an herb that resembles pot). She said you can use these seeds for making brownies, a favorite recipe used by nonsmokers who want to get stoned. The Smothers Brothers' patter is the last of a long chain of presentations to the white, educated middle-class public. They are singled out here only by way of example. By the end of 1967, faintly concealed pro-dope yak-yak could be heard and observed on almost any TV channel. Only the news programs and the cops and robbers remained mainly antidope.

The beginning might be dated from Aldous Huxley's publication of *The Doors of Perception* in 1954. Here we see dope in its elite stage as Huxley writes about the effect of mescaline on him as he examines Seurat's paintings and listens to Gesualdo's madrigals. At this stage, dope taking is restrained, exclusive, and associated with highly articulated sets of aesthetic ideas. Later, in the hands of Leary and Ginsberg, it becomes religious and political; the product is advertised in a way that will attract more people. It is hooked onto music—the singing commercial—but it is still limited in its appeal both because the religious ideas are exotically incomprehensible to most Americans and because the political ones seem rude and somehow subversive, even though they are based on ancient political slogans. It is during this period that Ken Kesey popularizes dope as an illuminated musical and terpsichorean happening—the famous "Acid Tests" from which the present-day psychedelic dance halls evolved; its next evolution is *Time* magazine, where dope is presented both as stuff kids use *à la* Wheaties and as mildly radical, but perhaps connected with the unpremeditated love of primitive Christianity.* Finally, the Smothers Brothers use the bland, undifferentiated message of the ordinary TV commercial: for a headache, take aspirin; for tension, take Compoz; and for a low, take pot.

For the elitist faction of the hip world, this vulgarization, this

*See, for example, *Time's* cover story of July 7, 1967, "The Hippies: Philosophy of a Subculture."

denaturing of the product of all its grander social and ethical meaning was infuriating enough to cause them to publicly mourn the death of Hippy, devoted son of Mass Media. Yet what has happened to pot and, to a lesser extent, to LSD also happened to the motor carriage. Henry Ford turned that aristocratic vehicle into the American family car and changed its social meaning too. Because of this change in meaning, it now can be said that while most hippies take dope, only a minority of dope takers are hippies. Students, professionals, the middle class, and the rich are turning on but not dropping out. Why should they? Pot has been sold to them not as a way to overthrow the government and see God but as a new, improved product that's better than liquor; you get high but not hung over.

The society is beginning to regulate and institutionalize usage just as it did thousands of years ago with alcohol. There are already signs that America is rediscovering that dope is handy-dandy for social control.

Not long ago, in one of the rock dance halls, a bunch of weekend hippies from the suburbs were causing trouble. Instead of threatening to toss them out if they didn't behave, one of the private policemen who was trying to calm them suggested, "Why don't you boys go off in the corner there and smoke a joint? You'll feel better and so will I."

It has taken considerable finagling of facts and people for dope to be presented in the attractive light it has been. This hasn't been easy with photographs because pictures don't lie; but liars take pictures. The ones that came out of the Haight of lovely, otherworldly girls floating in flowers and pastel butterflies have as much relationship to what goes on there as a shot of Bob Hope entertaining the troops does to the war in Vietnam.

One Sunday morning a wildly painted bus stopped in front of Betty Gips's house on Ashbury Street, high up on the hill overlooking the Haight. Betty owns Happiness Unlimited, a psychedelic supermarket that sells trinkets to the tourists, while she herself and three or four young men live the life of well-to-do hips with Nancy, an all-American blonde from Rutgers University.

"Nancy," says Betty, "is the house lay. She's also the girl who gave away the five thousand free STP tabs in the park on the Fourth of July."

Betty has an old man named Wil Garet, and Wil is making a documentary movie of the drug scene. To make this sequence, forty or so hippies have been rounded up to take the bus some miles south to an obscure commune at Ben Lomond, California, where, once in the mountainous countryside, they will be supplied by Wil with music, food, and acid. After they're thoroughly stoned, he will photograph them.

When they arrive the day is so beautiful, and Wil is so happy that these are the last shots for his picture that he not only gives out sixty-five acid tabs (his count) but takes one himself. He's foresighted enough to have hired a regular, turned-off TV cameraman, so there is somebody with the presence of mind to make the shutter adjustments when the boys and girls, now spaced out of *their* heads, wander down to the brook, strip, and swim naked in the waters. As they do, Wil photographs this spontaneous, unstaged scene for the documentary. The girls seem reluctant to take off their clothes, but a few do and the rest are shamed into following. Most of them hide in the water, but the boys are bold and exhibitionist. They prance in the shallows of the green-and-yellow-flecked stream, bending backward to show their genitalia to the sun and the camera until there is a sharp whistle from offstage.

"You are trespassing on private property which doesn't belong to you," the unscripted voice of a deputy sheriff calls. "You have five minutes to remove yourselves."

The party moves downstream and the photography continues under the direction of the happy Wil, happy because he's sure the movie will be a commercial success, happy because his lawyer has got him out of jail on his dope charges and because he's with Betty and all the beautiful young people. Wil, naked, walks into the water with the synchronized microphone in one hand and something invisibly small in the other. "I know," he says in a gentle, calling, almost wooing voice, "there is somebody here who needs two more acid tabs before the heat gets to them, and I don't mean the sun." The tabs are snatched away.

"Will the real John the Baptist please stand up," somebody says to the bearded men, who are now floating neck high in water, like so many decapitated faces on a watery platter.

"I'm still flashing on the sheriff's whistle," Wil remarks simultaneously with the arrival of a man high on the hill across the stream. He's standing on the terrace leading to his house, flashing on them. "I have witnesses here. I'll have you arrested if you don't put your clothes on," he shouts down to them.

"We love you very much! Honestly, we do," they call back in honeyed voices of sweetest aggression.

"John, John!" the man says, calling to somebody behind him and out of sight. "Come out here and identify these men—and, my God! women too!"

They saunter out of the water, unperturbed, and move to the main house of the commune, where bad musicians are playing astral-rock-twang on instruments of their own making. The results sound like the frightened lowing of a hundred bronchial cows. Walking around in the middle of them is another John—John the ex-cook at the clinic. He says he dropped acid about an hour before. "But when you've had your own religious experience and your own love experience, it'll have to show me more than it has. It hasn't shown me anything. They don't show me anything. I've been listening to their music. They have boys playing men's instruments and men playing boys' instruments. That's their trouble. I don't get any insight or life out of this. If this is their ultimate experience then I'll still say genuflecting and sliding into a pew is best; but for a generation that's never had that experience, this expresses the natural religious feeling that's in all of us." The special expression of sorrow and dignity that he showed when he talked about Shirley, his dead wife, or the day he quit at Macy's, comes on his face and he ambles off.

The noise subsides. The acid-powered dancers are running out of fuel. One fifteen-year-old boy, who has been doing a flat-footed

269

Indian stomping dance, grows rigid, leans back on his heels, and falls straight as a ruler into the dust. He is unconscious, but in his oblivion he carries on the dance, his feet twitching in time to the electrified sounds. He will regain consciousness after a while, find a fifth for himself, and do it all over again before the night's out.

In the lull of the dusk, Malachi, who often beds down in the basement of Betty's house back in the Haight, performs an eerie service of his own devising, based on the *Tibetan Book of the Dead,* which mystical heads use as a guide to their acid trips. He sits among candles and small statues surrounded by high pines. The pot pipe is passed. He twangs his instrument, an accomplished musician, and makes the steely strings reverberate and form, out of their vibrations, pictures of the saffron monks of the high Himalayas. He chants of spirits Westerners have spent centuries interring in the ground, sealing up in wells and hidden springs, and driving back east of the Oxus; but a memory remains and the chant is more frightening because the memory is garbled and only half-realized.

> *O ye Conquerors and your Sons, abiding in the*
> *Ten Directions,*
> *O ye ocean-like Congregation of the All-Good Conquerors,*
> *the peaceful and the wrathful*
> *. . .*
> *Out of your great love, lead us along the Path*
> *. . .*
> *May we be saved from the fearful narrow passage-way*
> *of the* Bardo,
> *May we be placed in the state of the perfect Buddahood*
> *. . .*
> *May the ethereal elements not rise up as enemies;*
> *May it come that we shall see the Realm of the Blue Buddha.*
> *May the watery elements not rise up as enemies;*
> *May it come that we shall see the Realm of the*
> *White Buddha.**

*W. Y. Evans-Wentz, ed., *The Tibetan Book of the Dead,* New York, 1960.

270

The mass media are intrepid; no spirits, however powerful, can make them hesitate. MGM Verve Records is coming out with a recording of Malachi playing his holy music.

The dancing resumes in the main house. It is dark outside; a sheet has been hung on an outside wall for a light show. Betty is having the discussion about dropping out; everything is repetitious now. The Haight is over, the summer is over, invention and novelty are lost.

John, the cook, is back in view. He's still studying the effects of the acid. "I've forgotten the time. I can't keep track of it," he says. "If I went off by myself I'd see the colors move the way they say they can. I think I would now. But I don't want to see the colors move, that doesn't show me anything. I've had my love experience. I've had my————," he breaks off, and then resumes walking off into the darkness. *"Introibo ad altare Dei. Ad Deum qui laetificat juventutem meam. Judica me, Deus, judica me, judica . . ."*

### PEOPLE DIE OF GRIEF

**London, Oct. 7 (Times-Post Service)—A new and careful survey has confirmed old concepts, both folk and medical, that people do indeed die of broken hearts.**

The first rain came. It went on for hours. The kids who lived on the streets had been warned that in the fall the cold mists give way to downpours, but they had no money to provide against the bad weather. When the rain came it washed the kids out of the parks, off the rooftops, into storefronts, and out of town.

The first rain did bring back Black Preacher. He materialized out of a passageway on Page Street. Somewhere back there they were selling smack and crystal. He'd been in jail and looked very drawn. "I'm shooting smack to get back into condition . . . Hmmm ummm, I'm not dealing. They busted thirty last night and forty the night before. They got a nark pointing out every dealer walking the streets. I'm so clean I'm afraid to wipe my glasses . . . I'll sell you an American Express card. It's almost cool. The owner didn't sign it. I'd use it myself, but I don't have the threads you need to flash one of these. Sell it to you for $50. You could charge a couple of thousand on it and then throw it away."

He moved off, unhurried, through the rain in the general direction of the Drogstore, where the kids who had the price were sitting out the weather. Benches had closed its sitting section, and Tracy's never had much capacity. Bonnie, Mona's roommate, was in the Drogstore, very dispirited. "Mona's gone crazy, man. She's dealing again. I told her I don't want any part of it. I got one bust already an' I don't want to get busted again before I gotta go to court, but she's flipped out. She broke my tamboura, an', man, that cost $300. I'm gonna split. I'm looking for a furnished house, but it's gotta have a garage so Fish has got a place for his bike. I can't pay more than $135, though. Yeah, ya know Mona, nobody can control her exceptin' maybe Crazy Bob, but he's been busted again. Gee, man, when Mona deals she can't keep her mouth shut. I don't wanta have my baby in jail. Anyway, dealin's not my thing. Clothes are my thing, man . . . Yeah, I guess Fish is my thing too . . . Well, he said he was going to marry me. He better, 'cause I know the guy he cops from real well, and if Fish don't marry me, this guy isn't gonna let him cop from him no more."

The first rain ended in a day or so. But the devolution continued. The cops were putting on heavy pressure. Dope busts all the time, and street sweeps. At the summer's height they came predictably at two o'clock in the morning and they were easy to elude, but now they might come any time. Every underage juvenile became a fugitive, yet the old impulses were not utterly exhausted. Larry Burton made one last push and established his Love Center.

The Love Center was to be open every night at All Saints Church, where Papa Al had his headquarters. There would be counselors there waiting to talk to you if you had a problem. Everyone got on the therapy jag sooner or later. The proximate cause for Larry appeared to be his girl friend, Saqui. "Saqui tried to commit suicide three times. Once she shot herself in the belly when she was eight months pregnant. The baby only lived three days," Larry said, recapitulating the facts of the case. He had no sense of the need so many of the kids had for inventing these tragic histories. She had told him and he believed that "she gave her brother a gun, which he put in his mouth to use to blow the top of his head off. She was catatonic for three days after that. He had to kill himself, as I see it, because they were too close for both of them to live. She's also bisexual. Her parents wanted a boy. The first time she even wore dresses was when she was twelve or so."

"Basically, I'm putting her through a therapy thing. I've done this with other girls. After I'm finished, we split. Sometimes I work as a Zen master, which means working very strictly at the verbal level. I won't let her play games, let her do things that are self-destructive. But at an emotional level I give her support, so from her innermost being she knows I really like her. The one thing I can say that acid has done for me is give me an understanding of people, so I can work with them. Without it, I wouldn't be able to help Saqui, but what I've learned under acid shows me why she had to expose the pain and heal it. It's like she has this big shell around her. You crack off a little, let it heal, then crack off some more. You know she's a retired speed freak, so she's rap, rap, rap, rapping all the time, but it's all intellectual. I'm teaching her how to be spontaneous and live her feelings. I've already done some interesting things in therapy. Somebody ought to write my biography some day. I'll bet by the time I'm forty I'll have lived a fascinating life."

Jolly West introduced Larry to one of the best-known and most respected orthodox psychiatrists in the Bay Area, who agreed to meet the Love Center's counselors and perhaps give them advice. The doctors winced at the project but seemed to feel they could curtail its mischief more by sticking around than ignoring it. They needn't have worried. In a couple of weeks, everybody associated with the center had either forgotten about it and drifted away or was too busy with cops and the district attorney to play.

It came Cowboy's turn to go. He'd been up at Morningstar camping out and avoiding deputy sheriffs and raiding parties from the Department of Health. When he got back to the street he found the crippled boy, Sam, in his wheelchair in front of Tracy's, turning on. Cowboy took a couple of tokes and announced he'd been meditating, thinking about what he was going to do with his future. Before he could tell them, he was interrupted by the hysterical Lollipop.

"Sam, you're gonna get us all busted turning on like that. Don't ya know the heat's all over? It's not like the summer anymore."

"Paranoid heads attract narks like shit does flies," Sam replied, quoting an old Haight-Ashbury proverb. "You know once I took sixteen kilos of grass across the border in this little briefcase, right on my lap, in this very wheelchair, with no more protection than having one of these crippled toy legs of mine slung over it," Sam continued, exaggerating a little. "The border guard asked me what was in it. I told 'im. Sixteen keys of grass. He let me through. You won't get caught if you tell the truth. I was in that big bust at 526 Cole. I was there on a mattress sleeping, and then I woke up looking at the longest cannon you ever saw. There was a piece of fuzz at the far end of it. He tells me to get up, and I tell 'im I will just as soon as he wheels my chariot back to me from across the room. They asked me if I had any dope on me. I told 'em sure I do. I got smack in my right boot and hypodermic needles in my left one. He laughed and let me go."

"I was going to join the Marines and turn them on," Cowboy persisted.

"They're turned on already. That won't stop the war," somebody said.

"Yeah, that's what I thought," Cowboy agreed, "so I decided I'm going to Evansville, Indiana, to work in the mental hospital there. If you ever get to Evansville, look me up."

Not long afterward, Augie surfaced one more time. He was very down, the élan drained out of him. "My head's been all messed up by Raena. She told me she had syphilis, so I guess I have to have syphilis too," said the deflated and defreaked Boohoo of the Bethesda Bag. "I've got to go to the VD clinic, but I don't know where it is and I don't have carfare. I'm messed up. Raena's freaked completely. She's moving out of that place on Laguna. She threw me out, so I don't have a place to crash. She's really freaked. She ought to go to the funny farm . . . man, I'm way down. I'd like to drop a hundred thousand mikes and leave my body behind."

Augie must have taken his body off somewhere because it wasn't seen again, but Raena's was. It was sitting on top of a sleeping roll in front of Tracy's on one of the crowded Saturday nights. The spirit inside the body was agitated, for she kept calling out to everybody she knew who passed, "Have you seen Ego? D'ya know where Ego is?"

"Where did you leave him?"

"I left him with some friends for the afternoon, but then I lost —oh, it must be a couple of days or so. I don't know for sure. I went down to the Big Sur with Aaron and we dropped. We're going to New York to raise hell and sell dope. We made a beautiful star-net. It covered the whole sky, the whole world, a love-net protecting everything. When I got back they'd split."

"Who'd split?"

"My friends. They didn't split with Ego. They left him with some other people, but they gave him to somebody else, only that guy's so spaced he doesn't remember, an' his old lady isn't at their pad, so I don't know who they gave Ego to. If you see Ego, tell him I'm at Tracy's, or tell me—I jus' gotta find Ego."

An hour later she'd split from Tracy's and wasn't seen again. Every day the number of summer faces lessened. The regulars, those who weren't going into bankruptcy, said it was wonderful, that the old people were coming back and that it would be a quiet, groovy scene again. And there were a few like Gary Goldhill who were still operating in a now extinct bull market. He'd quit Grant and the *Haight-Ashbury Tribune* and could be seen moving around with a portfolio containing the prospectus for his new psychedelic magazine.

It was time for White Rabbit to go. He couldn't make it with a straight job and nobody would let him cop from them, so he couldn't make it as a dealer. The gas bill remained unpaid. His plans had fallen through and they were too difficult to formulate. People were leaving so he had fewer and fewer places to crash, and his parents had sent him air fare home. He no longer trusted Papa Al, but he couldn't face the meaning of his distrust. The night before he left he tried to dope it out: "I don't know which side to be on. I keep asking myself, 'Who is Papa Al, who is Papa Al?' Lee and Apache say Papa Al is a colonel in the CIA, that he's also chairman of the board of the Wells Fargo Bank. They say he was sent here to prevent acid from being distributed this summer."

"White Rabbit, there are no colonels in the CIA, and I'm sure the chairman of the board of Wells Fargo Bank, whoever he is, has got something else to do but chase around this freak show trying to stop the likes of you from pill-popping."

"Then why did Papa Al buy up all the acid he's bought? And why did he queer so many acid deals if he isn't a colonel in the CIA?"

"They don't have colonels in the CIA, and if they did, they wouldn't be here. The CIA is for spies and counterrevolutions—Cuba, Vietnam, the Dominican Republic! The CIA isn't interested in dope fiends. That's the FDA's jurisdiction."

"Then how about Leon?" White Rabbit asked.

"Now who in hell is Leon?"

"Leon was murdered. I never met Leon, but I knew about him. He was a fabulous chemist, a genius at it, who could make anything, acid, anything, but he was a fool about everything else. Leon was living in an apartment here, and he was told he was never to go out. Everything was brought to him—his food, his chicks, everything—but somehow he was lured away and killed. Papa Al had something to do with it."

"Look, White Rabbit, perk up your furry, smooth ears and get them parallel to each other so they hear straight. There never was a Leon. Don't you see who Leon was? What kind of a myth he was? There were a hundred stories in the Haight about miraculous chemists who make any kind of candy, cake, or ice cream for good little boy and girl dope fiends."

"I know Leon was killed. Papa Al must have had something

276

to do with it . . . Did you know that Papa Al is very rich? Look at that car he drives, and did you ever notice the whiplash antenna on the back of it?"

"Yes, I did notice the whiplash antenna on the back of Papa Al's car."

"What did you think it was? It's not for broadcasting, because there's no transmitter in the car. It's for something to do with the CIA."

The next day White Rabbit went home on his airplane, but Cowboy reappeared that night at All Saints Church in Papa Al's office. Apache had just run in from the recreation hall where Papa Al, the Dirty Dozen, and the church were combining to sponsor a clean-cut, constructive, anti–juvenile delinquency, straight dance and social hour for the benefit of the clinic. "Come out and see it! It's packed!" Apache announced.

"I don't want to see anybody being happy tonight."

"Awww, why not Al?"

"Why don't you just pass the hat around the dance floor for the clinic, and after everybody's contributed, steal the money? If you don't burn 'em, somebody else will."

"Awww, Papa Al," Apache sympathized, and that moment Cowboy made his return. Larry and Black Preacher didn't say anything, but Papa Al greeted him with, "Are the rest of you aware that Cowboy is back with us? He's only allowed three resurrections a month, but this month he's already on his fourth. Cowboy is the only male hippy in the Haight who has periods."

Cowboy laughed. The rest looked glum, except Saqui, who fidgeted.

"Let me tell you about the great burn artists and bums who live around here, or did until they'd double-crossed all their friends and split, which reminds me of Useless Reynolds, your friend, Larry. Great guy, Useless. When Useless didn't have a dime, he'd send his wife out to be a topless dancer."

Nobody but Al really thought that was so bad, but they looked serious because they knew he didn't like that kind of thing.

"We don't always dig you," Black Preacher said suddenly.

277

"I can't tell you how much that hurts me to hear you say that, Preacher," Papa Al answered him. They were irked at Black Preacher for the moment because he burned a black leather jacket over at the Dirty Dozen's. "What kinda trip you on, Preacher? Smack, isn't it? You're just like the rest of them."

"I haven't geezed tonight. I haven't geezed in two days. I'm down because on the way up here I ran into a kid who told me you've been having him snitch for you. Why should I trust you?"

"Why should I trust you, Preacher?"

"Aww, don't try that crap on the ol' preacher. You can't out-fake me like that. The preacher, he been on the streets so long he knows all the games; the preacher he knows every tactic, every ploy; so remember, man, when you play with the preacher, you ain't playing with a toy."

He walked out of the room, muttering the same question to himself. Larry stepped in to apologize for Preacher. "He's on a paranoid trip tonight. He'll be all right after he shoots up." Larry and Saqui were the only two in the room that Papa Al hadn't brought down, Larry because he was playing sympathetic friend and Saqui because she was grooving at having put a lid and a half of grass and an ounce of cocaine-cured hash in the bread she baked at the church that afternoon. Visions of turned-on sandwiches danced in her head.

"This comunity takes dope because it's on a perpetual downer," Papa Al told them.

"I've always dreamed of starting a regular dope exchange here," Larry said, as if that might be an upper. "A place where people would walk around buying and selling, and they'd shout things like 'International Pot at ⅜'s.' "

"This community should assemble in the Straight Theater where they should all give each other clap—and bring the drag queens up from the Tenderloin and give them clap too. Then they can exchange hepatitis needles and overamp on Drano and arsenic."

"Papa Al, you shouldn't talk like that, not you. If you go on a

278

bummer, what'll the community do? Man, don't give up, do your thing. This community depends on you."

"You're tired, you need a rest," Larry said, but Apache was pouring out more compassion and inspiration. "Papa Al, you're the only one we can all trust. If you don't do your thing, nobody else around here is going to be able to do his."

"Whatever's right," said Papa Al.

"Whatever's right," said Larry.

"Whatever's right," said Saqui, and Cowboy too.

### THE TRIP

The San Francisco Recreation and Park Commission is considering a proposal by sculptor Elizabeth Weistrop for the erection of a monument to the hippies. The statue is called The Trip.

—*Berkeley Barb*, December 15